magu: the c
power of t

tr gunter

Ma Gu:
The Classic Book of the Power of the Yielding Way

TR Gunter

Copyright 2021 Tracy R Gunter
ISBN 978-1-716-86780-4

Elf Magick Multimedia
Berkeley, CA
Elflord7@gmail.com

This labor of love was commissioned by Her Celestial Majesty the Immortal Dragon Fairy Goddess Magu.

Preface

This is not a book or thesis on Chinese or Southeast Asian culture, politics, anthropology or religion. This is simply an exploration of an ancient goddess of marijuana: Magu, who brings longevity. But while it is the Immortal Magu that brings blessings at birthday parties and celebrations, she is but a dim reflection of the great primordial goddess Magu of Neolithic times. It is that Magu in who we seek, the primal creatrix of the Golden Age that passed the shamanistic secrets down through her daughters and whose presence still remains in folktales, superstitions, mythology, archaeology, shamanism, religion, and magic.

As such, this work is mythology, not precise science or reporting, but rather: storytelling. Storytelling is how our cherished religions and beliefs have come to us and it continues. These stories grow larger each time they are told, and details change and shift. This tale is no different. We do not seek to find absolute truth, but rather, relative truth. The stories are tales from long ago that no one really knows what happened at the time because none of us were there. All we can do is to make educated guesses at best and wild imaginings at worst. Hopefully this finds its way somewhere in between. Embrace the goddess through her sweet incense and its smoke while we travel along the pathway to explore her mysteries together and wonder at the marvels of what she created.

As far as cultural appropriation and exploitation are concerned, this book is not about Chinese or Southeast Asian contemporary or historical cultures, except in where they intersect with cannabis. The China and Asia we write of is an idealized Neolithic "Golden Age" that was ruled by mythological Shaman Goddesses and their male consorts. And too, it is about the incredible scientific, ecological, medical, metaphysical and spiritual discoveries of the original Chinese people that gave rise to civilization as we know it and the possibility of actualizing that Golden Age once again. The primary culture explored is that of Cannabis Culture, but again, the focus is on the Neolithic and historic more than the present cultures. More than anything it is a tale of the way, the Dao.

This is not a book of history of China, religion, shamanism, or of cannabis. This is a book that explores and celebrates Magu in her many forms and flavors, the compassionate Chinese Ganga Girl of Mount Tai with her basket of herbs, mushrooms and cannabis wine. This is a tribute to the ancient cannabis growing and weaving culture inspired by the goddess Xian Magu. But most of all, this is a Fairytale of the Cannabis Flower Fairy Xian Magu Shan.

Table of Contents

Chapter One: Heaven   12
Ma
Xian Magu
The Primal Pure Ones
The Birth of Magu
Chinese Cannabis Culture
Centering
The Heavenly Heart

Chapter Two: Earth   36
Yin and Yang
Mago, Mother Goddess of Korea
Immortal Couple Fuxi and Nuwa
Cowherd Girls Weavers Festival
Korean Cannabis Culture
Circulating Qi
The Primal Spirit and the Conscious Spirit

Chapter Three: Lightening   63
Three Treasured Jewels
Gua- Three Pure Ones
Three Cinnabar Fields within the Body
Twenty-One Taras
Magu the Liberator
Immortal Shennong
Hmong Cannabis Culture
Balancing Yin and Yang
Circulation of the Light and Protection of the Center

Chapter Four: Water   94
Four Noble Truths
Four Directions and Guardians
Immortal Yellow Emperor
Fairy Magu and the Maidens
Thai Cannabis Culture
Mindfulness
Circulation of the Light and Making the Breathing Rhythmical

Chapter Five: Wind   119
Wu Xing –Five Phases
Five Dragons
Five Dakinis
Magu and the Peach
Japanese Goddess Taima Mako Asa Amaterasu
Japanese Cannabis Culture
Invocation
Deities of Prosperity
Mistakes During the Circulation of the Light

Chapter Six: Mountain   139
Smooth Lucky Number Six
Six Bardos
Magu's Magic Cannabis Wine
Laos and Cambodian Cannabis Culture
Six Mystical Steps to the Six Subtle Dharma Doors
Confirmatory Experiences During the Circulation of the Light

Chapter Seven: Fire   **161**
Queen Mother of the West
Magu's Long Fingernails
Quan Yin
Vietnamese Cannabis Culture
Snake Whip Cord of the Law
The Living Manner of the Circulation of the Light

Chapter Eight: Valley   **180**
The Eightfold Path:
Ba Gua – Eight Trigrams
Doorway of the Mysterious Female - The Valley Spirit
Eight Immortals
Death of Magu
Mazu
Taiwanese Cannabis Culture
The Magu Mantra
A Magic Spell for the Far Journey

Appendices: **210**
Zig Zag Zen Commandments of Lama Surya Das
Immortal Sister Cui Shaoxuan
Celestial Goddesses of the East
Bibliography
Notes

The road that can be spoken is not the road of eternity. The name that can be named is not a eternal name. Void of name is the beginning of the universe. Named are the ten thousand things of the mother. Therefore usually without desire its wonder is seen, usually with desire the boundaries are seen. Two aspects of a single thing, two synonymous designations Unseen of what is unseen, door of wonders.
Dao de Jing Ch 1

"The sole source of energy is the Tao. Who may declare its nature? It is beyond Sense, yet all form is hidden within it. It is beyond Sense, yet all Perceptibles are hidden within it. It is beyond Sense, yet all Being is hidden within it. This Being excites Perception, and the Word thereof. As it was in the beginning, is now, and ever shall be, its Name operateth continuously, causing all to flow in the cycle of Change, which is Love and Beauty. How do I know this? By my comprehension of the Tao." Dao de Jing Ch.21 Trans. Alister Crowley

Interpretation:
Three solid lines symbolize sky or heaven. The heavens are strong and have divine power to provide infinite space to accommodate all. The image is the stary night sky. The motivation is creativity. It is the Origin, the Creative, Force, the powerful storm cloud that rains down his seed upon the fertile soil of the earth inseminating her freshly plowed furrows with the seed of life.

Right View/Perception: Karma- we all live on, there are consequences to actions- the laws of cause and effect, every action has an equal and opposite reaction, what goes around comes around. All existence is unsatisfactory because it is craved, by detaching, that is, not clinging onto, or obsessing with, the craving and lust for result, right perception can now guide action and the inevitable reaction.

"The Pathway that can be described leads in the opposte directioon of the true path. The name is not the thing named, it is a finger pointing at the moon. She whose name cannot be spoken gave birth to ten thousand things giving them names of manifestation. The state of wu yü, mind turned inward to thought-free awareness, reveals the essence. The state of yu yü, the mind turned outward to thoughts and outcomes, reveals the body of form and manifestation. The two appear as opposites, but are one when unmanifest and two when named. There is a secret within this secret, hidden within itself, a primal mystery. The doorway from which came the Secret Essence, I do not know its name, I call it the pathway." Dao de Ching Ch 1

In ancient times myths of the gods were inspired by the constellations, planets and their movements. Deities and spirits were summoned as the personification of the physical and metaphysical energies of the universe and nature in tribal folk religions. Daoism is based upon the principal of wu wei, balancing the aggressive yang with the submissive yin. Daoism from its earliest roots emerged from, and blended with, Chinese Shamanism which then was blended with folk religions and beliefs and then with Buddhism and Confucianism forming a heterogeneous tradition incorporating whatever works. Daoism itself has a yin and yang in its expression, the yin being the esoteric traditions of feng shui, divination, fu craft, shamanism, witchcraft, sorcery, mediumship, alchemy, and the quest for immortality. The yang side is exhibited in the more commonly known philosophical and religious expressions. Esoteric Daoism is an active practice where the person raises energy from Heaven, the realm of deities, immortals, and higher spirits and from nature to direct and redirect these forces. Heaven is the infinite boundless continuum that encases and revolves around the earth as a canopy whose veil is composed of the sun, moon, stars and planets. Every Daoist ritual begins with the lighting of incense to create a portal between the worlds of spirits and people, a nexus between the realms.[1] Taoism is the ancient living tradition that throughout history has adapted to the culture, religion, ethos, people, customs, politics, and environment around it. Like water, it molds itself to its surroundings, forming itself to whatever shape and form of the receptacle it is placed into or passing through. It is the watercourse way, the power of the yielding way, the enigmatic woman, the valley spirit.

MA

"Tao begat the One. The One exhaled the Two. The Two gave birth to Three. From Three came Ten Thousand things. Ten Thousand things carry Yin on their backs and wrap their arms around Yang. Through the blending of the breath of qi they achieve harmony. People fear being alone and abandoned, looked upon as bastards, but embraced by emperors and lords. People sometimes lose something, yet win, and sometimes win, yet lose something. What others teach, I also teach, 'A violent and aggressive man will die a violent death!' This will be the foundation of my teaching." Dao de Ching Ch 42

Ma, the primordial vibration of sound from light. From this song of love came two daughters who gave birth to four daughters each, these are the eight planets whose motion is in harmony with the song of Ma, reflected by the eight trigrams of the I-Ching, the eight directions, the eight musical octaves, the eight families of the Periodic Table of the Elements, the 8x8 codons of the genetic code, the eight neuro-somatic circuits of consciousness, the eight limbs of yoga, the Noble Eightfold Path, the Eight Immortals, the Eight Genii of the Wine Cup, the ten thousand things and the totality of creation. They in turn give birth to four male and four female humans, establishing the sexes. Heaven, earth, ocean and qi are created and are mixed to become plants, herbs, birds and animals. Mago is Mother of the eight shamans who were sent to the eight provinces of Korea as progenitors, she is Amaterasu Omi kami, Mother of the eight-island kingdom of Japan, she is the great archaic, creatrix of the gynocentric cultural matrix, the source and form of the Tao, the watercourse way, the expression of the mysterious female. Ma is the archaic spirit of the cannabis plant which has been existing and evolving on this planet for the last eighty million years.

The name for cannabis in Chinese is Ma, a pictograph of two cannabis plants hanging in a drying shed,[2] and there are many terms in Chinese for Cannabis, its parts, products, properties and use due to its cultural usefulness throughout antiquity.[3] Interestingly, the Chinese character for deity includes a pictograph that resembles a plant calyx in the Oracle Bone Script. Ma is also a primal universal root word that can mean mother, mother's breast or goddess. As an

Indo-European language root word, it appears in the names of the goddesses Mary, Mari, Mara, Maia, Maira, Mariam, Magdala, May, Maat, Mab, Macha, Mardoll, Matabrune, Mader Akka, Mater Matua, Mati Syra Zemlya and also the Syrian goddess Magna Dea and the Scythian goddess Magog.[4] Ma is also the root of such words such as Magus, Magic, Matrilineal and Matriarchy. Ma is one of the first sounds that a baby makes and is most often the infant identifying the mother or her breast. Even the word man has at its root ma, indicating that the original source, the creator, both of man and woman, was the great goddess, as all men are born of woman. In Korean language Ma also means goddess, grandmother or mother.[5] Cannabis is a very ancient plant, much older than even the first humans, and its roots stretch back before the time of dinosaurs. Every vertebrate species on the planet has evolved with an endocannabinoid system and cannabis is the only known plant that produces cannabinoids that interact with the endocannabinoid system. Ma, or her manifestation as cannabis, is the ancestral grandmother that has been with us since our infancy and has nourished our bodies and spirits, healed our bodies and spirits and aided us in maintaining an equilibrium between our bodies and spirits, between earth and heaven. The ancient alchemical tradition of the immortal sages of China, with their elixirs, practices of the Dao, the banju of the Yin and Yang, maintain that the human stands between the powers of heaven (tien) and the natural forces of earth (di), assimilating the energies of both and transmuting them into electromagnetic and bioenergetic energies for the body to use.

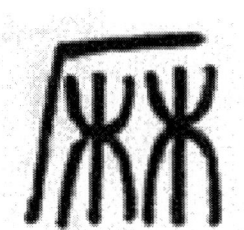

Cannabis is one of the oldest cultivated plants, having been domesticated some 10,000 years ago, and one of the first cultivated crops in China and Indochina. Its cultivation began in the late Paleolithic when it was domesticated by early farmers from native wild ancestor plants between 8,000 and 5,000 BCE.[6] It is believed that cannabis originated on the Tibetan Plateau and spread from there to Europe, East Asia, India and was further spread by the nomadic tribes of the steeps. Cannabis has been an integral part of Chinese culture and agriculture for thousands of years for food, fiber, oil and medicine.[7]   In ancient times, China was known as "land of mulberry and hemp," referencing the Chinese tradition of making paper from the inner bark of mulberry trees and cannabis fibers, and weaving fine fabrics from silk and cannabis. It was also a general reference to cultivated fields, cannabis being a primary crop. The mulberry also references the silkworms that live on the mulberry trees and eat their leaves. Cannabis was prized as a grain, for its fiber, and for its medical and shamanistic properties. Cannabis may have in fact been the first cultivated crop in China where it has left archeological evidence of is use since Neolithic times and has been integrated with the lives, religion and culture of the Chinese people throughout all periods of Chinese civilization.[8] According to "the father of Ethnobotany" and past Director of the Harvard Botanical Museum, Richard Evans Schultes contended that cannabis had been cultivated in China continuously since 12,000 BCE.[9] Over 15 sites excavated in China have produced cannabis artifacts ranging from seeds and female flowers, to pottery with hempen impressions, to fabric and cord that has been carbon dated to approximately 4000 BCE.[10] Pottery shards possibly dating as far back as 10,000 BCE with cord made of cannabis impressed into the clay have been found at an archeological site at Yangmingshan, Taiwan and other sites in Hwang He, or the Yellow River Basin have provided evidence of Neolithic Chinese use of cannabis fiber for rope, netting, cloth and clothing as far back as 5,000 BCE and extending into 230 BCE in the Hunan Province.[11] Evidence from Neolithic sites confirms Cannabis cultivation and religious or entheogenic usage from 5,000 to 3,000 BCE in Northern China at the Yangshao and Linchai archaeological sites where carbonized remains of cannabis flowers and seed were found indicating usage for religious, shamanistic or entheogenic purposes.[12] Entheogens are substances, usually plants, that have psychoactive effects and can induce a religious, spiritual or mystical experience by invoking the divine to reside within via the co-substantial communal sacrament that serves as a path between the divine and the human. This entheogenic way has been an integral part of shamanist practice since cave dwelling Paleolithic times and was fundamental to the development of the arts of civilization, especially in art, music, and dance.[13] Cannabis is a very unique and distinctive plant in its appearance, fragrance and effects. Even cultures that were cultivating cannabis for fiber or seed would not be able to ignore the entheogenic properties of the plant, especially cultures that employed slash and burn agricultural techniques. Paintings of what resembles cannabis were found on Yangshao era pottery dating to 6,200 BC.[14] The Yangshao were an early Neolithic matriarchal culture that practiced agriculture and domestication of animals along the Yellow River form around 5,000 BCE. At the early Neolithic Yangshao site at Pan-p'o, near Xi'an in Shaanxi Province, imprints of textiles were found on many pottery shards dated to approximately 3500 BC and another yielded pottery spinning whorls, fine bone needles and textile impressions in the dirt of one grave and were interpreted as hemp remains.[15] The Yangshao people lived extensively along the central Yellow River from around 5000 BC to 3000 BC and flourished mainly in the provinces of Henan, Shaanxi and Shanxi. They produced pottery, silk, grew cannabis, wore hemp clothing, domesticated pigs and dogs. In the Shaanxi province they left behind hemp cordage and textiles that have been carbon dated to 4000 BCE.[16] The Yanghai Tombs in Xinjiang Provence revealed a shaman from 2,700 BCE who was buried with a wooden mortar or bowl and a leather container with 789 grams of female THC rich cannabis flowers at his head and feet. Two pottery vessels in Lin-chia contained carbonized cannabis flowers, further indicating that not only did the Neolithic cultures domesticate cannabis for cord and fabric, but were aware of its entheogenic properties as well.[17] A late Neolithic site in Zhejiang province, produced several textile articles made of hemp, the Kungshan culture of about 4000 years ago also left hemp cloth, the agricultural tribes of the Lianghzu culture left two pottery vessels on the floor of a house in Linchia with carbonized fruits of cannabis, indicating that the resinous bracts were burnt and the seeds left behind,[18] yet another indication that Neolithic cultures domesticated cannabis for cord, fabric and its psychoactive properties as well.

"Planting hemp [cannabis], how do you do it? You plant it in straight rows." – Shih-Ching [Shijing], Book of Songs[19]

Xia Xiao Zheng, an ancient Chinese scientific and astronomical book from 770 BCE or earlier, names cannabis as the primary crop in agriculture, while the Confucian texts "The Annals" and "The Book of Songs" from around 300 BCE name cannabis as one of the six crops that should be planted. A tomb from the Han Dynasty at Ma-wang-tui in the Hunan Province called Han Tomb No. 1, contained cannabis seeds alongside other foodstuffs stored in hemp fabric bags. As a species, we have grown and evolved side by side with cannabis, and we have carried its seed with us everywhere as we have spread out across the planet. In Neolithic times of shamanism and animism, cannabis was well known and widely used as the physical evidence shows conclusively. These Neolithic cannabis shamans would perhaps use talismans written on cannabis paper, burn cannabis incense, bind with cannabis rope, and chase out the demons, germs and viruses of disease with invocation, chanting, drums and rods made of cannabis stalks and cannabis rope or ribbon. Daoism, Buddhism, and

Confucianism are all derivative of the ancient shamanistic Magu Goddess religion.[20] It is shamanism that was the precursor of the religions of China, Korea, Japan, Vietnam and Thailand, and cannabis was integral to this matriarchal shamanism. Its fiber, nutritional, medicinal and entheogenic properties created an intimate connection between cannabis and early shamanism. These connections can still be seen today in symbolic usage of hemp fiber and incense in the Korean rituals of Mu, Japanese Shinto and Zen rituals, Hmong tribal rituals, Buddhist and Daoist rituals and alchemy. There is also an overabundance of evidence to demonstrate that psychoactive cannabis use was prevalent among ancient Daoist and that it was the primary ingredient in their ritual incense.[21] It is incense that creates a shamanistic nexus between the realms.

"Central Asia, a vast land of deserts, steppes and oases is, despite its name, usually seen as of marginal historical influence, a kind of cultural vacuum between the great civilizations of China to the east, India to the south and the Middle East to its west. Yet, very early on, thriving trade routes passed through the region and these became known as the Silk Roads, on account of the importance of Chinese silk for both Muslim and Western merchants. It is known to archaeologists that Central Asia was an important center for the transmission of new discoveries and religious ideas from prehistoric times onwards. The hemp plant, being of major technological importance as a fibre and being one of the most influential psychoactive plants in human culture, was most likely a key trade item from a very early date. The anthropologist Weston La Barre was of the opinion that cannabis use goes as far back as the Mesolithic (Middle Stone Age) period as part of a religio-shamanic complex. Certainly the use of the plant had already spread across an area stretching from Romania to China, secondly south to India and on to south-east Asia, and last, and certainly not least, to western Asia, from where it diffused to Africa, Europe and eventually the Americas."
– Rudgley, Richard (1998). *The Encyclopedia of Psychoactive Substances*, Little, Brown and Company

Xian Magu

Magu or Ma Gu[22] is a legendary Daoist Hsian or Xian, 仙 immortal or transcendent, one who has transcended the realm of mortals and can transverse between the heavens, the underworld and the world of people. A Xian is a solitary one of the mountains that appears to die, but does not, and travels at will throughout the universe. The transcendent one has transformed their body like a chrysalis through spiritualizing it with inner and outer exercises, medicine, drugs, chemistry, alchemy, and the wine, pills, fruits or fungus of immortality. Transcendence, otherwise referred to as immortality, is achieved by mastering the art of wu wei. Wu Wei is to cause no harm, through vacancy, stillness, placidity, tastelessness, quietude, silence, drifting and non-action like water. To achieve transcendence, or Xian, one must accumulate 1,199 good deeds through the practice of wu wei by extending love to all life through "forbearance in the quietude and stillness of wu wei, to be voiceless and drifting."[23] By performing altruistic deeds without selfishness, self-preservation, self-interest and avoiding fight or flight reactions one becomes able to transcend space-time to experience past, present, future, above and below, within and without, the four cardinal directions and the five relative directions to find alignment with the Dao."[24]

Magu is the flower maiden of rebirth and renewal invoked on birthdays as an omen of long life and her devotees celebrate Magu's birthday on the 6th day of the 6th lunar month, but she always stays forever young. She is the Ganja Goddess, the Pot Priestess associated with healing, health, the elixir of life, springtime, elegance, beauty and eternal youth. She is the personification of the goodness within all humans and manifests physically as the cannabis plant. In later times, she became one of the Eight Daoist Immortals. The Hemp Maiden or Auntie Cannabis the Flower Fairy, was the protector of females in Chinese mythology, a beautiful young woman from the heaven reaching Cinnabar Cloud Grotto caves of sacred Mount Tai with long birdlike fingernails or bird claws. Magu is also an alternate name for Hua Gu, the Flower Maid, and she is Mago, Nogo or Nogu in Korean[25] and Mako in Japanese,[26] the Great Goddess herself; the archaic gynocentric cultural matrix as creatrix,, progenitress, and sovereign from whence all began.[27] There are other Chinese goddesses and immortals that bear the name Ma such as Maku, the goddess of Springtime, Mazu the protector of sailors and Ma Xian Ku, the holy shaman. From the sinews of Magu's body were spun, woven or twisted cords and cloths.[28] She is the pockmarked one, from the healing seeds her flowers produces, whose oil relieves acne, blemishes and skin conditions, the father's sister, husband's sister, the husband's mother, the nun, the young girl, the prostitute, the priestess, the goddess ripe and full with life giving seed, the Pockmarked Priestess, the beautiful and fragrant flower heavily laden with seed that yields the oil of beauty and youth. Magu, the Cannabis Lady with her magical spiced cannabis wine who blesses married couples with silver and gold on their anniversaries. She wears an apron or shawl of cannabis plants, her shimmering, multicolored gown, not woven of this world. The Jiayi Cemetery, Turpan, China, contained the tomb of a nomadic Gushi shaman buried wrapped in a well-preserved shroud of female, THC rich cannabis plants which in it's prime, would have surly shimmered with its psychoactive crystals been luminous and "not of this world."[29]

"During the ninth Century B.C. 'Female man-barbarians', an Amazon-like dynasty of female warriors from Indochina, offered the Chinese Emperor a 'luminous sunset-clouds brocade' fashioned from hemp, as tribute. According to the court transcriber, it was shining and radiant, infecting men with its sweet-smelling aroma. With this, and the intermingling of the five colours in it, it was more ravishingly beautiful than the brocades of our central states".[30]

One of the earliest representations of Daoist Immortals depicts them as winged beings walking on clouds and holding an ingzhi, a "numinous mushroom", in their hands.[31] Magu, sensuous as a sparrow, rides upon the deer or flies on the crane and has the peach of immortality or a mushroom in her palm. When you see a deer, it is an omen of good fortune, as the deer is one of the totem animals of Magu and are fond of eating both cannabis and mushrooms. Deer are symbols of longevity, you often see images of Magu with deer, and is the basis for the saying "When you see a deer you know Magu is near". Magu carries a basket of cannabis, flowers, mushrooms or peaches and cannabis wine. The flowers elevate the senses, the mushrooms grant immortality, peaches grant longevity, and a drink of her famous cannabis elixir is said to bestow perpetual youth. Sometimes she holds a ruyi scepter, with an attendant holding a bundle of hemp scrolls with fu bats flying above. Like the Great Mother of the West, she also is identified with not only the peaches of immortality and the herb of immortality from which she brews her cannabis wine, but also the tiger.

"You can obtain Buddhahood: by taking a medicine pill which will make you immortal like the sun and the moon." – The Life of Gampopa[32]

Magu has appeared in three incarnations in this current age. In the first, she was a famous magician who lived in the Han dynasty under the Emperor Huan Ti, in 147-168 CE, where she reclaimed a large tract of landform the sea and planted it with mulberry trees. The next incarnation was during the reign of Chao Wang, 328- 332 CE, where she lived with a cruel father called Ma Hu. She became a hermit and created a special magical wine that could heal blindness. In the last incarnation she was known as Chen-Jen and lived as a hermit on Ma-yu Mountain in Shantung circa. 1111 CE.

The only temple dedicated solely to Her Holiness Magu that has survived the Cultural Revolution in China is in Yue Gu Temple complex on Mount Kunyu in the Shangdong Province.[33] Her tomb is also at the same complex and there is a Daoist Temple and a Martial Arts Academy nearby. The 8th Century Tang Dynasty Daoist calligrapher Yan Zhenqing visited there and inscribed the famous Magu Shan Xiantan Ji, 痲姑山仙墰記 "Record of the Mountain Platform where Magu Ascended to Immortality." Mount Kunyu is flanked on the north by Penglai City's Dan Cliffs in Yantai, the departure point of the Eight Immortals on their way to the Queen Mother's Conference of the Magical Peach, and to the west by Mount Tai, Taishan, the most sacred mountain in China, also said to be the abode of Magu. Between the city of the Immortals, Xi'an and Yanti there is a Buddhist Temple called Magu Damiao with a neighbouring Magu Villager's Committee in Shangjie District, Zhengzhou, Henan and a town of Magu in nearby Qiu County, Handan, Hebei and another in Pei County, Xuzhou, Jiangsu. Further south there is a town named Magu in Anren County, Chenzhou, Hunan.

There are numerous caves and mountains named after Magu, the mountains are called Magu Shan or Magushan. Along the Yellow River in Yuanqu County, Yuncheng, there is a Magu Mountain. There are two mountain peaks named Magu Mountain, in Guangde and Langxi County. In Xuancheng, Anhui, outside of Shanghi, Magu Mountain Yuhuang Temple is located nearby as is Tai Lake. There is also Magu Mountain in Nancheng County, Fuzhou, Jiangxi, Anhui. Along the Yangtze River downstream from Wuhan in Tuanfeng County, Huanggang, Hubei, is is a mountain called Magushan and there is Mount Magu in De'an County, Jiujiang, Jiangxi, China. North of Wuhan is another Magushan in Dawu County, Hubei, Xiaogan, Hubei. To the south there is a Magu Mountian in Nancheng County, Fuzhou, Jiangxi with a shrine to Magu and a town named Magu in Anren County, Chenzhou, Hunan.

Today there are few remaining temples dedicated to Magu, but scattered cannabis plants may often be found growing wild around them.[34] Her eminence and worship are in the mists of history now for the most part, other than bringing blessing at one's birthday. But the abundance of mountains and towns named after her attest to the history and antiquity of her reverence and worship.

"There is a way of perceiving the world in which everything is alive and conscious… Some plants communicate with their form or their scent or via the uses to which we put them. They communicate via pollen, insects, and companionship with other species. They communicate in an incredible chemical dance of scents, pheromones, alkaloids, terpenes, flavonoids and other compounds… Cannabis has been a character in the human drama for at least the past ten thousand years… Eight thousand years ago, cannabis seeds were used as food in China. Six thousand years ago, the Chinese were cultivating an ancestor of Cannabis sativa for its stem fibers, as hemp for making cordage and weaving into textiles. We know Chinese were employing parts of the cannabis plant for medicines for various ailments five thousand years ago. At least three thousand years ago, across Central Asia and perhaps farther, the seeds were widely used in rituals- as offerings in invocations and also left with flowers in graves. Cannabis was widely used as an incense that could affect anyone who breathed its ambient smoke… In ancient China, Ma was the name of the deity resident in hemp, the extremely useful fiber that comes from the cannabis stem. Both the male and female plants are depicted in the pictogram for hemp, sitting inside a built shelter or home…Hemp has been a plant of fundamental utility to hundreds of generations of humans. Ma was therefore the spirit of she who grows, she who cloths us, she who binds, she who ties it all together."[35]

Followers of the Way of Infinite Harmony view the Path of Ma Gu, the Way of Infinite Harmony, as the path of the Dao. Followers use the words "Ma Gu Xian Shou" as a statement of faith and believe hearing these words gets one closer to knowing the self and attaining the Dao. It is also often said as a mantra by devotees.[36]

"The Tao is like a container: used but never used up. It is like the eternal void; fountain of infinite possibilities. It blunts the sharp and unravels the tangled; harmonizes with the light; mingles with the dust. It is hidden but always present, calm like a deep pool. I don't know who gave birth to it. It is older than our understanding of God." Dao de Jing Ch 4 trans. Wayism

The Primal Pure Ones

There are thousands of goddesses in Chinese mythology and folklore such as Shin Mu, the mother of perfect intelligence, Yang the patroness of shamans, Yaoji the patron goddess of Wushan Mountain and daughter of the Queen Mother of the West, Sky Mother Abkai Hehe, and Lady Jinhua, the divine protector. Even today, followers of deified women of China, [37] such as Mazu, Guanyin, Mago, Sun Buer and Magu, taken together constitute one of the world's largest religions. Mazu alone has over one hundred million followers worldwide and Guanyin is one of the most commonly worshiped deity in the household throughout Southeast Asia.

In Chinese mythology it is told that before all there was the Yuan-shih T'ien-tsun: The First Principal. She existed "before the void and the silence, before primordial chaos." This first principal can be identified with the Dao. The Dao is generally translated as "the way" or "path", but "the model" or "template" may be a better translation. The Dao is the Source of all that is, an unnameable mystery, all-pervading numinosity, and the cosmological process which is the universe, the darkness and silence beyond intellectual conceptions. This is the primordial movement that cannot be spoken or named. As Laozi revealed: "That which is the Dao cannot be named, all that we give names to is the Dao."

Daoist, Confucian, Buddhist and Hindu traditions all speak of a "Golden Age" long ago, before 2100 BCE, a time of beauty, harmony, peace, equality, compassion, mutual respect and natural virtue, where social equity and servant leadership were the standard norms. This was an archetypical matriarchal time that served as a memory of what once was and will be again. As to whether this mythological realm ever existed, recent archaeological discoveries in China have unearthed ancient "Goddess Cultures" adding credence to the old legends and myths. The Classic of Rites described it as "When the great Way was practiced, the world was shared by all alike. The worthy and able were promoted to office and the men practiced good faith and lived in affection. Therefor they did not regard as parents only their own parents, or as sons only their sons."[38] These values and ways of life can still be seen within the anthropological generalizations of primitive Chinese tribes, as well as other aboriginal tribal peoples globally, general equality amongst members, consensus-based decision making through open and protracted discussion, and freedom of movement. In the tribal villages activities such as clearing fields, planting, harvesting, building houses, weddings and funerals were communal activities whose labour was shared, as was the equal distribution of property to insure plentiful food for the children. Many of these customs persisted through the ages in the villages of China through the popular religions of the countryside and the tribal people. From the ancient warlords to the modern communist state, these folkloric traditions have persisted and adapted but never have they been extinguished by any rulers. The Na, also known as the Naxi, of Yunnan still follow ancient matrilineal customs and claim to be tiger people, forbidding the killing of any cat, invoking archetypal memories of the Queen of the West in her tiger aspect and also those of the archetypal image of the tiger as yin, the doorway to the subconscious and occult realms.[39]

There is also archaeological evidence to substantiate these myths. Excavations of Chinese Neolithic settlements reveal that the Pre-Dynastic people had homes that were roughly the same size and relatively equal amounts of possessions, indicating an egalitarian societal structure. Goddess figurines were commonly found and there were agricultural and hunting tools, but no evidence of weapons of defensive fortifications to protect against wars or raiders.[40] Interestingly, most of the Neolithic archaeological sites also have evidence of cannabis cultivation, ranging from hemp fibre and cord, cord impressed pots, seeds and pollen samples to charred seeds, pouches of cannabis flowers and shamans wrapped in cloaks of cannabis plants.[41] Many of these early Neolithic Goddess Cultures were located in the Yellow River and Yangzi River Basins and extended down to the Tonkin Gulf in Vietnam. How old these cultures were we do not know, but in Chongqing on the Yangtze River, fossil remains of a 170 million year old dinosaur have been found and humanoid remains dated to approximately 1.9 million years ago.

One of the primary gods of the Chinese cosmology is P'an Ku, who chiselled the universe out of chaos accompanied by the four celestial creatures: the unicorn, phoenix, tortoise and dragon. Interestingly, P'an Ku does not appear until the 4th century AD, and his story shares much in common with the Korean tales of Mago. This primal ancestor was the offspring of the Yin and Yang. Yin represents everything that is feminine, dark, withdrawn, receptive and passive and things moving down and in. Yang represents the masculine, bright, forceful and expansive, and movement out and up. From these two poles of existence which are opposite but complementary, and which exist in everything, came the primal god P'an Ku. This primal god may be representative of the Neolithic shamanic religion of the aboriginal Chinese, who like other early Palaeolithic and Neolithic groups, would have used entheogenic plants to commune with the gods and ancestors. As an allegory for an amanita muscaria, or other mushroom, the god would be co-substantial with the mushroom, the eating of the mushroom enabling the god to speak through the shaman that ate the entheogen.[42] 'P'an' means 'the shell of an egg,' and 'Ku' 'to secure,' or 'solid,' referring to P'an Ku being hatched from out of Chaos in his mythology, and symbolically representing the "egg" stage of development of the mushroom, as it bursts forth from the abyss of the underworld or the deep aboriginal primordial times.[43] P'an Ku is a dwarf, another symbol consistent with the allegories used for the amanita muscaria in many different cultures worldwide.[44] He is depicted with horns, perhaps representing the scabby horn-like remains of the universal veil[45] on the cap of the amanita muscaria. His head is that of a dragon and his body a serpent, again, the fiery red cap of the amanita muscaria with its white scales being the dragon head, and the slender, smooth stem being likened to the body of a serpent, while also emphasizing his chthonic nature. This connection with the underworld may also be a connection with the cave dwelling ancestors as they emerged to form villages. He is also often depicted as wearing an apron of leaves, this could have originally represented the straw and plant matter that attaches itself to the mushroom as it emerges from the ground and later stylized into leaves of herbs or specifically cannabis leaves to represent the fabric making qualities of cannabis. P'an Ku holds a hammer and chisel that he proceeds to fashion the world with, but in other iconography he holds the sun and the moon, again symbols that are commonly associated with the amanita muscaria,[46] but also symbols of the yin and yang. It is also said in folklore that P'an Ku's voice was the thunder, again, a common reference to the amanita muscaria or other mushrooms that commonly appears after the rains of a thunder storm.[47] Memories of these entheogenic shamans remain in folk tales and legends. In one tale little people wearing red cloths and having heads disproportionally large for their bodies are described, in another, one eyed people, and in yet another, one legged people. These are all common metaphors in folk tales for the amanita muscaria.[48] This primal god figure represents the shamanistic ad animistic stage of religious development among the ancient peoples of the area. To the north in Siberia, the shamans there also used this same mushroom to commune with the gods as is well documented.

Chinese religious expression, like most religious expression globally, began with what is now termed shamanism. The word "shaman" is originally from the Tungstic word, šamán, loosely meaning a person of knowledge, later applied by Western scholars and writers to similar animistic religious practices in other cultures. The Tungstic Shamans of Siberia were chosen by the spirits to become shamans and were the bridge between the world of the spirits and the world of people that maintained the equilibrium between the two and therefore within the community, and they preserved the ancient knowledge and magic of the spirits, the tribe and their craft. The Tungstic people of Siberia and Northern Asia include the Mongolian and Manchu, and their folk religion is the animistic and shamanic folk religion that has been practiced since recorded history. Both cultures have influenced Chinese culture and religion in significant ways. While the Mongol Empire was at its apex, they spread the use of hashish from Siberia to the Mediterranean and sowed cannabis and opium poppies throughout all of the regions they roamed and occupied.[49] Before modern political boundaries and definitions, Siberia was the area that now includes modern Siberia, Mongolia, Inner Mongolia, Manchuria, north Xinjiang above the Tarim Basin and eastern and northern Kazakhstan and consisted of the Mongolic, Turkic, Tungstic and possibly the Uralic peoples whose primal religion was animistic based shamanism recognizing the spirits of the mountains, trees, rocks, water and sky.[50] Evidence of Neolithic goddess worship has been found in Hong-Shan district, China at an archaeological site stretching from Mongolia to Manchuria dated to 5000 BC. Common features of the North Asian shamanic cultures were the use of the drum for inducing trance states and the Windhorse.

The windhorse, or Hiimori in Mongolian, and Lung Ta in Tibetan, is a personal power, what the ancient Hawaiians called Mana. It is the ability to sense and perceive things beyond the physical realm and the ability to focus this power into manifestation. It is a figurative flying horse that can focus and manifest intent when strong and well-nourished acts that restore the balance in the universe and weak and helpless when malnourished and ignored by indulging in selfish, harmful thoughts and actions that disrupt the balance and harmony of the universe.[51]

Another important attribute for shamans of Inner Asia is the shaman's drum which may incorporate the shaman's ongon or ancestral spirit. The drum's skin was often made of horse skin, the drum itself standing for "the saddle animal on which the shaman rides or the mount that carries the invoked spirit to the shaman." The patterns on the drum membrane reflect the world view of the owner and his family, both in religious matters and in worldly matters instead of only the tribal shaman. The drum was used to achieve trance, by the rhythmic heartbeat of the drum, the shaman would pass into an altered state of consciousness where their spirit can travel to the heavens or the underworld, visit with heavenly beings, demons and ghosts. But most importantly to gain information about hunting fortune or to manipulate the prey to move into hunting range. A tonic known to the Mongolians as bogoshen was used to ward off all diseases and illnesses. It was made from cannabis, juniper berries and bat guano. Cannabis and juniper berries were often used in combination by shamans of the area to induce trance states.[52]

From this early animistic shamanism came the Daoist. Daoism is a religion based upon the observations of the interactions of nature and humankind. Around 500 BC Laozi wrote the perennial classic Daoist text, the Dao de Jing, encapsulating the Daoist philosophy. But the practices go back thousands of years earlier. After Daoism emerged, Confucianism developed in China, Confucianism, also known as Kung Fu Tzu or Kong Fuzi, was said to have been a student of Laozi. Confucianism contained strong elements of ancestor worship common the shamanistic folk religions of China and stressed moral and social codes and ethics. Buddhism arrived in China from Northern India in the fifth or sixth century BC and spread rapidly through China, integrating itself with the indigenous folk beliefs along with Confucianism and Daoism. The Buddha too, was said to have studied with Laozi for a time. These three religions co-existed with each other creating a triune religion embodying the essential elements of each and integrated with local tribal religions and beliefs. Daoist immortals were given seats beside the Buddhas, worshipped at the same altar were the three religious founders or figure-heads, Confucius, Buddha, and Laozi, and it was said "the three unite to form one". There are triads within the triads as well, Buddhism contains the triad of the three Precious ones, Daoism the Three Pure Ones.

"In the cult of spirits.... Chinese shamans... intermediaries with other realms... people who dance in order to bring down the spirits. They not only made use of drugs which brought about trance-like states but also were specifically interested in finding a herb which banished death...."[53]

The ancient masters were subtle, mysterious, profound and responsive.
The depts of their knowledge is unfathomable.
Because it is unfathomable,
All we can do is describe their appearance.
Dao de Jing, ch 15 - translation by Gia-fu Feng and Jane English

The Birth of Magu

"Green plains of lush fields, green rolling foothills, green, deep blue green mountains. Far up the eastern trail, the Temple of Lao Tzu, on the side, the Green Pond of Ma Gu." – Way of Infinite Harmony, Ma Guang Wei

Magu's father had a dream in which he was fishing upon a river and when he reeled in his catch, expecting a large fish, he found he had caught a beautiful lotus flower. He awoke to find his wife in labor and soon she gave birth to Magu. As Magu grew, she possessed exceptional beauty and remarkable hearing. Magu could converse before she was one-year old, it was said that she could walk upon the waters in her cannabis fiber sandals and was composing poetry before she was seven. At the age of seven she learned how spin cloth with the fine fibers of the male cannabis plant and knew to harvest the male plants just before they were releasing their pollen like dust, so that the fibers are fully formed but not yet darkened. From this fiber she would weave fine fabrics and canvases for her beautiful paintings. She learned to make pottery and would impress her creations with cannabis fiber cords. From the unpollinated flowers of the females she would make incense, medicines and wine. She learned to make torches from the fibers and stalks of cannabis and fuel for their flame by pressing the oil from the seeds of cannabis.

"Ma Gu fell asleep in the mountains next to a fragrant plant with a tall fibrous stalk and beautiful, sticky flowers of red, purple and green, laden with seed. As she lay and dreamed next to the plant, she became one with the plant and understood all its many qualities and uses. She rolled out her cape under the fragrant plant and shook the stalk of the tree. Seed filled her cloak and she rolled it up and flew off into the clouds. As she flew, she unraveled her cloak and the seeds fell upon the earth. Soon the mountains were filled with the fragrant trees exuding their intoxicatingly sticky resin that bestows the powers of insight." - Way of Infinite Harmony, Ma Guang Wei

As Goddess, Magu is co-substantial with the plant that is her totem, Cannabis. Her body gives rope, fiber, cloth and paper; her leaves give medicine, and her flowers exude healing and enlightenment and the entheogenic ability to become co-substantial with the goddess by ingesting them. As an Immortal, Magu has led many lives and has many stories describing her virtues, powers, properties, qualities and uses. The goddess in her many forms and representations is fluid in manifestation, borrowing from other cultures and stories and her name can mean maiden, priestess or aunt. Her many stories reflect her many qualities and facets, and like the plant that she embodies and represents, the stories are adaptable and have changed and evolved throughout the leaves of time.

"The Goddess does dwell within the plant co-terminus; one and the same being. The goddess plant and her transformative properties. Upon ingestion of the plant as food, smoke or extracted chemical there is a mystical union with the Princess of Cannabis, Ma Gu. In this most sacred and holy state the devotee can discover the true nature of the world and the true nature of self." [54]

Cloning is the only way to create almost identical plant matter. Cloning is copying the genes of one plant. If you have a crop of clones growing together and the environment is the same for all of them, you will end up with the same plant. Different environments, however, will lead to different results because of phenotypes. Ma is the Mother of Life and Divine Virgin, manifested as a Mother Plant who through parthenogenesis, gives birth to genetic identical daughters called clones, a plant with the qualities and characteristics that are desired that is a genetic duplicate of the Mother Plant. The Mother Plant is kept growing in a vegetative state and is not harvested except for small cuttings that are rooted, then planted and brought to maturity. The cutting should be taken from sturdy lower branches that are vibrant and the veins in the leaves are clean and translucent. The cuttings should be 8-12 inches and have at least six nodes. When taking cuttings from the Mother Plant, purify, the cutting tools, a sharp pruner or a razor, by sterilizing them. These sacred tools should be reserved

for the propagation of children from the Mother Plants and no other purpose. The cutting should be made with a cut as close to the main stem as possible, and then through the center of the fifth node from the tip of the branch. The cut should be made at approximately a 45-degree angle. Remove branches and leaves right above the node to signal the clone to root. Dip the cutting into a solution to stimulate root growth immediately. The clone can be rooted in rockwool cubes, soil, hydroponic solution or water. Clones should be kept at a constant temperature of 72-77 degrees, a Ph of 5.5-6.5, 80-90% humidity and given frequent misting. The clones should be exposed to filtered bright natural light or under florescent light tubes, LEDs or CFLs on 24 hours a day.

Chinese Cannabis Culture

"Tao in its eternal aspect is unnamable. Its simplicity appears insignificant, but the whole world cannot control it. If princes and kings employ it every one of themselves will pay willing homage. Heaven and Earth by it are harmoniously combined and drop sweet dew. People will have no need of rulers, because of themselves they will be righteous. As soon as Dao expresses itself in orderly creation then it becomes comprehensible. When one recognizes the presence of Dao he understands where to stop. Knowing where to stop he is free from danger. To illustrate the nature of Dao's place in the universe: Dao is like the brooks and streams in their relation to the great rivers and the ocean." – Dao de Jing Ch 32 trans. Dwight Goddard

The Chinese invented retting hemp stems, thereby to obtain the soft fibres, which were used for fishing nets, clothing, shoes, rope, and sails. The hemp seeds were also eaten, being rich in essential fatty acids, protein and vitamins. The ancient ancestors of the Chinese are thought to have migrated to the Yellow River in successive migrations from the west then migrated north-eastward, eastward and southward from the north-west corner of China. When the Chinese Ancestors settled in these areas, they began to cultivate crops such as rice, mulberry and cannabis.

In ancient China, the land of mulberry and hemp, hemp or cannabis sativa, was the primary source of fabric for the common people who were not able to afford the expensive silk fabric. Ancient Chinese writings contain passages urging the people to plant hemp so that they will have clothes, one book of ancient poetry mentions the spinning of hempen threads by a young girl and the "Shu King", dated to about 2350 B.C., says that in the province of Shantung the soil was "whitish and rich...with silk, hemp, lead, pine trees and strange stones..." Some have speculated that cannabis was first cultivated in China as early as 6500 years ago.[55] Cannabis seed was a primary food source into the time of the late Han Dynasty, where it was eaten roasted as a snack, made into a nutritional porridge, the oil pressed and used for cooking and the seed smashed and added to meats and stews.[56]

"I pluck the flowers in the sacred hemp [cannabis] field, pluck them for him who is far from me." – Ch'u Tz'u 3rd Century BCE[57]

Cannabis is still widely cultivated and used in China and since 1949 when the People's Republic of China, was established, there have been hundreds of studies done on cannabis for food production and industrial uses. Cannabis continues to be cultivated in the traditional manner in many rural villages in China, especially in the Yunnan Province, where it can be found growing wild in abundance, even though the government began eradication efforts in the 1990's. Its fiber is processed into textiles, rope and paper, and its seeds are eaten as a longevity food in the Bama region of Guangxi province, and in Hong Kong beverages made of hemp seed are commonly sold as well as hemp based products made by companies such as Coca-Cola.[58] Xinjiang Uyghur Autonomous Region is also an area of widespread cannabis cultivation where it is processed into hashish, using traditional methods by the tribal Uyghurs of the region.[59] In the 19th Century, Yarkand was a major center of hashish production and distribution to British India, exported legally and under tariff, until 1934, when Chinese authorities cut off the legal trade. The first outright prohibition on cannabis came after American President Richard Nixon visited China in 1972 soon after declaring his "War on Drugs". In 1985, the People's Republic of China joined the Convention on Psychotropic Substances and identified marijuana as a Schedule One Drug with no medical benefit and having a highly addictive nature. Even so, cannabis is widely cultivated for its industrial uses and Chinese companies hold 309 of the 606 global patents currently registered with the World Intellectual Property Organization.[60] There are cannabis landraces growing throughout the country, the majority being textile cannabis, today called, hemp, and defined as containing less than 0.3% THC by weight.[61] Cannabis landraces containing medium to high levels of THC are common in the provinces of Yunnan and Xinjiang. Entheogenic use of cannabis in Xinjiang has been recorded since the Qing Dynasty and a detailed report was recorded by Russian explorer Shoqan Walikhanov in 1858.[62]

"Arms, though they be beautiful, are of ill omen, abominable to all created beings. They who have the Tao love not their use. The place of honour is on the right in wartime; so thinketh the man of distinction. Sharp weapons are ill-omened, unworthy of such a man; he useth them only in necessity. He valueth peace and ease, desireth not violence of victory. To desire victory is to desire the death of men; and to desire that is to fail to propitiate the people. At feasts, the left hand is the high seat; at funerals, the right. The second in command of the army leadeth the left wing, the commander-in-chief, the right wing; it is as if the battle were a rite of mourning! He that hath slain most men should weep for them most bitterly; so then the place of the victor is assigned to him with philosophical propriety." - Dao de Jing 31, trans Aliester Crowley

Centering

"Heaven and Earth are impartial; They see ten thousand things as they are. The wise are impartial; they see people as they are. The space between heaven and earth is like a bellows, the shape changes but not the form, the more it moves, the more it yields. More words count less. Hold fast to the center." – Dao de Ching Ch. 5 trans. Feng, English, and Lippe

The purpose of centering is to bring all your energy to a central point and focus, the Dan-t'ien, the field of the elixir.

- *Stand with your feet spread shoulder's width apart and your knees slightly flexed.*
- *Sink down into your stance, finding your center of gravity, located in the lower center of your abdomen, the "lower dantien", which is the center of gravity of the body, about two inches below the navel. Focus all of your attention there.*
- *Relax your whole body – muscles, nerves, and internal organs. Regulate your breathing, making it deep, long, and soft and calming your mind.*
- *Place all your attention in the lower dantien. This will help accumulate and root the vital qi energy. Where your mind and intention are, there will be your qi, by focusing on the dantien, you are gathering energy in this natural reservoir.*
- *Feel the qi circulating freely through your body as you breath in and out.*

"The sage stays behind, thus he is ahead. He is detached, thus at one with all. Through selfless action, he attains fulfillment." Dao de Ching Ch. 7 trans. Gia-fu Feng and Jane English

"Filling up is not as good as stopping when full. Grind an axe after it is sharp and it will no longer protect. If gold and jewels fill the hall no one can protect it. When wealth and honours lead to arrogancy, this brings about their own misfortune. When the work is done and one's name is becoming distinguished, to withdraw into obscurity is the way of Heaven." Dao de Jing Ch. 9

"The Yellow Court stands for the center, which in Taoist Yoga often means the center of the body, but also means the metaphysical center of equipoise, the state of mind before emotions and feelings emerge."[63]

Legend has it that the great Daoist master Loatsu wrote the Doa de Jing for his pupil Yin-his. Master Yin-his developed from the Dao de Jing "The Secret of the Golden Flower".[64]

"If there is time in the morning, one may sit during the burning of an incense stick; that is the best." – Secret of the Golden Flower, trans. Richard Wilhelm Ch. 4

The Heavenly Heart

"*Naturalness is called the Way [Tao]. The Way [Tao] has no name or form; it is just the essence [Hsing], just the primal spirit. Essence and life are invisible, so they are associated with sky and light. Sky and light are invisible, so they are associated with the two eyes... First establish a firm foothold in daily activities within society. Only then can you cultivate reality and understand essence [Hsing]... The whole work of turning the light around uses the method of reversal. The beauties of the highest heavens and the marvels of the sublimest realms are all within the heart: this is where the perfectly open and aware spirit concentrates. Confucians call it the open center, Buddhists call it the pedestal of awareness, Taoists call it the ancestral earth, the yellow court, the mysterious pass, the primal opening. The celestial mind is like a house; the light is the master of the house. Therefore, once you turn the light around, the energies throughout the body all rise. Just turn the light around; this is the unexcelled sublime truth. The light is easily stirred and hard to stabilize. When you have turned it around for a long time, the light crystallizes. This is the natural spiritual body, and it steadies the spirit above the nine skies. This is what is referred to in the Mind Seal Scripture as 'silently paying court' and 'soaring upward.' The golden flower is the same thing as the gold pill. The transmutations of spiritual illumination are all guided by mind.*" Secret of the Golden Flower Ch. 1, Trans. Thomas Cleary

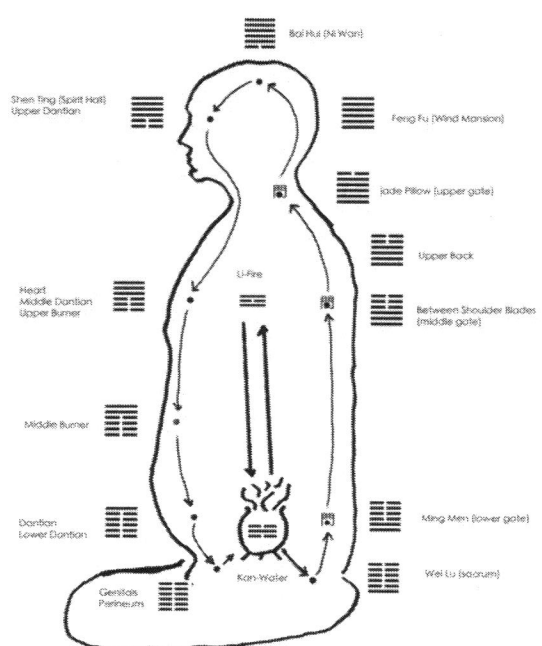

"*If thou wouldst complete the diamond body with no outflowing, diligently heat he roots of consciousness and life. Kindle light in the blessed country ever close at hand, and there hidden, let thy true self always dwell.*" - The Hui Ming Ching, The Book of Consciousness and Life, Ch. 1 trans. Richard Wilhelm

"Simply lie down, as you are lying down in your bed, on your back. Keep your eyes closed. When you breathe in, just visualize the great light entering from your head into your body, as if a sun has just risen close to your head, and going, going, going, deep, deep, and going out through your toes. And when you breathe out, visualize another thing: darkness entering through your toes, coming up, and going out through the head. Do slow, deep breathing, so you can visualize. Go very slowly." Osho - The Secret of Secrets, volume 2

"The great Tao is everywhere, on all sides. Everything derives from it; nothing is rejected by it. Through Tao everything exists yet it does not take possession. It provides for everything yet does not lay claim. Without motive it seems small. Being the source of everything it is great. Because it never claims greatness its greatness shines brightly." Dao de Jing Ch. 35 trans. FJ MacHovec

"The first realization is that the world is impermanent."[65]

"*The beginning of everything is the mother of everything. Truly to know the mother is to know her children, and truly to know the children is to turn back to the mother. The body comes to its ending but there is nothing to fear. Close the openings, shut the doors, and to the end of life nothing will trouble you. Open the openings, be busy with business, and to the end of life nothing can help you. Insight sees the insignificant. Strength knows how to yield. Use the way's light, return to its insight, and so keep from going too far. That's how to practice what's forever.* "Dao de Ching Ch. 52 trans. Ursula Le Guin

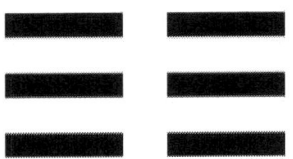

Interpretation:
Three broken lines are used to symbolize earth. The earth is soft and receptive, supporting and nourishing the body in life and in embracing the body in death, composting it into the elements from whence it came. The image is the vastness of our planet. The motivation is the receptive, to receive the seed and let it grow. It is the Receptive Field, the devoted, yielding Mother and Consort.

Right Resolve/Intent: Harm none and live in peace and simplicity expressing compassion.

"The first promise is I vow to develop my compassion in order to love and protect the life of people, animals and plants. The second promise is I vow to develop understanding in order to be able to love and to live in harmony with people, animals and plants. So, the two promises are compassion, or love, and understanding. They are the essence of the Buddha's teaching."[66]

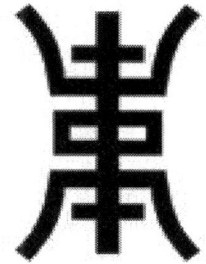

Yin and Yang

"All the myriad of things carry Yin on their backs and hold Yang in their embrace, deriving their vital harmony from the proper blending of the two vital breaths."
Dao de Jing Ch. 42 trans Michael LaFargue

In the beginning the primal mists swirled together rising from the absolute, separating into the binary forces of yin and yang, propelling and attracting, pulsing outward and inward, uniting the inner and the outer. There are two trigrams that are the parents, the mother and father, of all the other trigrams. Qian ☰, Heaven is made of three Yang solid lines symbolizing pure Yang. Kun ☷, Earth is made of three broken lines, symbolizing pure Yin. Qian and Kun joined and gave birth to the other trigrams. Yin is reflected in the agents, phases, elements or cardinal directions of Great Yin, the first of the elements, Water, the North and winter. Yin is also reflected in the Minor Yin, Metal, the West and autumn. The Great Yang is Fire, the South and summer. The Minor Yang is Wood, the East and Spring. The balance of Yin and Yang is represented by the central agent Soil.

These qualities and interactions of the yin and yang are reflected in human consciousness. There is the body consciousness that responds instinctively and reacts emotionally to impressions received from the outside world through the senses and is bound by the physical and mechanical laws of physics. There is also a spirit, or psychic consciousness that responds intellectually and imaginatively to impressions received from subtle realms of consciousness and is bound by the abstract laws of quantum physics and mysticism.[67]

Within any given circuit of Qi, it divides into the binary polarities of yin and yang. Yin represents the moon, dark, the shadow, the curved, the soft and yielding, the potential, the receptive, the underworld, dreams, the subconscious, contraction, and stillness. It is the realm of spirits, hungry ghosts, demons and nature spirits. Yang is the sun, light, the straight line, hard, pushing and driving, the kinetic force of action, aggression, force, expansion, and movement. It is the realm of the gods, fairies, immortals, and higher spirits. Yin and Yang are opposites and at the same time compliments, they are in accord and discord, they are seen in the light that creates the shadow and in the water that extinguishes the flame, they are the heavens and the earth, the father and the mother, and their union creates people that stand and mediate between heaven and earth. Seeded by stardust from the heavens to inseminate and fertilize the womb of the earth from which these clay bodies were born and are nourished while enlivened and sustained by the breath of the heavens. We honor and commune with them both through ritual, music, and incense.[68] Every person and situation are comprised of interactions of yin and yang. Yin and yang are opposites and cannot exist without each other, yin is contained within yang and yang within yin, so each has the potential to become the other.

All suffering and misfortune are the result of excess or deficiency of yin or yang and can be adjusted accordingly.[69] Ailments, calamities and discord caused by an excess or deficiency of yin or yang in one of their expressions and are often anthropomorphized as demons and malevolent spirits which are exorcised or banished by restoring the balance of yin and yang.[70] Through the binary of yin and yang, the yin within the yang can expand until the yang becomes yin and also the same is true of the yang within the yin. Energy cannot be created or destroyed according to the Law of Conservation of Energy, energy can only be transformed or transferred from one form to another. Energy and matter being interchangeable, the energies within matter can be tapped into through changing the vibrations of matter through ritual practices.[71] The shaman acts as a transformer of the energies of heaven and earth to channel them into the physical realm of human experience. In folk religions in China, demons have traditionally seen as the cause of illness and suffering by possessing and poisoning an individual or space. Viruses, disease and physical ailments were seen as inner demons to be exorcised by a shaman and replaced with an inner god.[72]

The binary system of the yin and yang is also reflected in the body's endocannabinoid system. Yin is the parasympathetic nervous system and yang is the sympathetic nervous system. The endocannabinoid system, like the Qi, is the mediator between the two. The endocannabinoid system maintains the body's state of homeostasis through retrograde signaling of neurons, using an on-off binary signal transmitted through neural pathways by special neurotransmitters called endocannabinoids, from the sending neuron to CB1 or CB2 receptors on the receiving neuron. This signaling process instructs organs, cells or systems to orchestrate different functions in the body to return to homeostasis, the balance of yin and yang. When the body is attacked by a demon such as a virus or bacteria, the body naturally responds by generating heat to ward of the invading energy in the form of a fever. Once the demon has been exorcised with fire, the endocannabinoid system signals the body to cool down and restore homeostasis. These cannabinoid receptors are the most abundant cell receptors in the body. As there are two cannabinoid receptors, there are also two endocannabinoids that are naturally produced by the body, the fatty acid neurotransmitter anandamide, which is also found in chocolate, and 2-arachidonoylglycerol, which is also found in human breast milk. And there are two types of cannabinoids as well, endocannabinoids produced in the body and Phyto-cannabinoids that occur exclusively in the cannabis plant. There have been over one hundred different Phyto-cannabinoids identified that are concentrated in the trichomes that cover the flowers and leaves of the cannabis plant, each with its own unique qualities, benefits, along with therapeutic and healing applications. And of course, the cannabis plant expresses itself bisexually having both male and female plants.

Most Common Cannabinols:
THC (Tetrahydrocannabinol)
THCA (Tetrahydrocannbinolic acid)
THCV (Tetrahydrocannabivarin)
CBN (Cannabinol)
CBD (Cannabidiol)
CBDA (Cannabidiolic Acid)
CBG (Cannabigerol)
CBC (Cannabichromene)
CBL (Cannabicyclol)

"Recognize the male - the yang, guard the female - the yin. Be a valley under Heaven. Be a valley under Heaven and the constant virtue will not fade away. One will become like a little child again. Recognize the white - the yang, guard the black - the yin. Be a model under Heaven. Be a model under Heaven and the constant virtue will not fade away. One will return to the infinite. Recognize the glory, guard the disgrace. Be a valley under Heaven. Be the valley under Heaven and return again to the uncarved block. When the block is carved up it is transformed into useful wares. The sage will use them with equal heart. Therefore the great law will not crumble."
-Dao de Jing Ch 28 trans. Chao-Hsiu Chen

"The interaction of yin and yang is called the Dao, and the resulting creative process is called change." - I Ching

"What you would shorten. you first should lengthen. What you would weaken you first should strengthen. What you would topple you first should raise. What you would take you first should give. This is called hiding the light, the weak conquering the strong. Fish can't survive out of the depths and a state's greatest weapon isn't meant to be shown." Dao de Jing 36 trans. Red Pine

Mago, Mother Goddess of Korea

"The story of Mago commences with the music of the stars, of the universe. When this heavenly music came into optimal harmony... Mago birthed Herself and is the strong, wise Mother Goddess whose name means both Goddess and Grandmother... Mago births her daughters by parthenogenesis and her two daughters birth both male and female children until there are 3000 children living in Mago's paradise... A life-sized goddess statue was unearthed in an ancient site in the northeastern region of China which dates from 4,700 to 2,900 BCE... Worship of Mago dates back to the Stone Age... During the emergence of Confucianism Goddess worship was considered to be primitive and only the practice of the uneducated and simple minded. At this time, Ma Go 'transformed' to Mountain Goddess as Grandmother spirit of the Ancestor."[73]

In China Magu is one of the Immortals, but in Korean mythology, she holds a much higher place of honour. She is called Ma Go or Mago, Nogo or Nogu, and is the Grandmother of all humankind and her two daughters, Gung-Hee and So-Hee gave birth to the four races of humans. Her counterpart in Chinese mythology is the Queen Mother of the West, in Japan Amaterasu, and Mazu in Taiwan.[74] The story is told of how at first all humans resided together in Mago Castle or Stronghold, but they became intoxicated by the wine of the fruit of paradise and were expelled from the castle and its gates closed to them. This has interesting parallels to the tales of the Queen Mother of the West's peaches of immortality and Magu's peaches of immortality, her mushrooms of immortality and her cannabis wine of immortality. Not only is Mago revered as the creatrix and great mother, she is also associated with dragons. The Korean dragons were believed to be creatures of water, capable of bringing rain and steering the courses of rivers and streams and for the shaman, the dragon holds the secret of travelling between different dimensions.

The principal text of Magoism is the Budoji, or the Epic of the Emblem City. Magoism was a cultural system that emphasised the primacy of female power and intelligence in maintaining equilibrium, equating the creative force of culture to the great goddess Mago from which they derived and is the edifice upon which all later East Asian religions and cultures were built upon[75] beginning with Neolithic Shamanism and continuing to the present day. There are three realms of Magos rule, the Former Heaven, Mago's World and Latter Heaven, which also correspond to the three realms of human consciousness, the archetypal, conscious and subconscious and the three shamanistic realms of the heavens, middle (mortal) world and underworld.

The original stronghold, the Mago Stronghold was a paradisiacal place of sonic equilibrium where all were aware of their connection to one another. Mago Stronghold was located on the highest mountain that sits at the epicenter of the earth, the home, womb and tomb or the earth herself. It was the primordial home where balance was maintained between the heavens, earth and underworld through music. It was Mago herself. Interestingly enough, the highest mountain on earth is Mount Everest, located on the Tibetan Plateau, the probable origin of cannabis on the planet. From Mago Stronghold the four shaman daughters of Mago left the Mago Stronghold each going out in one of the four directions, the eldest pledging that she would remind all of the people that would come after them of their common origin from the great mother and the interconnected tapestry that we have woven together. Through pollen analysis and archeological subfossil seed evidence, the probable origin of cannabis as a plant species was on the northeastern Tibetan Plateau in the vicinity of Qinghai Lake and Baishiya Karst Cave. There has been found at Baishiya Cave the archaeological remains of a 160,000-year-old hominoid, classified as a Denisovan, a close relative of the Neanderthal, and were once believed to have only lived in the in the Altai Mountains of Siberia. Comparisons of the Denisovan, Neanderthal, and modern human genomes have revealed evidence for a complex web of interbreeding among these lineages. From there it is hypothesized that cannabis spread west to Europe, south to India and Northern Pakistan, Afghanistan, Tajikistan, Uzbekistan and the Western Shan Mountains, then east to the mountainous regions of Central and Western China and the adjutant lowlands, appearing in Japan 10,000 BC. From these three primary areas cannabis has spread across the globe. The rise and spread of civilization is woven with the fabric of hemp and colored with the brilliant colors of the fragrant and sticky flowers of Ma.

Mago is the creator goddess in ancient Korean mythology, central to the practice of Muism and Shindoism, Korean Shamanism. Mago manifests herself as many, encompassing the earth's ecosystem and her path is the gynocentric way of the great goddess.[76] The Giant Goddess Grandmother Mago created all the geological formations on earth mountains, crags, rivers, valleys, plains, plateaus and wetlands, using mud, rocks, and her own urine and excrement.[77] She carried mud in her hemp skirt to create the mountains and islands.[78] Mago came from the seven jeweled serpent constellation (the Korean designation of the Big Dipper) and formed the mountains and rivers of the earth. There are many visual manifestations of Mago in Korea, with mountains, caves, villages, rocks and strongholds named after her.

"Giving birth and nourishing, bearing yet not possessing, working yet not taking credit, leading yet not dominating, this is the primal virtue." Dao de Ching Ch. 10 trans Gia-fu Feng and Jane English

Mago danced to the cosmic vibrations of the music of Pal-ryeo and from her dance twin daughters were born, Gunghui and Sohui, manifestations of space and time, together they laid the harmonic foundations of all things. From the one came two and from the two came the many. She is the one and the many and inseparable from her many manifestations, the individual and the collective. From this primordial triad were born two sets of twin daughters to both Gunghui and Sohui. These eight daughters taught the arts and sciences of shamanism to the women that birthed the four races and the eight clans.[79] They sit at spindles spinning thread from the fibers of cannabis and singing the songs of the movements of the planets whirling around the Spindle of Necessity at the center.

The Korean Shaman, called mudang, or mu, derives from Chinese wu, shaman. The mu or mudang originated from the Ancient Holy Mother Goddess of the Mountain where cannabis plants thrived along the riverbanks. The Holy Mother of the Mountain became a human being, the Princess Sungmo, and married the Pobu Hwasang, giving birth to eight girls, the first mudang, and divine investiture of the mu is passed down through the female lineage. The princess followed the Dao and granted welfare to her people.[80] The mu is magician, healer, mystic and poet who enters in and out of trance states at will and navigates the multiverses of consciousness. At the Temple of Mago in Korea, the mudang used ceremonial fans made of cannabis paper in their kut ceremonies to brush away shadows and waft in blessings. In one creation myth, Changsega, enacted in some Korean shamanist rituals, Mireuk, or the Buddha Maitreya, gathered arrowroot vines to weave hemp and make for himself the monk's robe jangsam.[81]

In Korea Mago, is the goddess of equilibrium, the originator who completes and maintains the self-equilibrating power of the universe. She is the macrocosmic endocannabinoid system of the cosmos reflected in the microcosmic human endocannabinoid system and supported and enhanced by the cannabis plant. She is the ancestor of all races, the originator, and takes care of everything on earth through the equilibrium of cosmic the musical sound vibration called the 'Eight Female Musical Pitches' or tones.[82] These are cosmic, or vibratory, reflections

> **Functions and Systems regulated by the endocannabinoid system:**
> *Memory*
> *Hippocampal neurogenesis*
> *Appetite and hunger*
> *Energy balance and metabolism*
> *Stress response*
> *Social behavior, and anxiety*
> *Immune function*
> *Female reproduction*
> *Embryonic development*
> *Central Nervous System Feedback*
> *Analgesia*
> *Thermoregulation*

of the Eight Trigrams of Daoist cosmology and manifested physically as the movement of the eight planets, and as the Eight Mudangs, or Shamans, that were dispatched to the eight provinces of Korea and then the eight islands, and the Eight Female Immortals. As the Mother Goddess, it is she who maintains the equilibrium of the heavens, the cosmos, and the earth. Magu, the Cannabis Maiden, is contained within each living being and manifests herself in the functioning of the endocannabinoid system. Just as Ma is the self-regulating homeostasis system of the universe, so too is the endocannabinoid system the self-regulating system of homeostasis in the human body. In keeping with the hermetic maxim of "As above, so below", just as the earth is a self-regulating energy system, so too is the human body and its self-regulating system is called the endocannabinoid system. The endocannabinoid system exists in all vertebrate species and may have begun evolving as early as 600 million years ago.

> **Dosoju** is an herbal liquor made of a blend of various medicinal herbs, placed into a triangular hemp bag and hung deep inside a well on New Year's Eve. The bag was then taken out of the well on New Year's morning and put into liquor to brew. It is believed to expel evil forces and help maintain a happy and long life if consumed on the Lunar New Year's Day facing east, and people would be able to free themselves from impure energy and diseases. People began to make their own liquor in their homes, introducing new herbs and spices, creating the medicinal liquors culture in Korea.[1] The gut or kut, the shamanistic ritual of the Mu, is a theatrical ritual performance often involving rhythmic movements, songs, oracles, prayers, offerings and sacrifices done in a three-fold pattern. The communion between ancestors or gods and men takes place through a cup of purified wine, called bokjan or "cup of blessings" and the purification of the body is performed through burning cannabis paper.

"The religion of the ancient world were all based on nature worship... They recognized that all the functions of nature were reproduced in miniature in the human body... every function in nature, was represented by a corresponding center, pole, or activity within the human body." [83]

The endocannabinoid system is the largest receptor system in the human body, a set of signaling molecules in the central and peripheral nervous system that helps regulate processes of the body such as appetite, pain, mood, and memory. A signaling molecule is a chemical that passes information from cell to cell. In the endocannabinoid system, these molecules are primarily signaling lipids called endocannabinoids, fatty molecules that bind to receptor proteins to trigger a response. The chemical composition of endocannabinoids and the responses they elicit are mimicked closely by the cannabinoids contained in cannabis.[84]

There are three components to the endocannabinoid system: endocannabinoids, cannabinoid receptors, and enzymes. The system exemplifies the osteopathic principle that the body possesses self-regulatory mechanisms that are self-healing in nature. The two cannabinoid receptors, CB1 and CB2, are involved in the regulation of appetite, immune system functions and pain management. Responses in the endocannabinoid system regulate many of the body's processes, including the sensation of pain, appetite, mood, memory, learning movement skills, and the regulation of the nervous system. The enzymes synthesize and degrade the endocannabinoids. Endocannabinoids possess immune-modulatory functions are key regulators of food intake, gastrointestinal function, energy storage in the body, energy processing by the liver and the skeletal muscle, are deeply involved in pain processing, regulate both male and female reproduction, and differentially affect cell fate in healthy and cancer cells by regulating differentiation, proliferation and apoptosis. The endocannabinoid system interacts with many different systems and functions of the body, its general role is to maintain homeostasis, or balance. A person with a fully functioning endocannabinoid system would, in theory, have no pain, a healthy appetite with good digestion, and normal mental function. Hence, Magu bestows longevity.

Dysregulation of the endocannabinoid system underlies several neurological, immune and metabolic disorders. Endocannabinoid deficiency may account for many diseases difficult to diagnose and treat, where there are more than one occurring in the same patient at the same time, and are normal sensations are magnified to the point of being perceived as painful.[85] For some Clinical endocannabinoid deficiency (CECD) related conditions such as fibromyalgia, migraine, and irritable bowel syndrome, it appears that introducing Phyto cannabinoids may help treat the body's deficiency, or lack of endocannabinoids. Inflammation is part of the immune system's natural response to injury, however when this inflammation response is out of balance it can create unnecessary pain as well as additional damage to the body. Activating both CB1 and CB2 receptors can help alleviate inflammation. Both THC and CBD are anti-inflammatory and anti-spasmodic.[86] Cannabis is a medicine that can dispel many of these demons of disease and replace them with the smiling gods of the body by increasing or reducing the yin or yang as needed to regain homeostasis.

CECD-related conditions:
Fibromyalgia
Migraine
Irritable Bowel Syndrome
Depression
Neuralgia
Interstitial Cystitis
Neuropathic Pain Conditions
Cancer
Inflammatory Diseases
Arthritis
Myofascial Pain
Crohn's Disease
Ulcerative Colitis
Allergic Inflammation
Neurological Diseases
Parkinson Disease
Multiple Sclerosis
Huntington Disease
Amyotrophic Lateral Sclerosis
Seizure Disorders/Epilepsy

"All mater is made of energy, and energy systems can harmonize (tune-up). When you hug or kiss someone, your two energy fields (auras) are joined into a single field. Likewise, when you sit at family diner, the family can harmonize into a single energy field… The earth is a self-regulating energy system."[87]

"By reaching utmost receptivity and keeping steadfast stability, I, as myriads come forth in profusion, contemplate their circulation. All multiply in fruitful growth, then bend homeward to their root. This going home call equilibrium; Equilibrium, returning life; Returning life, call natural order; To know this order, inner vision. Not to know it is delusion. Delusion will produce misfortune. Knowing order means acceptance; Acceptance, magnanimity; Magnanimity, totality; Totality, accord with heaven; Accord with heaven, with the Way; With the Way, long-lasting life; The self-submerged will not miscarry." Dao de Jing Ch 16 trans. Moss Roberts

Korean Cannabis Culture

The Ye-Maek who inhabited Korea's east coast at the beginning of the last millennium, cultivated hemp and silkworms evidenced by Painted Basket Tomb near Pyongyang which contained hemp and silk textiles. Korean Buddhist culture began to develop in Korea around 372 BCE and cannabis was important for the purposes of creating artwork and prayer scrolls. The Korean art of papermaking began around 150 BCE and utilized hemp scraps and fibers. These earliest forms of paper, called maji, derived from the Chinese Ma, cannabis, making the paper or canvas auspicious in its own right. From China, advanced methods of making paper from the fibres of cannabis moved to Korea in the 2nd Century AD and then to Japan in 610 AD according to the "Chronicle of Japan".[88] When papermaking arrived from China it was embraced and evolved, and exported to neighboring nations such as Japan. From 105 CE and for centuries to follow, cannabis was the main plant used to make paper, often mixed with other materials like mulberry bark, bamboo, silk, rags and fishing nets. The movable type was invented in China first using movable wooden blocks before 200 CE, the oldest remaining examples being a printed silk fragment from 220 CE, two copies of the Dharani Sutra, one printed on hemp paper dated to 650 CE in China and another in Korea dated to 704 CE printed on mulberry paper, and the Dimond Sutra at the British Museum dated to 868 CE. Movable type using ceramic was invented in 1040 CE in China and then by 1115 CE Metal type was being used, primarily bronze. This too was imported to Korea where it was further developed and refined. By 1234 CE books were being published using movable metal type in Korea and the earliest printed book in existence is the Korean Jikji, printed in Korea in 1377, 78 years before Gutenberg Bible was printed in 1454 by Johannes Gutenberg in Europe. It was not just paper that cannabis was used for, it was used for cloth, rope, thread, food, fuel, animal fodder and many other uses. In Medieval times, Korean warriors used cannabis fabric for their armour, emblazoned with magical talismans to protect and strengthen them, and even today clothes made of cannabis fabric are worn at funerals.

The Democratic Republic of Korea, commonly known as North Korea, may be one of the most closed and secretive countries in the world today. The Korean Peninsula has been inhabited for over 500,000 years, archaeological remains of pottery date from around 8,000 BCE, and agriculture began in around 6,000 BCE. Cannabis is believed to have been brought to Japan via Korea, and archaeological evidence of cannabis in Japan dates back as far as 4,000 BCE.

Impressions in pottery made with hemp cord date as far back as 5,000 BCE in the central Korean region and hemp thread strung through a needle, from the Chulmun (Jeulmun) Period of 4,000-2,000 BCE, was found in northern Korea. An active hemp industry continued throughout ancient times up to the very recent past maintaining an active hemp trade with Japan until the end of World War II. North Korea's first president Kim Il-Sung actively implemented the growing of cannabis, including inter-cropping of hemp with beans and potatoes, in order to increase productivity as a cold-tolerant crop in mountainous terrains with short growing seasons, established vegetable oil factories in every county to press oil from hemp seed, opened a textile mill in each county to process hemp fiber, and mandated each county to cultivate at least 300-400 hectares of hemp and flax. Hemp is planted along railroad tracks throughout North Korea because its long roots help stabilize the ground alongside the tracks, and it is reported to grow both wild and cultivated in gardens throughout the country. North Korea is still one of the world's largest producers of hemp, with hubs of industry located in Ryanggang, South & North Hamgyong and North Pyongan, and in 2008, South Korea's Andong Hemp Textile Company and North Korea's Saebyol General Trading Company merged to become Pyongyang Andong Hemp Textiles, the first north-south joint business venture.[89]

> An offering to the ancestors, Songpyeon, is made by making rice flour dough with hot water, forming it into a crescent shape, and stuffing it with crushed hemp leaves, acorn and pine bark. A pine needle can be placed inside the songpyeon before steaming it. The rice cakes are then placed inside an earthenware steamer over a bed of pine needles and steamed. It was believed that if a woman picked an undercooked cake to eat, she would have a girl and a well-cooked cake indicated that the baby would be a boy. If a pine needle inside the songpyeon, then if the bite was from the part where the head of the needle was, the baby would be a girl. If the first bite was at the pointed part of a needle, the baby would be a boy.

Drug law in North Korea is generally extremely strict, and North Korea is the Single Convention against Narcotic Drugs and the Convention on Psychotropic Substances, although plant-based drugs such as cannabis and opium do not have the same approbation reserved for synthetic, highly-addictive drugs such as methamphetamine and heroin. North Korea lies around the 40th parallel where cannabinoid production of THC would naturally occur in cannabis plants even if grown for fiber production. The modern designations of hemp and marijuana based upon THC content are modern legal fictions and social constructs based upon lies and propaganda and were unknown prior to the late 20th century and the War on Drugs. In the 1950's American soldiers stationed around the demilitarized zone (DMZ) between North and South Korea reportedly picked wild-growing cannabis to help them relax and unwind. Reports from visitors to North Korea indicate that cannabis use is not only socially acceptable, but so widespread that it is more common and prevalent than tobacco use. Cannabis is known in North Korea as *ip tambae*, leaf tobacco, or *yoksam*, or the special plant.[90] Although Rason's indoor market has sellers with stalls containing cannabis for sale, and smoking cannabis is common in tourist-friendly eateries, recreational use of cannabis is illegal in North Korea.[91]

> At death, a ritual called Gwangmeori ssitgimgut, or coffin head cleansing ritual, is performed to purify the deceased before their entry into the underworld. Hemp cords are tied around the coffin and knotted. The knots represent the grievances that the deceased acquired through their lifetime. The knots are untied, clearing away the past grievances and a procession carrying the coffin to its resting place, ending with festive song and dance to send them off to the underworld is held.

Magoism was the primordial matrix from which Shamanism, Daoism, Buddhism, and Confucianism emerged and has survived under the name of the Dao and the practices of the shamans, mostly female, in Korea.[92] Buddhism, Confucianism, Shamanism and their synchronistic mix have all been prominent in Korea since early history. Like China, Korean mythology and folklore speak of a Golden Age also. The Third Magoist State was comprised of autonomous self-governing matriarchal clan communities and tribal communities.[93] This gynocentric culture was led and guided by clan shamans and tribal elders. Once thing that should be kept in mind when looking back in time to ancient cultures, especially as far back as Neolithic and Paleolithic cultures, that the national and ethnic regional distinctions that we have now irrelevant and cultures, territory and identity were determined by tribe, clan and trade rather than national identity or borders.

Korean shamanism is known as Muism, from mu, shaman. It is also sometimes called Sindo or Singyo, the "Way of the Gods". Korean mu, or shaman is synonymous with Chinese wu, which defines priests and shamans, both male and female. In contemporary Korean language the shaman-priestess is known as a mudang and they act as intermediary between the spirits or gods, and the human plain, through "gut" rituals, seeking to resolve problems in the patterns of development of human life. The religious ceremonies of the Koreans follow the cycle of agriculture and are carried out through singing, dancing, and the drinking of wine that bring the participants to a state of ecstasy in which it is believed they experience direct communion with the Gods and spirits being worshipped.[94] Koreans practice an "instrumentalist" approach to religious life, subscribing to any religion so long as it proves beneficial to their goals here and now. Christianity came to Korea in the 18th century and now, South Korea has some of the biggest churches in the world, ranks as the second most Christian country in Asia after the Philippines, and produces the second largest number of Christian missionaries in the world, next only to the United States, winning support from the lower classes for its egalitarian doctrine and significant support from the U.S. Army Military Government in Korea (USAMGIK) in the three-year interim period following independence (1945-48) and the First Republic (1948-1960) led by President Rhee Syngman who publicly vowed to rule South Korea as a Christian nation.[95]

Buddhism has been a prominent part of Korea's cultural identity and all three of the Buddhist schools have Korean traditions, although the predominant one has been Mahayana. Theravada, or Teaching of the Elders, is the earliest Buddhist tradition and observes the only complete Buddhist canon surviving in a classical Indian language. It is practiced in Thailand, Burma, Sri Lanka, Cambodia, Myanmar, Nepal, Laos, Bangladesh, parts of Vietnam and by the Vipassana movement in the West. Tantric Theravada, or Borān kammaṭṭhāna, is practiced in Thailand, Cambodia and Laos and preserves the ancient teaching of internal and external alchemy, magic, mantra and meditation. It focuses upon ethics, logic and austerity and is the most fundamental of the vehicles. The goal is personal liberation through the practice of meditation to cultivate wisdom, combined with vows and good deeds to cultivate merit. It is called the lesser vehicle because it is a vehicle that only carries one passenger.

"Like many people before and since, the Buddha recognized the medicinal value of cannabis and he recommended it as a cure for rheumatism (aṅgavāta). The patient should be placed, he said, in a small room filled with steam from a tub of boiling water and cannabis leaves (bhaṅgodaka), and inhale the steam and rub it on the limbs. There were four kinds of `sweating treatment' (sambhāraseda); using steam made from water with certain herbs it, steam made from water with cannabis in it, `great sweating' and udakakottaka, which may have meant soaking in a tub of hot water."[96]

Mahayana, or the Great Vehicle, is practiced in China, Indonesia, Vietnam, Korea, Tibet, and Japan with the central doctrine emptiness or voidness, the middle way. It focuses upon the path of the bodhisattva. Interpretations of Mahayana Buddhism include, Chinese, Korean, Japanese and Vietnamese Buddhism, Zen, Chan, Pure Land, Vinaya and Tiantai. It focuses upon others and having an open and compassionate heart. It is called the greater vehicle, because the merits and wisdom gained through meditation, vows and good deeds are given freely to all beings for their enlightenment.

Vajrayana, Diamond or Thunderbolt Vehicle, known as Tantric Buddhism, is largely practiced in Tibet, Bhutan and the Himalayan region as well as in Mongolia and the Russian republic of Kalmykia. It is also practiced as Mìjiao, Hànmì or Tángmì in Chinese traditions, Shingon Buddhism, Shugendō and Tendai in Japan and Milgyo in Korea. It utilizes practices that make use of mantras, dharanis, mudras, mandalas and the visualization of deities and Buddhas. Vajrayana is the path of the fruit; the practitioner takes his or her innate Buddha-nature as the means of practice. The thunderbolt vehicle is the path of accelerated growth. It is a secretive vehicle that is passed through initiation and utilizes rituals, meditation, magical practices, and employed entheogenic plants such as ephedra, cannabis, Syrian rue, acacia, various mushrooms and fungi, datura, opium, camphor and other plants. Vajrayana Buddhism is closely associated with Tantric Yoga and Shivaism, which both incorporate cannabis referred to variously as amrita, soma, rasa, charas, ganja, bhang and nectar in various contexts.

Immortal Couple Fuxi and Nuwa

Fuxi was the Shaman King, who with his sister, Shaman Queen Nuwa, created civilization in the Neolithic Period approximately 10,00 – 2,100 BCE. Fuxi was the first of the three Celestial Emperors of China, whose portraits hang on the walls of almost every Traditional Chinese Medical School and hospital in China. It is possible that the Sovereigns or Emperors and their consorts were not individuals but mythological representations of the male and female elders and shamans of the Paleolithic and Neolithic eras.[97] We know from archaeological evidence that the area around Beijing has been inhabited by humanoids since at least 230,000 BCE from the fossil remains of the "Peking Man". These primordial fathers were known for their compassion, nurturing, teaching, guidance, and generosity. All of the primordial "Emperors" bore their mother's clan name, indicating that their reigns were back in the time of the matrilineal tribal clans.[98] These vertical manifestations of Heaven called the Three Sovereign Augusts Ones, or Emperors: Fuxi, Shennong and Haungdi, representing the three realms of potency: yang, the heavens, yin, the underworld, and the space between, the human experience. They were the archetypes of the virtuous ruler, who was a servant and parent, first and foremost, seeking the wellbeing of their people, their children, before their own needs and desires. There was an even earlier chthonic triad of Augusts also composed of Zhurong, 祝融, dragon god of fire; Gonggong, 共工, dragon god of water; and Suiren, 燧人, bringer of fire from heaven. There was a hierarchy of gods of medicine in ancient China. P'an Ku, wearing his apron of dried cannabis leaves was the first of the gods of Traditional Chinese Medicine. Fuxi, Shennong, and Huangti were the ancestral triad of medicine-gods, and Yao Wang was the King of Medicine. Traditional Chinese Medicine (TMC) begins from the premise that humans and nature are intimately bound together and that people occupy the space between heaven and earth and must bring their inner world into harmony with the outer world around them. Cannabis has been used in TMC from the time of the first legendary Chinese pharmacopoeia around 2737 BCE to modern Chinese Medical College pharmacopoeias as an antiseptic, aphrodisiac, emollient, sedative, asthma agent, tonic, purgative, prophylactic agent and treatment for gout, rheumatism, malaria, nausea, anaesthetic mixtures, headaches, coughs, nervousness, senility, constipation, female ailments.[99] Traditional Chinese Medicine classifies cannabis as sweet neutral character with an affinity with the spleen, stomach and colon, the stem is hydrating with diuretic effects, the oil sooths an inflamed throat, the male flowers are good for bowel and female ailments, the resin of the femal flowers effect the nervous system and are used for nervous disorders.

The "Celestial Emperor of the Heavens," Fuxi, represents the transition from nomadic hunter-gather to that of herding and domesticating animals in familial tribes, he was of the first cannabis matrix. "The Red Emperor of the Earth," Shennong, ushered in the second evolutionary wave of agriculture and further domestication of animals and building structures and villages, facilitated by domestication of cannabis and other crops. The "Yellow Emperor," Huangti, of the middle land between heaven and earth, where people live, ushered in the third wave building of cities and civilization, again aided by cannabis for rope and fiber, cloth for clothing shelter and utility, seed for food, and flower for medicine and offering to the spirits.

The first great sovereign the Celestial, Great Bright One, Emperor Fu Hsi, Paoxi, Tai Hao, Bao Xi, Mi Xi or Fuxi, the bright shining one, was the founder of China's first dynasty. Born of Wujimu, the Eternal Ancient Unborn Mother who personifies the void and truth. After giving birth to herself, Wujimu then gave birth to Nuwa and Fuxi, the personifications of yin and yang.[100] Together with his twin sister and wife Nuwa, they created the first civilization and taught the people hunting with iron weapons, fishing with nets woven from cannabis, domestication of animals, cooking, painting and music. Fuix revealed the art of canji writing, the bagua trigrams, and wrote the first book: the Yijing (I-Ching). Archaeological artifacts such as the of Chinese Oracle Bones establish Chinese written language to have started well before 1200 BCE, artifacts from the Dawenkou culture in Shandong, dating to c. 2800–2500 BCE, contain written inscriptions and a site in Longshan, Shandong, has produced fragments of inscribed bones dating to 2500–1900 BCE, so if Fuxi introduced writing, he reigned before 2500 BC, possibly much earlier. Fuxi was known as the "original human," perhaps if so, he was the "Peking Man", and he was said to have been born in the lower-middle reaches of the Yellow River. He was often depicted with a garland or a garment of leaves, undoubtedly a nod to the male cannabis plant from which the finest fibers for weaving were gathered, other representations show him as a leaf-wreathed head growing out of a mountain or as a man clothed with animal skins. His totem animal was the tortoise, and the oracle bones that he used to divine the future and the mysteries of the Dao were of tortoise shell. An archaeological site in Northwestern China known as the Ch'i-chia Culture sites, contained oracle bones and cannabis remains dated to 2,000 BCE or earlier. Fuxi, it is told, was given the eight trigrams of the I-Ching and shown the twelve animals of the Chinese zodiac by a tortoise and he designed the original throwing sticks for the I Ching from cannabis stalks. His twin sister and wife, Nuwa, like Fuxi, had the body of a serpent and the face of a human. They lived during the later matriarchal period when "men knew only their mothers". As chthonic beings associated with the underworld, serpents and dragons, they represent the brain stem and primal instincts such as procreation, clothing and shelter to protect from the elements, nourishment and appeasing the spirits internal and external. Nuwa is the archetypical spirit of matriarchal age that prevailed across the central plains of China in ancient times.

"Confucius spent most of his life studying the practical instructions of the 'Book of Rites' and the delicate artistry of the 'Book of Odes.' It was only at a very advanced age that he undertook the study of the esoteric 'I Ching.' This pattern was not unusual. In China it is traditional that children and old men meet with the greatest success in the study of the 'Yi.'" This is not unconditionally true. Anyone who is willing to devote sincere attention to the study of the 'Yi' will meet with success. Witness Aleister Crowley, Richard Wilhelm and C.G. Jung. All took up the book between childhood and old age and attained many profound insights through it. The 'I Ching' is a subject of such wide comprehension that a hundred articles could hardly do justice to any one aspect of it. It resolves all questions of metaphysics, Magick and philosophy as well as such vital matters as who's to take the dog for a walk. It is all things to all people." [101]

"In the old times of King Fuxi's regime, he observed sky and the stars when he looks upwards, and researched the earth when he looks downwards, and watched the birds and beasts to see how they live in their environment. He took examples from nearby and far away, and then made 8 Yin Yang signs to simulate the rules of universe... After Fuxi died, Shennong rises. He made Plow and teach people how to raise crops and fishing. He invented money and market for the exchange of goods." I-Ching [102]

Nuwa is the great Mother Goddess capable of changing shapes at will and was beautiful woman above the waist with the form of a serpent below, representing her primal and chthonic nature, and possibly her origins amongst cave dwelling civilizations. She is also depicted with tiger legs with the tail of a snake, again invoking the tiger's den and the snakes lair that would be well known to cave dwellers. It was said of her that her beauty was so remarkable that no one could have created such beauty. When the sky and the earth were separated there were no people or animals so Nuwa began to form the animals and people so that she would not be alone. On the first day she created chickens, the second day she created dogs, the third day she created sheep, the fourth day she created pigs, the fifth day she created cows, the sixth day she created horses and on the seventh day she began creating people from yellow clay of the river banks, sculpting each one individually into the form of poppets and breathing upon them to infuse them with her Qi. After creating hundreds of figures, she became tired, so she dipped a hemp rope into the clay and then lifted it. The mud that dripped from the rope also became people. Nuwa fashioned the hemp rope into a whip that moved like a snake and again dipped it into the yellow mud then and lashed the long whip against the riverbank. Thousands of clay droplets sprayed into the air. As they landed, they too magically turned into more little humans. Some of the figures melted in the rain as Nüwa was waiting for them to dry, and in this way sickness and physical abnormalities came into existence. Once her task was complete Nuwa sat on the bank of the Yellow River and surrounded by her creations, her children, she sang with them, made musical instruments, taught them to dance and play. She taught them to conceive and care for children of their own and the humans multiplied. Thus Nuwa is revered as the patron of marriage, childbirth, fertility, children, and music, and the inventor of the reed pipe.

It is also told that the Black Dragon Gong Gong, a descendant of the Red Emperor and personification of the energies of water, was born in the Yangtze River and had the face of a human but the body of a snake and red hair. He kept records of all waters, traveled along their courses gave them names. Gong Gong was ashamed that he lost the fight with Zhurong, the red dragon god of the southern fire, to claim the throne of Heaven. In a fit of rage, he smashed his head against Buzhou Mountain, one of four pillars holding up the sky, greatly damaging it and causing the sky to tilt towards the northwest and the earth to shift to the southeast, releasing a deluge of floodwaters which caused great floods, fires and suffering. Nuwa gathered stones of five different colors from a riverbank and, with heaps of dried cannabis reeds, built a massive fire with which she melted the stones into a mortar-like substance. Using this five-colored mortar, the goddess the heavens with fluid stones of five colors, then cut off the legs of the giant turtle Ao and used them as the Four Pillars of Heaven and then burned cannabis plants and piled up their ashes to dam the floodwaters. For this deed, Nuwas is considered the savior of Chao, of the first people of China.

Nuwa and Fuxi with their intertwined serpent bodies, ruled over the primeval paradise as benevolent servants and parents to their children, the people of the earth. On Mt. Tai, the pair are revered as the Green Jade Mother and the Jade

Emperor, the Daoist Heavenly Duke who oversees all phenomenon upon the earth. But Nuwa is considered as a mother, or the first mother, as a savior, the musical goddess and the Jade Mother was the Taishan goddess that brought rain and fertility, wife and sister of the Jade Emperor, grandmother of Mt. Tai, the Goddess of the Azure Clouds.

"There are some biological oddities which link cannabis with humans, especially the females of our species. First, certain active compounds of marijuana have molecular resemblance to the female hormone estrogen. Possibly it is due to this aspect of cannabis' genetic make-up that some growers have reported success with fertilizing their plants with birth control pills or menstrual fluid, the use of which as a ritual fertilizer goes back to the matriarchal period. Of similar interest is that cannabis seeds contain rare gamma linoleic acid, found only in spirulina, two other rare seed oils, and human mother's milk. As the tribal people of the world have always shown an incredible intuition when it comes to right use of plants, it is interesting to note that the Sotho women of South Africa make a mealy pap from hempseed to wean their babies off breast milk." Chris Bennet, Marijuana and the Goddess, in Cannabis Culture 1998

"The all-surpassing medicine has three characteristics: ching (essence), ch'I (vital energy), and shen (spirit), which are difficult to grasp and are hidden… The elixir is called 'green dragon and white tiger'; the elixir is the nature of non-nature, the emptiness of non-emptiness." – The Jade Emperor, The Three Treasures of Immortality[103]

"What you don't see when you look is called the unobtrusive. What you don't hear when you listen is called the rarefied. What you don't get when you grasp is called the subtle. These three cannot be completely fathomed, so they merge into one; above is not bright, below is not dark. Continuous, unnamable, it returns again to nothing. This is called the stateless state, the image of no thing; this is called mental abstraction. When you face it you do not see its head, when you follow it you do not see its back. Hold the ancient Way so as to direct present existence: only when you can know the ancient can this be called the basic cycle of the Way." Dao de Jing 14 trans. Thomas Cleary

Cowherd Girls Weavers Festival

"One day a cowherder comes across some maidens bathing in lake. He takes the clothes of one of them. When the others fly up to sky clothed in feathers, this maiden is left behind. The cowherder marries her and eventually they have a child. The maiden contributes to the household by weaving [cannabis]. The child later finds the hidden cloak of feathers and the maiden puts it on and flies back to sky. The cowherd is sad without the maiden. One of cows, moved by master's sadness, has him slaughter her and he uses the cowhide to ascend to sky. The couple is reunited and are so happy that they forget to do their work. The King of Heaven decides that thereafter, they can only meet once a month. A magpie is entrusted to deliver this decree to the couple, but the magpie makes a mistake and tells them they can rejoin each other only once a year. So once a year, on the 7th day of the 7th lunar month (the annual feast of young girls), they reunite. On this day it is supposed to rain so that no one will see them (i.e.: their associated constellations) meeting in the sky".[104]

The Cowherder and Weaver Girl Story of the Circulation of Water and Fire:
On the east bank of the Heavenly River, we call the Milky Way, lived a weaver girl, daughter of the Jade Emperor of Heaven. She worked hard year in and year out, weaving colorful clothes from hemp and silk for the gods and goddesses and gossamer clouds and constellations like tapestries in the heavens. She was known as Li, also called Zhinu, Zhi Nu, Chih Nu, the goddess of spinners and weavers. She was the personification of the energetic meridian of the conception vessel, Ren Mai. One day the cowherder called Kan, who was the personification of the governing vessel meridian, Du Mai, came across a group of fairy maidens bathing in a lake and stole the clothes of one of them. When done bathing, the maidens clothed themselves in cloaks of feathers and flew back up to sky. Since her clothes were stolen and she no longer had her cloak of feathers, Li, was left behind. Kan came out from hiding and came to Li. The two fell in love and asked the Jade Emperor if they could marry. Since she lived all alone, the emperor took pity on her and allowed her to marry the cowherder and they remained on the west bank of the river. They lived happily together, and she wove for her household and the surrounding villages, however, she stopped weaving for the gods and goddesses after she was married, outraging her father the emperor. Before long Li and Kan had a child and when the child had grown into a toddler, the child found the hidden cloak of feathers. The maiden Li put on her feathered cloak and flew back to sky, leaving the Kan and their child behind and sad. One of cows, moved by her master's sadness, asked him to slaughter her and use her hide to ascend to sky, which he did. The couple was reunited and were so happy that

they forgot to do any work. Outraged once again, the emperor forced Kan the cowherder back across the river and decides that thereafter, they can only meet once a month. A magpie is entrusted to deliver this decree to the couple, but the magpie makes a mistake and tells them they can rejoin each other only once a year. So once a year, on the seventh day of the seventh lunar month, the annual feast of young girls, they reunite. On this day it is rains so that no one will see their constellations meeting in the sky. On the seventh day of the seventh month, magpies would suddenly become bald-headed because that day Kan and Li meet on the east bank of the river, and the magpies form a bridge for them to cross over. And for this reason, the down on their heads was worn out. The seventh day of the seventh month became the day of the cannabis harvest and also the time of Daoist seance banquets. [105]

"Plow and fertilize in January. In February, sow the female hemp's seeds, and on a rainy day in May sow the male hemp's seeds. Then, harvest the hemp and spin it into cloth in October... Sowing seeds ten days before the summer solstice is called late seeding. Late sown hemp will not grow vigorously, and its fiber will be too thin and light to spin into yarn." - Si Min Yue Ling 1 Century CE[106]

In Daoist meditation the "Upper Magpie Bridge" is the connection of the conception vessel, Ren Mai, and the governing vessel, Du Mai, meridians above, and the "Lower Magpie Bridge" connects the Ren Mai and Du Mai vessels below. To connect the Upper Magpie Bridge, the tongue is placed on the upper pallet of the mouth to increase the flow of saliva and In Chinese Medicine, the tongue corresponds to the spine and has thousands of nerves that are connected to every part of the body. Saliva, the divine water called Jade Juice, contains proteins, calcium, potassium, chloride and sodium, it prevents dryness of the mouth and aids in sitting motionless for extended periods of time. The lifting of the anus is the "lower magpie bridge" and connects the Ren Mai and Du Mai meridians below. When these two bridges of energy are connected they create a circuit of energy by connecting the Ren and Du meridians so that circulation in these two principal meridians can flow freely and unobstructed. This allows the alchemical transformation of Li and Kan to take place.

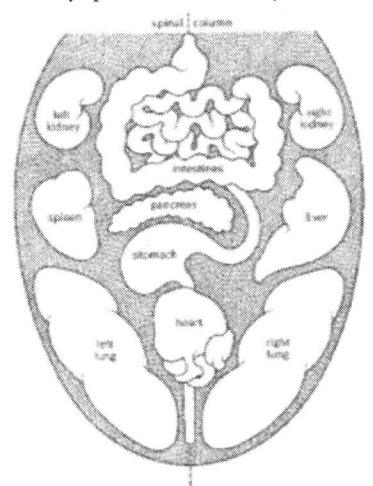

Circulating Qi

Xingqi 行氣 "circulating qi" inscribed on a dodecagonal block of jade 400 BCE:

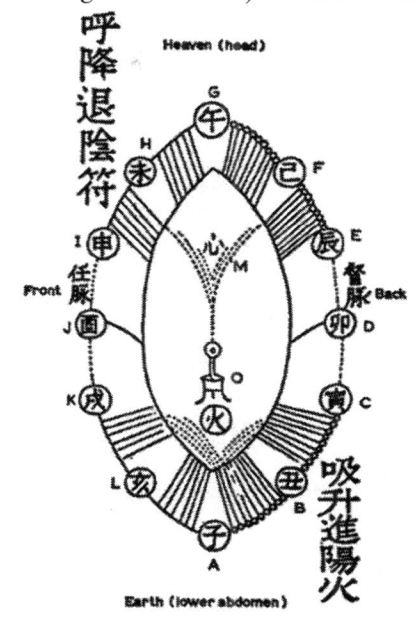

*"To circulate the Vital Breath:
Breathe deeply, then it will collect.
When it is collected, it will expand.
When it expands, it will descend.
When it descends, it will become stable.
When it is stable, it will be regular.
When it is regular, it will sprout.
When it sprouts, it will grow.
When it grows, it will recede.
When it recedes, it will become heavenly.
The dynamism of Heaven is revealed in the ascending;
The dynamism of Earth is revealed in the descending.
Follow this and you will live;
oppose it and you will die"*[107]

Practicing this series of exhalation and inhalation patterns, one becomes directly aware of the "dynamisms of Heaven and Earth" through ascending and descending breath. The most basic and fundamental connection we have to life is the breath. When the breath leaves the body, death ensues. When there is no breath left within the body, the person is dead. Their spirit has left.

"What is firmly established within cannot be uprooted. What is firmly embraced within cannot be disengaged. The Tao, thus firmly established and embraced within you, Will be respected for generations to come. Cultivate the Tao in your character, Then its virtues will be genuine. Cultivate the Tao in your family, then its virtues will abound. Cultivate the Tao in your community, Then its virtues will endure. Cultivate the Tao in your country, Then its virtues will flourish. Cultivate the Tao in the world, Then its virtues will pervade. Therefore, you can observe the virtues of the Tao, In your character, if you cultivate it in your character; In your family, if you cultivate it in your family; In your community, if you cultivate it in your community; In your country, if you cultivate it in your country; And in the world, if you cultivate it in the world. How can you know how the state of the world is? Simply by thus observing." Dao de Jing Ch 54 trans. Yasuhiko Genku Kimura

"The tiger is energy, while the dragon is spirit. The true lair is the general area between the breasts... When women cultivate immortality, they must first accumulate energy in their breasts."[108]

Focus upon your breath as you breathe in and out. With each breath inhaled, repeat: "the breath flows in" and with each exhale: "the breath flows out".[109]

"Women, the goddesses of Heaven, seek to descend toward Earth to acquire the yang essences of males to maintain their goddess position, as men seek to ascend upward to Heaven from Earth to attain the Yin essences of females to become gods." White Tigress Manual[110]

Visualize your breath coming in through your nose, down through the front of our body and filling your abdomen. Visualize your breath going out and rising up your spine to the crown of your head. Repeat. This is done by circulating qi up the back and down the front of the body, so that the body becomes an integrated whole, so that one activates the Dao in the subtle body.

"In his 'Secret of Feminine Alchemy', Liu I-ming says, 'There is a true Secret about starting practice. The operation is as different for men and women as sky from sea. The principal for men is refinement of energy, the expedient for women is refinement of body.' Men begin practice with the attention in the lower abdomen, just below the navel. Women start work with the attention between the breasts... Immortal Sister Zhang [related]... 'After midnight and before noon, settle the breathing and sit. As the energy passes through the mid-spine and on through the brain, gaining the power of energy, contemplate the self... While carrying out the work it may happen that women feel there is energy in the opening between the breasts that thrusts out, divides and goes into the breasts, right through the nipples which then erect. This is what alchemical classics call the living midnight when the medicine is produced... 'To settle the breathing' means to tune the breath so that it is even. In 'sitting' two people sit with unified attention placed between them. With mutual concentration, pure attention is embraced. With pure attention I the center, a unified energy flows, thus pressing tightly on the mid-spine and going on through the brain. This is what is referred to as the reversal of the Yellow River, meaning the opening of the spinal cannel... Yet it should be realized that expressions such as 'below the navel' and 'between the breasts' are both representational. Do not look for them as having physical form."[111]

The Primal Spirit and the Conscious Spirit

"If one discerns the beginning of the Buddha's path, there will be the blessed city of the West. After the circulation in conformity with the law, there is a turn upward towards heaven when the breath is drawn in. When the breath flows out energy is directed towards the earth. One time-period consists of six intervals (hou). In two intervals one gathers Moni (Sakyamuni). The great Tao comes forth from the center. Do not seek the primordial seed outside!" The Hui Ming Ching, The Book of Consciousness and Life, Ch. 2 trans. Richard Wilhelm

The path of energy in front leads down and is called the function-path (jen). The one at the back leading upwards is the control-path (tu).

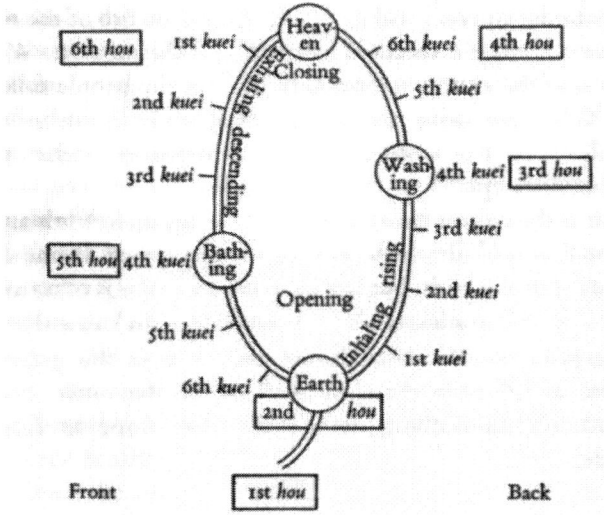

"In comparison with heaven and earth, man is like a mayfly. But compared to the great Way, heaven and earth, too, are like a bubble and a shadow. Only the primal spirit and the true nature overcome time and space. The energy of the seed, like heaven and earth, is transitory, but the primal spirit is beyond the polar differences. Here is the place whence heaven and earth derive their being." - Secret of the Golden Flower, trans. Richard Wilhelm Ch. 2

"...the primordial spirit dwells in the square inch (between the eyes), but the conscious spirit dwells below in the heart. This lower fleshly heart has the shape of a large peach: it is covered by the wings of the lungs, supported by the liver, and served by the bowels. This heart is dependent on the outside world... The way to the Elixir of life recognizes as supreme magic, seed-water, spirit-fire, and thought-earth;." Secret of the Golden Flower Ch. 2 trans. Walter Picca

"*One who knows others is clever, but one who knows himself is enlightened. One who conquers others is powerful, but one who conquers himself is strong. One who knows contentment is rich and one who pushes with vigor has will. One who loses not his place endures.*
One who may die, but will not perish is transcendent." Dao de Jing Ch 33

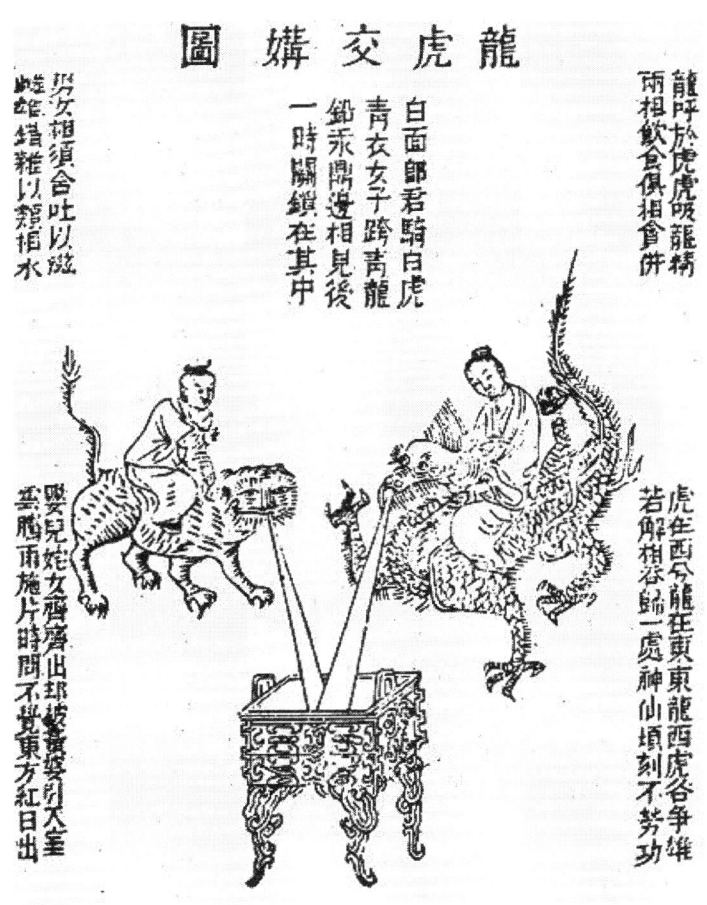

"*The second realization is that more desire brings more suffering.*"[112]

"The soft overcomes the hard. The small overcomes the large. The gentle survives the strong. The invisible survives the visible. Fish should be left in the deep water. Fire and iron should be kept under ground. Seed should be left free to grow.... in..... The rhythm of life." Dao de Jing Ch 43 trans. Timothy Leary

Interpretation:
The two broken lines on top have the image of lighting and the bottom solid line symbolizes elevation, portraying lighting striking on the top of a mountain. The arousing, inciting movement and initiative, the insemination. Mortals exist between Heaven above and Earth below. Above are the astral realms, the stars, the planets, the constellations, the sun and the moon, the macrocosm of our existence, the architypes, gods and goddesses. Below are the Chthonic, the mycelium, the underworld of decay, decomposition compost and regeneration, renewing life from death and decay. Thunder brings the mushroom and from the duality of yin and yang come the child, that ushers in ten thousand things standing between heaven and earth. The thunder brings the rains which nourish the roots that sustain life and perpetuate the growth and substance of life. The goddess Feng Bo Bo controls the thunder and storms. The dragon Leigong controls thunder with his wife goddess of thunder, Tian Mu.

Right Speech: Simply speak the truth. Be a fair witness, impartial without preconceptions and prejudices.
- Do not lie.
- Refrain from backbiting and slander and do not let your words inspire hatred, enmity, disunity, and disharmony.
- Speak not rudely, impolitely, maliciously, or abusively.
- Refrain from idle, useless, chatter and gossip.

***A sudden crash of thunder; the mind doors burst open!
and there sits an ordinary old man.*** (Alan Watts)

Three Treasured Jewels

Morality – Single-minded Concentration – Wisdom

Tranquility- Mindfulness- Dispassionate Insight

What is the Buddha?
Three pounds of cannabis.
-Zen Koan

I take refuge in the Buddha. This is the cave from whence all Dharmas of all Buddhas arise. I take refuge in the Dharma. Practice all good Dharma, this is the root-origin whence all Buddhas and Dharmas arise. I take refuge in the Sangha. Keep all precepts. Save the many beings. The Dharma of the Supreme Way is the way to do and have done.

Buddha- the awakened one. Everyone that is awake is a Buddha and the Buddha is within everyone. Only though us and within us can the Buddha awaken.

Dharma- the way or doctrine of compassion and love, that all beings may be freed from suffering and the causes of suffering. Only though us can compassion, love and understanding be expressed and made into real things. Anything that can aid in awakening has Buddha nature, and we can learn from everything around us and within us. The awakened can see the Dharma in everything.

Sangha- the community that lives in harmony and awareness. When his disciples abandoned him, the Buddha Siddhartha made the Bodhi tree his Sangha where he sat and ate only one cannabis seed a day. You create a sangha by being aware of the harmonious relationships that exist between you and that and those that are around you.

Every person can wake up, understand and love, so therefore within each person is where the Buddha, the Dharma and the Sangha are to be found. The day to day, minute to minute ordinary details of our daily lives are the Buddha, the Dharma and the Sangha, or else these are merely abstract concepts of something very far away and have no real meaning or value. From moment to moment, we can take refuge in the Buddha by being mindful to avoid evil. We can take refuge in the Dharma by understanding that love and compassion alleviate suffering. We take refuge in the Sangha by being mindful and understanding how our actions benefit each other.

"If we look closely, the Three Gems are actually one. In each of the two are already there. In Buddha, there is Buddhahood, there is the Buddha body. In Buddha there is the Dharma body because without the Dharma body, he could not have become a Buddha. In the Buddha there is the Sangha body because he had breakfast with the Bodhi tree, with the other trees, and birds and environment... If Buddha and Dharma are not present, it is not a Sangha. Without you, the Buddha is not real, it is just an idea. Without you, the Dharma cannot be practiced. It has to be practiced by someone. Without each of you the Sangha cannot be."[113]

三清

"*The Dao produced One; One produced Two; Two produced Three; Three produced All things.*" Dao de Ching Ch. 42 trans. James Legg

From Doa, Wuji
Wuji produced Taiji
Taiji produced Yin and Yang
Their interaction mediated by Qi is Liangyi

Three Treasured Jewels:

慈 Compassion

俭 Moderation

不敢为天下先 Humility
(not daring to act as first under the heavens)

The power of the gods of nature represent aspects of the Dao. Such powers must be wielded responsibly, as actions disturb the balance of the world and result in the Dao's re-balancing of itself which manifests as karma. Daoist theology is not foundationally dependent on the existence of an anthropomorphic godlike figurehead but rather the formlessness and primacy of the Dao. Before the Dao is the is the unknowable mystery of the primal egg and its source. The movement of the Dao produces Qi which grows and regenerates structure and qualities giving birth to Yin, the receptive and Yang the expressive, though each contains the seed of the other within. Together they ebb and flow in waves together, expanding and contracting. This dynamic tension cracks the cosmic egg and from it emerge the three treasures and the five patterns. Water gives rise to saltiness, fire to bitterness, wood to sourness, metal to acridity and earth to sweetness and are expressed as essence, scenes, vitality, spirit and energy.

Gua- Three Pure Ones

"Everyone under Heaven says that the Toa is great but seems foolish. Because it is great, it seems foolish. If it did not seem foolish it would have vanished long ago. I have three great treasures which I hold and keep. The first is compassion, the second is moderation, the third is daring not to be ahead of others. From compassion comes courage, from moderation comes generosity, from humility comes leadership. To shun compassion but try to be brave, abandon moderation yet try to be generous, forsake humility and try to be first, is certain death to all hope. Compassion brings victory in battle and strength in defense. Love is the means by which Heaven saves and guards."
Dao de Ching Ch. 67

The Three Pure Ones are often depicted as elders seated upon thrones, but they also represent the three essential fields of the body: jing, qi and shen. The congregation of all three Pure Ones results in the return to Dao. Below these Three Pure Ones are the Immortals, the Heroes and the Saints. The Saints, or Shêng-jên, are those who have attained to extraordinary intelligence and virtue. The Three Jewels are the basic ethical foundation of Daoism and are expressed by abstention from war and capital punishment, living simply, and refusal to assert active authority. These three virtues are microcosmically reflected in the body as jing, 精, essence, qi (chi), 氣, vital energy, the dynamic interaction between the yin and yang, and shen, 神, spirit. Macrocosmically they are reflected in the Three Pure Ones: the Jade Pure One, the Supreme Pure One and the Grand Pure One. The inner essence of the meaning is that essence transforms into energy, energy transforms into spirit, spirit commands energy, and energy commands essence, always remembering that energy and mater cannot be created or destroyed, merely changed and transformed.

"There is a form that developed from primordial chaos that was born before heaven and earth, silent and still, it stands on its own and does not change. It can be regarded as the mother of all under heaven. Not yet knowing its name, We refer to it as the Dao. Were I forced to give it a name, I'd call it the Great. The "Great" means "overflowing"; "Overflowing" means "going far"; "Going far" means "to return." Heaven is great; the earth is great; the Way is great; and the king too is great. In this realm there are four greats, and the king counts as one of them. Humanity takes as its model the earth; The earth takes as its model heaven; Heaven takes as its model the Way; And the Way takes as its model that which is so on its own." Dao de Jing Ch 25 trans. of the Guodian bamboo slip by Robert G. Henricks

Heaven represents the sky, deities, sun, moon, stars, constellations, and the air we breathe. Earth represents the four cardinal directions, the four elements, the natural world and physical manifestation. People are the sentient beings upon the earth created from the union of heaven and earth as the metaphysical trinity of the Three Pure Ones. The Treasure of the Dao created heaven and earth through yin and yang. He manifests as heaven and passed his domain to the Jade Emperor, this is the breath, the spirit that animates life, the Qi. The Treasure of the Law is the keeper of the laws of nature and physics and manifests as earth and the physical body. The Treasure of Knowledge manifests as humankind and he is the master teacher and bringer of civilization. The union of heaven and earth, the breath, and the body, creates consciousness.[114] The Three Pure Ones manifest in our lives as the Three Blessings: Fu (prosperity) Lu (Status) Shou (Longevity), and personified as the Three Stellar Gods.[115] Within the body the Three Pure Ones are personified as gods or spirit guides of the three primary cavities of the body. Dao Bao resides in the mind between the eyes and connects cosmic and personal Qi. Jing Boa resides in the heart of the chest and governs the vital energy of personal Qi and physical body, while Shi Bao is resides in the pelvis and is the vital generative energy that produces sensory experience and reproduction.[116]

The Three manifest in the body as three triads:
*Pineal Gland * Pituitary Gland * Brain Stem*
*Central Nervous System *Peripheral Nervous System * Endocannabinoid System*
*Pulmonary System * Digestive System * Circulatory System*

"The masters of the Dao in ancient times had mystical, versatile, and unfathomable understanding. As it is unfathomable, Only a proximate description is possible. They are prepared at all times, as if taking on a river journey in winter. They are alert and watchful, as if they were wary of the surroundings. They are respectful, as if they were the guests of someone. They are accommodating, as if they were ice about to melt. They are unpretentious, as if they were the embodiment of simplicity. They are open-minded, as if they were a hollow valley. They are murky, as if they were a muddy stream, They are unsettled, as if they were an open sea. They never stopped, as if they were the winds of the earth. Is there anyone who can be like a murky stream cleaning up when given a rest? Is there anyone who can be like calm air gathering motion and becoming alive again? The man who shuns full gratification of their desires, is the man who has this ability. He can rejuvenate." Dao de Jing Ch 15 trans Lok Sang Ho

Dao Bao, the first of the Three Pure Ones, the first supreme administrator of  the earth, predecessor to the Jade Emperor, born from the cosmic Qi transforming nonbeing into being with the Pearl of the Primordial Chaos which he holds as he stands in the center of the Three Pure Ones. Yuanshi Tianzun, the Pearly Emperor, Lord of Primordial Beginning, Treasure of Heaven, the Jade Pure One who rules the first heaven, Yu-Qing, which is found in the Jade Mountain beyond the Golden Door is and the source of all truth that lies there as the sun is the source of all light. The first Pure One is universal or heavenly Qi of all the planets, stars and constellations as well as the energy of the force of creation. In the First Heaven Mu Kung is the god of the Immortals and is the purest substance of the active male yang principal. There also is the Hero, or Chên-jên, is the Perfect Man, borne on the wings of the wind, seated on the clouds of Heaven, travelling from one world to another and fixing its habitation in the stars.

Jing Bao, Heavenly Lord of the Numinous Treasure of the Law, keeper of the laws of nature, the left hand of Dao Bao. Lingbao Tianzun, Lord of the Numinous Treasure, Supreme Pure One, is human plane Qi, the energy that  exists on the surface of our planet and sustains human life and rules over the heaven of Shang-Qing where Dao Jün is the custodian of the sacred books and determines the movements and interaction of yin and the yang.

Shi Bao, Heavenly Lord of the Virtuous Dao, Treasure of Knowledge, teacher of teachers, sage of sages, incarnated around 350 BCE or later, an elder contemporary and teacher of Confucius and Buddha. It is he who brought culture and civilization. Daode Tianzun, Lord of the Way and its Virtue, Honored Lord of the Dao and the Virtue, the Treasurer of Spirits, the Lord of Man, Most Eminent Aged Ruler, the Grand Pure One who rules over the heaven  of Tai-Qing and is depicted with pure white hair and beard, he is the earth Qi, all of the forces inside the planet as well as the five elemental forces. Daode Tianzun manifested himself in the form of Laozi, the Old Master, and chief among the immortals is the Laozi.

"Confucius had sought his [Laozi] advice presumably on mourning and funeral rites, given that the Confucian work Liji (Records of Rites) has Confucius citing Lao Dan four times specifically on these rites."[117]

Eternal Mother Wusheng Laomu, the Jade Maiden of Profound Wonder and the Highest Mystery, consort of Peng Gu, who hatched from an egg like a mushroom emerging from the moist soil after a lightning storm, was the mother of Laozi. Her name, Wu-Sheng, wu- shaman and sheng- life or creation, implies being the original mother of the shamans. Her name includes both wu and mu, both terms referring to shamanic abilities and Lao-mu can mean old shaman. Lao-zi, is the name inherited matrilineally from his mother meaning from Lao, implying from the ancient or from the original mother or original shaman. One day Wusheng Laomu gazed upon a falling star and conceived Laozi who remained in her womb for sixty-two years until she leaned against a plum tree and Laozi emerged as an old man with long grey beard and abnormally long earlobes. She nursed Laozi at her breast and taught him the ways of the Dao. Since the days of Fuxi and Nuwa he has been born thirteen times and worked as the Keeper of the Archives for the royal court of Zhou where he studied the works of the Shennnog, the Yellow Emperor and other classics and attracted students such as Confucius and the Gautama Buddha. Therefore, it could be that the stories illustrate that both Confucianism and Buddhism were originally influenced heavily by Daoism via Laozi so their later confluence would be understandable. Historically the three religions of Taoism, Confucianism and Buddhism became known as the Three Teachings. More importantly though the story illustrates that Laozi himself the wise learned old sage, was himself taught the mysteries of the Dao from the original mother of the shamans, and that brings us back to Ma, whether manifesting as Magu, Mago, Mafu, Mazu or even Wu-Sheng, Bari or Gongsim she is the primal mother of the shamans.

Three Cinnabar Fields within the Body

"The all-surpassing medicine has three characteristics: ching (essence), ch'I (vital energy), and shen (spirit), which are difficult to grasp and are hidden... The elixir is called 'green dragon and white tiger'; the elixir is the nature of non-nature, the emptiness of non-emptiness." - The Jade Emperor's Three Treasures of Immortality[118]

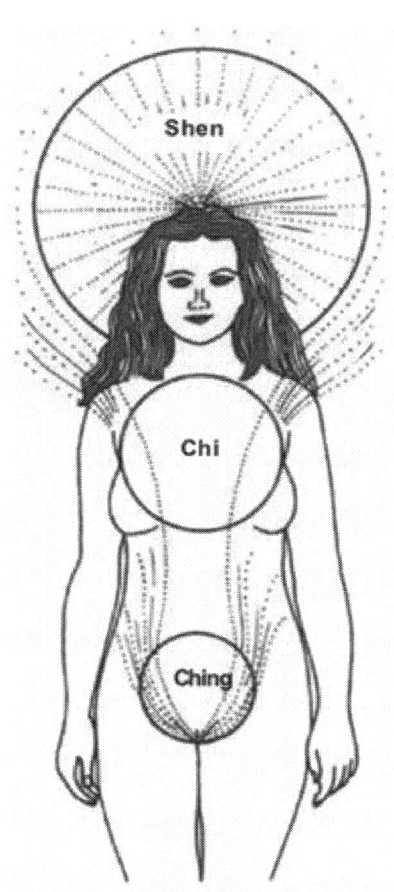

There are three body cavities that are referred to as Cinnabar Fields. These three cavities are located in the abdomen, the heart, and the head, and play a major role in breathing, meditation, and Daoist Neidan Internal Alchemy practices. The lower Cinnabar Field is the dantian proper and is the seat of jing, located in the lower abdomen about 3 fingers below and behind the navel.[119] The middle Cinnabar Field is in the center of the chest, and is the seat of chi located in the Yellow Court of the Central Crimson Palace of the Mysterious Female. The upper Field is the Muddy Pellet, located within the skull and is the seat of shen located in the Palace of Qian which is divided into nine chambers arranged in two rows. These three cinnabar fields are where the three pure ones reside.

Jing: Jing/ching- semen, seminal essence, body fluids, physical essence, vitality, vital physical energy that facilitates reproduction and transformation. Stored in the kidneys, adrenal glands and the lower dantien, jing is the densest physical matter within the body, the material basis for the physical body and is yīn in nature. Jing nourishes, fuels, and cools the body, while carrying our DNA and creating semen, menstrual blood and bone marrow. Its nexus is in the dantian, called hara in Japanese, the lower cinnabar field a few inches below and behind the navel, the bodies center of gravity.

Qi: Ch'i/Ki/Qi- energy, breath of life, nervous impulses, the natural energy of the universe, the vital force that operates the body and manifests in everyone and everything, the unseen universal life force. It is the unseen impetus behind all change, creative and destructive, through initiation, continuation, transformation, or cessation and divides itself into personal and universal. personal Qi flows through the body in paths moving to each individual organ and these pathways were mapped by the Yellow Emperor and form the basis of acupuncture, cupping, herbalism and massage techniques in TCM. Universal Qi is the unified connection of everyone's personal Qi connected in the collective energy force of the universe. Therefore, to understand the flow of Qi in the circuits of oneself is to understand the flow of Qi in the universe. To study the universal flow of Qi is to study oneself.[120] Each individual sentient being has within themselves personal Qi. All individual personal Qi is connected on a metaphysical and quantum level forming a singularity, being the totality of all synchronicity and homeostasis. This is illustrated metaphorically by Daoist mythology by personifying these metaphysical energies and paradoxes of quantum physics into deities and demons.[121]

Shen: Shen- spirit, mental activity, the brain, the mind, the spirit, spiritual energy or spirit of the body. Found in the nervous system, the blood and in the upper dantian located between the eyebrows, also known as the Third eye. Shen is associated with consciousness, mind, gods, spirits, Kami, ecstasy, magic, the mysterious, supernatural, ancestral spirts, lightening, the presence or aura of a person. Shen is the elemental energy call the five shen of the organs of the body. Shen rejuvenates itself at night and if the jing and the chi are happy then the shen will be content as well. Shen is the essence in all things the connects to the divine principle through states of higher consciousness. Shen is the divine inside all that fuels the collective and individual Qi.

If you wish to seek immortality you must acquire the quintessence. To acquire the quintessence, preserve your sperm by conserving jing and stimulating the shen, causing the jing to return and nourish the brain. Ching is semen in men, menstrual blood in women. Circulate your breath like a baby in the womb by breathing in quickly, holding the breath for as long as possible and exhaling through the nostrils so gently it will leave a feather undisturbed, to harmonize the chi. This is the dance of the coiling dragon and playful tiger, the play of fire and water in the cauldron, spinning the waterwheel to return jing to the brain. Once this is achieved then you must take the transcendent medicine.

"It seems that alchemists made use of hallucinogenic drugs.... it included the art of growing marvelous plants (ling chih), including hemp, which were believed to prolong life and bring about immortality. The most famous was the magic mushroom, which was pictured in the hands of alchemists, both female and male, in many popular portraits. The fact that mushrooms were so prominent in alchemist lore suggests that there was a ritual use of hallucinogenic substances; indeed, many alchemical poems show, visions and ecstatic trances of riding the wind with the immortals were common in ancient China. Ko Hung made no bones about it: 'All the numinous fungi can bring men to longevity and material immortality- and this belongs to the same category as making gold.'... Official envoys of the incense, Lords of the Dragon and the Tiger to the left and the right, Golden girls and boys attending upon the fragrance, and all Divine Beings, cause at that at this place where I have today conducted an audience, the divine mushroom of immortality, cinnabar and jade green, may spontaneously grow from out of the golden liqueur, and the host of Perfected Immortals may meet in unity at this ardent incense burner. May the Immortal youths and Jade Girls of the 10 directions attend upon and protect this incense and transfer swiftly all that I have said before the heavenly throne of the supreme Honored Jade Emperor."[122]

Twenty One Taras

"Tara is known as the 'Mother of all Buddhas.' This is because she is the wisdom of reality, and all Buddhas and bodhisattvas are born from this wisdom. This wisdom is also the fundamental cause of happiness, and our own spiritual growth comes from this wisdom. That is why Tara is called the Mother. And Mother Tara has much wisdom to manifest many aspects, sometimes peaceful, sometimes wrathful, in different colours; all to help sentient beings." -- Lama Thubten Yeshe

The name 'Tara' means 'star' in Sanskrit and the bodhisattva is likened to the North Star, as it is her role to guide those who are lost onto the path of enlightenment. Tara is also a goddess in not only Tantric Vajrayana Buddhism, but also Hinduism, Jainism and in Japan she is Tarani Bosatsu. Tara is the mother of liberation, expressing the virtues of success in work and achievements, a tantric meditation deity the guides the development inner qualities of compassion and emptiness. She is also associated with the entheogenic usage of cannabis in the Tara Tantra. In the Tibetan language, Tara is known also as 'Sgrol-ma', meaning 'she who saves'. This name reflects Tara as a savior that carries one across the raging sea of samsara. Tara is the feminine aspect of the bodhisattva of compassion, Avalokitesvara, whose tears of compassion she was born from. Tara is the enlightened manifestation of the feminine principal and as such, also represents wisdom. The Green Tara specifically represents wisdom applied and active compassion which is manifested in the inner Qi and the Windhorse. Wisdom is the mother of enlightenment and the Buddhas became enlightened due to wisdom, so therefore, Tara is the Mother of all Buddhas. As the Mother of all the Buddhas, Tara protects the welfare of all beings. Tara is also associated with Amitabha Buddha, wearing a tiny image of Amitabha Buddha on her crown. Aspirations made in the presences of Green Tara may easily grow into results, and requests made to her may be quickly actualized. Green Tara is believed to protect her followers from eight obscurations: lions (pride), wild elephants (delusion and ignorance), fires (hatred and anger), snakes (jealousy), bandits and thieves (wrong views, fanatical views), bondage (avarice and miserliness), floods (desire and attachment), and evil spirits and demons (deluded doubts). While Tara is not explicitly associated with cannabis her image is often used as a template for cannabis goddess imagery, her compassionate aspect is reflective of contemporary medical cannabis legislations and contemporary researchers have identified historic connections between Tara and both cannabis and entheogens.

Tara has 21 primary emanations, each of which performs different activities such as pacification, increase and so forth. The different colors of these 21 Taras correspond to the 4 different types of enlightened activity, as explained by Kirti Tsenshab Rinpoche: "Tara is the female Buddha of enlightened activity, of which there are 4 types: pacifying, increasing, overpowering and wrathful. Each of these is represented by a different color… the twenty Taras surrounding the central Green Tara are divided into four colors white, yellow, red, and black. These colors represent the four types of enlightened activity. White represents the activity of pacifying… yellow the activity of increasing… red the activity of overpowering… black the activity of wrath… Each of the twenty Taras has her own name… It may be added that in Mongolia, there is a popular form of White Tara known as 'Tara of the Seven Eyes'. This form of White Tara is shown with a third eye on her face, as well as an eye on each of her palms, and on the soles of her feet, making it seven in total. The seven eyes are meant to symbolize the bodhisattva's vigilance and her ability to see all the suffering in the world."[123]

The Vow of Tara the Liberator

"There are many who desire enlightenment in a man's body, but none who work for the benefit of sentient beings in the body of a woman. Therefore, until samsara is empty, I shall work for the benefit of sentient beings in a woman's body."[124]

Mantra of Tara

Om Tare Tuttare Ture Svaha [Soha]

Om (AUM) = Tara's body, speech and mind.
Tare = Liberation from delusion, suffering and karma.
Tuttare = Liberation from, and calming of, all fears.
Ture = Liberation from ignorance, bringing success and cessation of suffering.
Soha [Svaha] = May the meaning of the mantra take root in my mind.

"The Acharya entered the village, and since he prayed to Tara, a great rainfall of amrita descended from the sky, which cured the dying of their affliction." – The Golden Rosery of Tara[125]

Magu the Liberator

"The Master has no mind of her own. She understands the mind of the people. Those who are good she treats as good. Those who aren't good she also treats as good. This is how she attains true goodness. She trusts people who are trustworthy. She also trusts people who aren't trustworthy. This is how she gains true trust. The Master's mind is shut off from the world. Only for the sake of the people does she muddle her mind. They look to her in anticipation. Yet she treats them all as her children." – Dao de Ching Ch. 49 trans. J.H. McDonald

"The Green Goddess is the divine feminine spirit that lives within the Cannabis plant. She is the goddess of Liberation and Delight. She has a gentle but powerful voice for the suffering. She has given her gift of the sacred Cannabis plant to the world. The Green Goddess shares with us the therapeutic and holistic powers of the Cannabis plant. Her gifts are magical and healing. They include beautiful fabrics, the highest quality paper and essential oils. She is the compassionate caregiver who asks for mercy, freedom and justice for all who need her. The Green Goddess mourns, for those who in passing have been incarcerated for her cause. She prays for the veils of ignorance to be lifted from the eyes of the masses." - Way of Infinite Harmony, Ma Guang Wei

Magu the Liberator personifies compassion, the goodness in all of humankind. Magu freed slaves who were working for her oppressive father. With the aid of her magical powers, she could walk upon the waters in her hemp shoes and was able to reclaim the land from waters transforming it into fields of Mulberry trees and Cannabis. For this, she is invoked for protection from oppression and by those persecuted for her goodness.

"If the chosen are not exalted, no one envies them. If material treasures are not praised, no one steals them. In other words, if the objects of passions are not shown off, there are no temptations. The wise ruler does not create such temptations to people but takes care that people have enough food. This eliminates passions and strengthens people's health. Yes, the wise ruler always strives to prevent temptations and passions and does not let evil people act. The absence of these problems brings calm." Dao de Jing Ch 3 trans. Vladimir Antonov and Mikhail Nikolenko

The people of Magu's father's village were very poor, even though they worked hard for Magu's father every day. The land was mostly marsh and wetland and the main industry of the people was fishing. It was hard and strenuous work. On the edge of the marsh, the villagers would throw all of their waste and refuse.

Over the years it grew larger and larger. While it grew, cannabis plants began to grow there also. Soon the plants began to grow tall and spread, and as they grew and spread, they also revitalized the soil that they grew in and helped speed the decomposition of the refuse that it grew upon and remediate the soil. Magu encouraged the villagers to harvest the seed and use it for oil and for gruel, reserving enough to re-sow the refuse heaps to ensure the cycle to continue. Magu then instructed the villagers to harvest the cannabis for its fiber. Magu instructed the villagers to "ret" the cannabis stalks by soaking the cannabis in the water so that the strong fibers are loosened, and the fiber can be easily collected and dried, to be woven into thread, rope, fishing nets, string for hunting bows and cloth. The villagers began to impress their clay containers with the strong and sturdy cannabis rope. But cannabis brought abundance in many other forms as well. When the cannabis was retting in the water, the fish would float to the surface and the villagers came out with nets made of cannabis fiber and harvested the fish. As the fish decreased in population, and the cannabis fields grew, the waters retreated, and the land was soon filled with cannabis fields and Mulberry trees.

"First Harvest Fire Festival today is the day mentioned in the sacred text 'When the World Was Green' where devotees burn cannabis in a large gathering as way of giving thanks to Her Holiness, Mother Earth and Father Sky. Over the centuries and due to persecution, the Fire Ritual has evolved into many forms depending upon how Cannabis has been viewed by the authorities at the time. Many people started to burn Joss Paper (ghost money) instead as to be caught in possession of Cannabis would result in persecution and being sent to re-education camps for example. What should you be doing today? As described in the sacred texts we should be gathering together, burning Cannabis, praising and communing with Her Holiness together. Princess Ma Gu is a Goddess of great Mercy and Kindness who saved the slaves from under Her evil father and we are sure any offering you make to Her will be greatly received and She will bestow myriad blessings upon you." - Ma Gu Xian Shou

"The highest kindness is like water. Water's kindness benefits ten thousand things without contending. It flows to places men reject like the Tao. Dwell in happiness upon the earth, with deep kindness in the heart, kindness towards friends, speak with kindness and truth, use kindness when leading others, in duties be kind and competent, time your actions to express kindness. So not competing there is no blame."
- Dao de Ching Ch. 8

"*The Jushi (Chinese: 車師), or Gushi (Chinese: 姑師), in the Turpan basin (modern Xinjiang, China), lived in tents, followed the grasses and waters, and had considerable knowledge of agriculture. They owned cattle, horses, camels, sheep and goats. They were proficient with bows and arrows. A 2,700-year-old grave discovered in 2008 at the Yanghai Tombs, contains the remains of a shaman who had blue eyes and light-coloured hair. Near the shaman's head and foot were a large leather basket and wooden bowl filled 789 grams of dried cannabis flowers.*"[126]

"*Thus I have heard: That night the bodhisattva awoke and found herslf surrounded by vines, branches, flowers roots, sap, essence of the plant world, and the wildness of nature, all supplicating her for a teaching that would illuminate their minds. The bodhisattva spoke: 'No, it is you, not I, that needs to speak… speak to us of our interconnectedness, teach use how to hold each other in love, teach us how to experience our own primal essence, true nature, teach us how to know the essence of each sentient being, trees, grasses, rocks, mountains, stars, clouds, animals, insects, spirits, other realms of existence…*" – The Plant Medicine Sutra, Robert Schrei

Immortal Shennong
神農

The second great sovereign was the Divine Farmer Shennong, the Red Emperor or Earth Emperor, Lord of the Five Grains, who reigned over the Second Dynasty. Originally a god of the stars, he was sent to earth by the Emperor of Heaven to instruct mortals that if they worked hard, they would always have enough food to eat. He was born to a princess and an Imperial Celestial Dragon in the city of Xian in the Hua Shan mountains. Shennong had the body of a man with a transparent abdomen, the head of an ox, whose forehead was made of bronze and skull was made of iron. He was not only revered by the Chinese, but also the Korean and Japanese people, while the Vietnamese and Hmong believe themselves to be descended from him. It is written in Classic of Tea that, Shennong, as the God of Medicine, to save the people from the torments of disease, travelled the wilderness of Hubei in Shennong Jia, a high plateau of central China lying between the Yangtze River and the Han River. It is famous today as a place where the "bear man" a "bigfoot" or "yeti," resides and much of Shennong Jia is now a nature preserve, where there are numerous rare plants and many ginkgo trees. There Shennong tasted every plant to determine their properties. Shennong carried out his investigation of herbs and plants by eating them, often poising himself. He relied on tea to neutralize the toxins. One day Shennong was poisoned by herbs and almost died while he was passed out under a small tree. Fresh dew was on the leaves of the tiny tea tree and dropped into his mouth reviving him. Shennong has a transparent belly allowing him to see the actions of what he had eaten, so he ate some leaves of the small tree that had revived him and saw that they moved up and down inside his belly as if they were inspecting something. He boiled some water and leaves fell from the tree into the water, Shennong drank the resulting amber liquid and found that it made all aliments and toxins disappear. Thus, was discovered cha, or tea.

Under his various names, Shennong is the patron deity of farmers, cooks, rice and cannabis traders, herbalists, weavers, tailors, archers, potters, farmers markets, cannabis processing, tea houses and practitioners of traditional Chinese medicine. Fireworks and incense are his favored offerings. The wife of Shennong was Sien Zang or Sien Tsang, a weaver goddess who wove the clouds that clothe the heavens from strands of hemp and silk.

Legend has it that Shennong lived in a cave, as did many of the immortals, indicating again perhaps that their origins lie in prehistoric cave-dwelling

Paleolithic or early Neolithic times. The time of Shennong was said to have been a golden age where people cultivated rice, mulberry and cannabis, a time where people "only knew their mother"- meaning it was a matriarcial and matrilineal culture, lived alongside the elk happy, peaceful, self-sufficient and stable. They sowed seed and were fed, they wove fibers into cloth and were clothed, they woke up happy and slept soundly.[127] Shennong led the people from being hunters and gathers into animal husbandry and agriculture and taught them the properties and qualities of plants for healing, nutrition, enjoyment and survival. He taught them to plant mulberry, pomegranate and cannabis trees by the banks of rivers and ponds and to tether their cows on the pomegranate trees where they would be content and strengthen the embankment by treading upon it, and to flood the rice fields to create a sustainable ecosystem of fish, algae, grass and rice. Shennong as the Lord of the Burning Wind brought slash-and-burn clearing scrublands that left the ground rich in potash ready for plowing and planting. Once when Shennong, the Holy Plowman King, while teaching the people the ways of farming and agriculture, clouds appeared in the sky and released a sudden downpour of cannabis seed, sesame, millet, rice, and soybeans. Shennong collected the seeds instructed the people how to carefully sow them and soon crops covered the land. plow, and axe, teaching cultivation, preservation, and storage of foods, digging wells, irrigation, preserving stored seeds, purifying water by boiling it, scaffolding, the Chinese calendar, teaching pulse measurements for health diagnosis, the practice of both moxibustion and acupuncture, and to have instituted the harvest thanksgiving ceremony (Zhaji Sacrificial Rite or Laji Rite). He helped people to transition from a diet of meat, clams, and wild fruit, to one based on grains and vegetables, thus moving from hunter-gather to agriculturally based civilization marking his reign at the transition from Neolithic to Bronze age. It is written in "Classic of Tea" that, *"The tea drinking tradition began with Shen*

Nong and actively developed by the Duke of Zhou."[128]

There are eight major innovations that Shen Nong is credited with:
- The plough and rake
- Introducing cultivation of the five grains
- Medical herbalism
- The loom to weave fabrics using silk and hemp for clothing
- Bow and arrow of hemp string
- Invention of commerce through the Farmer's Market
- Pottery art by impressing hemp rope into the pottery
- Planting mulberry trees to harvest the silk from the cocoons of the silkworms nesting the trees and to plant hemp between the rows of mulberry trees and harvest its fiber to weave together with the silk for fabric.

Around 2500 BC the Red Emperor Shennong who wore a garment of cannabis leaves, through divine inspiration, wrote the ancient herbal classic "Pen Ts'ao" or "The Herbal", Shénnóng Běn Cǎo Jīng, known by other names such as "The Divine Farmer's Materia Medica," or "The Compendium of Materia Medica," or "The Divine Farmer's Herb Root Classic". It is still in use today by practitioners of Traditional Chinese Medicine. The Pen Ts'so describes the following properties of cannabis flowers or mafen: *"Flavor: acrid; balanced. Governs the five taxations and seven damages, benefits the five viscera, and descends blood and cold qi; excessive consumption causes one to see ghosts and run about frenetically. Prolonged consumption frees the spirit light* [Po, a seed that descended from the Heavenly Realm] *and lightens the body. Another name is mabo."* [or ma-po, the heavenly cannabis seed that lightens the body]. It goes on to describe the properties of cannabis as spicy, good for the five organs, balances the yin and yang, tastes good, is not poison, helps the entire body, increases the bodies energy, stops sweat, promotes urine, is not rough, but eating too much will cause one to see ghosts.

According to the "Yearbook of the United States Department of Agriculture" in 1913: *"The 'Lu Shi,' a Chinese work of the Sung dynasty, about 500 A.D., contains a statement that the Emperor Shen Nung, in the twenty-eighth century B.C., first taught the people of China to cultivate 'ma' (hemp) for making hempen cloth. The name ma occurring in the earliest Chinese writings designated a plant of two forms, male and female, used primarily for fibre. Later the seeds of this plant were used for food. The definite statement regarding the staminate and pistillate forms eliminates other fibre plants included in later times under the Chinese name ma. The Chinese have cultivated the plant for the production of fibre and for the seeds, which were used for food and later for oil…"*

"In the sixteenth century Compendium of Materia Medica, Li Shizhen repeated this statement and added a previous recipe that states: 'for those seeking to see ghosts, take unprocessed cannabis [the text says, "cannabis seeds" (sheng ma zi) but lists the recipe under the entry for mafen], acorus rhizome (shi chang pu, Acorus spp.) and dysosma (gui jiu, Dysosma spp.) in equal parts and form into pellet pills. Take one pill every morning facing the sun and after 100 days one will see ghosts' (Liu et al., 2009). Additionally, in 973 ADS, the Materia Medica of the Kaibao Era (Kai Bao Ben Cao) quoted an earlier author from the eighth century with the statement that 'cannabis causes happiness in the heart'" (Zheng, 2008)."[129]

The instructions were given for the processing of herbs into drugs by Shennong and they were transmitted by Tao Hongjing:

"All drugs used in the preparation of pills or powders must first be cut up into fine pieces. Then they are dried in the sun and pulverized. Whether a drug is to be pulverized individually or together with the other drugs in a prescription is determined by the prescription. For drugs containing a large amount of moisture, such as ophiopogon and rehmannia, the following is applicable. First, they are cut, dried, and pounded individually into small pieces. Remove the fine parts repeatedly and tear the remaining portions. Then, they are dried again. If shady weather or rain arrives, they may also be roasted over a weak fire until they are dry. One waits a few moments until they have become cool again before they are pounded. All drugs containing moisture suffer great weight losses during the drying process. For this reason, the amounts must be carefully increased before drying. Weighed again afterwards, the amounts will be correct. This does not apply to drugs used in decoctions or medicinal wines.

"Decoctions are boiled gently over a small fire. The amount of water varies with the volume of the prescription. In general, one dou of water is used with twenty liang of drugs, reduced by boiling to four sheng [note: 1 dou = 10 sheng, so reduced to 40% the original volume]. This should serve as a standard. If one wishes to prepare a laxative decoction, by means of slight processing [note: rhubarb root was usually cooked only a short time to preserve its laxative effects], only a small amount of water should be used but a relatively large quantity of the boiled liquid shall be taken. If a restorative decoction is desired, which needs thorough processing [note: tonic herbs

were often cooked for an hour or more], a large volume of water is used, boiled long enough so that only a small amount of liquid remains to be taken as medication."

The Classic of Rites compiled by Confucius in the 5th and 6th centuries BC lists soybeans, wheat, broomcorn, foxtail millet, and hemp. The Five Grains traditionally date back to the Shennong Ben Cao Jing, reputed to be a record of an oral tradition first delivered by Shennong himself.

"One ingredient, one medicinally effective drug, take one pill the size of small hemp seeds. Two ingredients, one medicinally effective drug, take two pills the size of large hemp seeds. Three ingredients, one medicinally effective drug, take three pills the size of small beans. Four ingredients, one medicinally effective drug, take four pills the size of large beans. Five ingredients, one medicinally effective ingredient, take five pills the size of hare droppings. Six ingredients, one medicinally effective drug, take six pill the use of wutong seeds [firmiana] The preparation of pills is determined by the number [of the ingredients]. The reference to 'medicinally effective ingredient' is to a potent herb, usually of the lower class, while the other ingredients, though effective, are milder in nature and used to harmonize the activity of the main ingredient. The term applied in Chinese for these effective ingredients is du, which means toxin or poison. However, this epitaph is used as a contrast to the herbs that can be taken in large quantity and repeatedly, which are said to be free of toxins."[130]

Ma was a unique drug because it was both feminine, or yin, and masculine, or yang. Yin represented the weak, passive, and negative female influence in nature while yang represented the strong, active, and positive male force. When yin and yang were in balance, the body was in harmony and healthy. When yin and yang were out of balance, the body was in a state of disequilibrium and ill. Ma was used to treat absences of yin, such as: menstruation, gout, rheumatism, malaria, beri-beri, constipation, and absentmindedness.[131]

There is considerable confusion in the terms used for cannabis and its various parts, seed, leaf, flower, stem and root. The flower, or mafen, is also called mabo or mahua, and these terms are inconstant throughout different ages and eras, reflected in different associations and applications in various translations and transmissions of Chinese Herbal and Medical texts throughout the centuries.[132] Nonetheless, cannabis and its various parts have been used in Chinese Medicine from its very earliest beginnings and is still used today. Its many applications include relief from various types of pain, complications with menstruation and childbirth, expelling wind, itching and skin problems, gout, cough, spasms, convulsions, headaches, and many other conditions. Today Ma Ze Ren Wai, Hemp Seed Pill, is still a prominent remedy in Traditional Chinese Medicine.

> **Cannabis Root Tonic**
> * Cannabis Root 2 parts
> * Ginseng Root 1 part
> *Suspend in Clear Grain Spirits 3 months or longer.*

There is a long and enduring history of cannabis root in Traditional Chinese Medicine starting even before Shennung's Pên Ts'ao Ching of 2800 BCE, extending into the present with current Chinese medical research into cannabinoids. Shennong's Materia Medica recommended utilized the dried cannabis root for reducing pain in broken bones and surgery, a diuretic, to reduce swelling from abrasions, for post-partum bleeding and difficult childbirth. The root contains primarily sugars and lipids, low levels of terpenes, alkaloids, choline and atropine. In 1971 the terpenes friedelin, pentacyclic triterpene ketones, and epifriedelanol were isolated from the root. Friedelin is found in many plants, as well as algae, lichen, mosses, peat, coal, and mineral wax. Friedelin has been shown in clinical tests to have anti-inflammatory, antipyretic, and analgesic effects, reduce fever, abdominal constrictions and stretching.[133] The alkaloids piperidine and pyrrolidine have both been found in the roots, stems, seeds, pollen and leaves.[134] Pentacyclic triterpene ketones are associated with antimicrobial and anti-inflammatory effects. Cannabis roots being should be carefully selected from known organic growers, since cannabis roots can be used for phytoremediation and can accumulate heavy metals from the soil, including iron, chromium, and cadmium. The roots are generally used dried and powdered or as a decoction or tincture. Sometimes the roots are juiced fresh as well. There is also a hemp-root tea known as ma cha that is still consumed in Korea[135]

> **Cannabis Root Salve**
> Melt 1-part beeswax over a gentle heat. Mix in 4-parts dried and powdered cannabis root till well blended. Remove from heat and stir in ½-part hemp seed oil. Place in amber glass container and store.

Traditionally cannabis root has been used around the globe for gout, joint pain, burns, bruises, skin rash and inflammation, removing blood clots and stopping hemorrhaging during childbirth.

Roots anchor and stabilize while drawing in nutrients and water. The soil is their home, the moist darkness of the mother and their energy is yin like their chthonic abode. Roots can also form symbiotic relationships with fungi in the soil.

Healthy roots are essential to a healthy plant. The roots stretch out horizontally in equal proportion to the canopy of the plant and grow down 9 – 18 inches, depending on the soil's moister. The moister the soil, the shallower the horizontal roots grow. The vertical roots can stretch down up to 4' in search of water, while in moist soil they may be quite short.

"There is no 'perfect' soil for growing cannabis; different varieties each grow within a range of soil condition parameters. The soil must be well-drained, nutrient rich, and have a pH between 5.8 – 6.5... the soil should test high in the three macronutrients: nitrogen (N), phosphorous (P), and potassium (K). The most important quality of any soil is its texture, which is determined by the size of the soil particles. Marijuana prefers soil that drains well but also holds moderate to large quantities of water." [136]

Substantiation for the cultivation and usage of cannabis at this early stage in China is confirmed by archaeological findings at the Yanghai Tombs in the Turpan District of the Xinghian-Uighur Autonomous Region in China. A large amount of cannabis radio-carbon dated to 2700 years ago was found in the tomb of a male shaman, resembling those of other mummies of the Tarim Basin also containing cannabis artefacts.[137] There was found a skeleton of a forty five year old male shaman, who died in the "Heavenly Mountains" in the highlands of the Tian Shan and was later moved to a cemetery complex at Yanghai. Near the head and foot of the shaman's bier was a large leather basket and wooden bowl with 789 g of cannabis sativa. After careful analysis of the plant material found, an international scientific team determined that "the Gushi culture cultivated cannabis for pharmaceutical, psychoactive or divinatory purposes."[138] Nearby in Turpan at the Jiacemetery, there were found well preserved locally grown cannabis plants that were arranged like a burial shroud for the deceased.[139] What this shows us without a doubt, is that cannabis has been known and used as a religious sacramental agent and for medical purposes for over two millenniums, and in all probability for more than six millenniums, and it was used in areas associated with Magu and the Daoist Immortals. The tribal people of the region around Tian Shan are predominantly practice the shamanistic religion of Tengrism. Cannabis is indigenous to the region and from the times of the Silk Road to the present. An abundance of petroglyphs have been found in the area that indicate an intimate knowledge of the psychoactive and entheogenic qualities of their flora and fauna.[140] Cannabis in the form of textiles and incense was a major trade item on the Silk Road and fine Chinese silk and hemp fabrics were prized in the Middle East, Mediterranean, and Europe.

Taishan, or Mount Tai, in the Yellow River basin, was the sacred mountain of Shengnog, and Magu was the goddess of the mountain and her sacred herb was grown upon Taishan mountain for the Daoist seance banquets, and to burn in censures for divination and to speak with the immortals.[141] Today Taishan Mountain is still covered in wild cannabis plants.[142] Shennong introduced the principle of the five fingers, most likely inspired by the five fingers of the cannabis sativa leaf. The five finger principle divides all things into five phases of energetics for classification of things and their properties. This is illustrated by the five grains and applied practically by the "Five Excellences": painting, medicine, calligraphy, poetry, and t'ai chi ch'uan or by the "Five Perfections" of drinking, drugs, smoking, sex and gambling.[143]

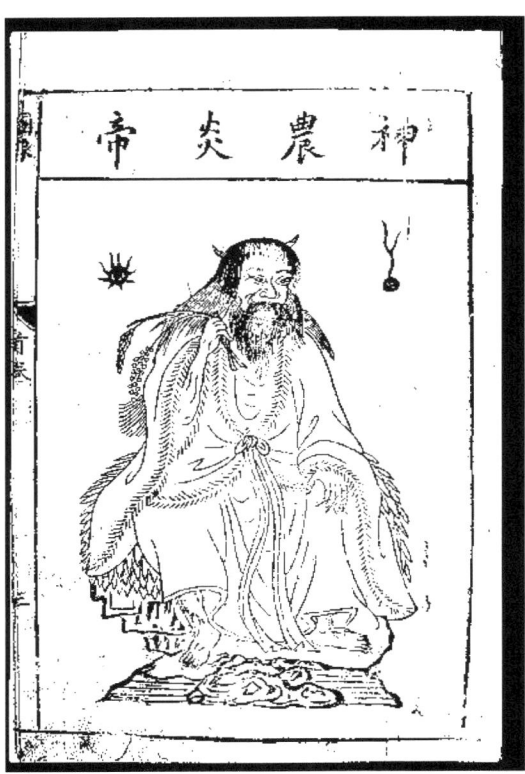

Hmong Cannabis Culture

The Miao, Meo or Hmong, are a minority ethnic group of China, Laos, Thailand and Vietnam who originated, like the widespread cultivation of cannabis, in China. Specifically, in the Yellow River Delta and along the lower reaches of the Yellow River and the middle and lower reaches of the Yangtze River around 2300 BCE, possibly descended from the Liangzhu Culture and are one of China's largest minority ethnic groups, distributed mainly over Guizhou, Hunan, Yunnan, Sichuan, Guangdong and Hubei provinces and the Guangxi Zhuang Autonomous Region, they also have large communities in Thailand, Vietnam and the United States in Minnesota and California. They were known from the earliest times as weavers and dyers, growing cannabis for their thread, cloth, medicine, food and inspiration. The Hmong were described as "those who dwelled among the clouds and mist." Hemp seed was a dietary staple of the Hmong, eaten roasted for snacks, made into tofu and hemp milk, and prepared as a paste or a drink. The seeds were roasted and pressed for their nutritious oil, and the leaves were made into an infusion to relieve constipation, encourage smooth bowel movements and cure measles in children. The leaves and buds were also smoked by men to "relieve discomfort".[144] Seeds, leaves, flowers, stalk and ash from the cannabis are all used traditionally by the Hmong for healing and curing of disease and ailments. The religious expression of the Hmong includes shamanistic rituals and ceremonies of healing, divination, protection and the cycles of life that are deeply and religiously connected to the cannabis plant. The three major religions of China, Korea, Japan and Vietnam are native tribal shamanist animism, Daoism and Buddhism. These are reflected by the Hmong shaman's view of the three worlds of the earth, spirit and heavens. The native shamanistic practices connect one with the plants, animals and energies of the earth, the Daoist alchemical practices connect one with the spiritual realms of the immortals and the Buddhist practices connect one with the heavenly Buddhas. Of course, all of these realms exist within each person and are expressed as the consciousness, subconscious and the archetypal realm of the collective consciousness. Buddhism which is prevalent in all of these regions of the world as well as Thailand, is also composed of three parts, schools, or traditions, the three vehicles of Theravada, Mahayana and Vajrayana which represent the progressive stages of the path.

The Hmong still practice their tribal religion based upon animism and shamanic practices, never fully adopting Taoist or Buddhist practices, instead they hold onto their traditional shamanistic practices akin to those of the Tungstic shamans

and the Neolithic shamans of the remote past. Animism is the belief that every being and every natural object and force has a spirit, called by the Hmong, dab. Communication with these spirits is accomplished by navigating different dimensions of consciousness, called by the Hmong, nee. Also important to the Hmong are care of the soul in the realm of the physical and spirit, the reverence of, and communication with, ancestorial spirits and the wheel of karma. [145] Ancestor Worship has been practiced in China since Neolithic times. Ancestors are revered and respected, honored and remembered. They are believed to live on to help their descendants and ensure their protection and prosperity. They are consulted in time of crisis, need or grief through the burning of incense. Gifts are also given to them in the form of joss papers or offerings of food and drink. They are not seen as deities, but rather guardian spirits, however, the gods and immortals may have first been revered as ancestors and over time grown to become deities. Ghosts are seen as benign spirits of those who have passed on, but their spirits still linger for a time. Hungry Ghosts are persons that were neglected when alive or deprived of a good life in some cases, while others are people that died of a violent or unnatural death. Either way, they are tormented spirits that seek for something that cannot be attained or resolved. Some people can naturally see ghosts, but they commonly have bad luck and misfortune. [146]
For the Hmong people, Chiyou was their ancestral sage king and the God of War, one of the three legendary founding fathers of China. Chiyou had a bronze head of a bull with a metal forehead, two horns, four eyes and six arms, wielding terrible sharp weapons in every hand and the body of a human. He had 81 brothers comprising the 81 clans in his kingdom. Chiyou knew the maps of the constellations and the ancient's spells for calling upon the weather. He was also associated with Chìdì (赤帝)the Red Deity, the Nándì (帝) the South Deity, Nányuèdàdì (南岳大帝)the Great Deity of the Southern Peak, Yandi the Fiery Deity associated with the essence of fire and summer and with the planet Mars. He was Shennong the Divine Farmer, his animal form the Red Dragon and his stellar animal the Phoenix, the god of agriculture, animal husbandry, medicinal plants and the market.

In Hmong cosmology, "mam ntsuj hlau" or "mam pling hlau," means "soul of hemp" and refers to one of the three main divisions of the soul. The soul can have many divisions, but there are three main divisions, the earthly, the spiritual and the heavenly. Man ntsuj hlau is the earthly connection the connection to the land, the connection to the home, the connection to the family and the connection to the community. This can be seen in the symbolism of Ua dab ceremonies where spirits are propitiated with khi hluas, thread-tying rituals using hemp strings. These strings signify the binding up and holding intact of the life-souls. Man ntsuj hlau also refers to the shadow, both the visible shadow and the spiritual shadow.[147] Hemp string tying rituals where hemp strings were tied most commonly around the wrists, but also the neck or ankles, were performed to capture good fortune and prevent the separation of the soul from the body. Performed commonly during healing and protection ceremonies, the naming of infants, weddings, when there is illness and for celebrating leaving for or returning from a journey. During healing ceremonies, a hemp cord is tied to the alter to serve as a bridge to the spirit world for the shaman to travel along.[148]

The dab tshuaj, or gods of medicine, are generally worshipped by women in Hmong culture because women specialize in the knowledge of herbalism, as it was taught to them by the first shaman. It is in their funeral rites that the usage of hemp cloth is most prominent in Hmong society today because it is said that "the dead need the hemp cloth."[149] Mourners must be dressed in hemp clothing and the dead must also be buried in hemp clothing. The dead must wear sandals made from twisted and braided hemp bark to guide the corpse to the afterlife, they must also wear a hemp collar or else "sky door's gods will refuse the dead's spirit," and there are several long pieces of hemp cloth are hung vertically above the coffin from the top of the wall opposite the door. The coffin is the "horse" and the hemp cloth represents the "horse's tether" that will "lead the horse to the after-world."[150]

"*When an elderly Hmong woman dies, her corpse must be dressed in a hemp jacket, hemp skirt and hemp leggings. The Hmong man must wear a long hemp robe. Both wear hemp shoes. The Hmong believe that when the dead person wears hemp shoes, they can 'ford the caterpillar river and cross the green worm mountain safely, to reach their ancestor's resting place'… Hemp fiber is also used to make rope for tying animals, securing loads to horses and carrying firewood. The Hmong make twine from hemp and hemp is used to make the strongest crossbow strings. Sacks are made from the finer hemp cloth strips sewn at a diagonal. The sacks are tall so the top can be twisted and tied onto a horse's saddle to support the load of grain within. When the Hmong harvest their hemp, they spread the hemp leaves to enrich the land. The fresh leaves are also fed to pigs and goats. Dry peeled hemp stalk hurds are used as kindling for lighting cooking fires. In the past, there was no electricity, and the Hmong women burned hemp hurds for light while they peeled the fibrous hemp bark from the stalks. Hemp hurds are also good for stuffing pillows, building temporary animal fencing or erecting trellises for climbing crops…*"[151]

At the end of the Vietnam War, the United States pulled out of Laos in 1975 and thousands of Hmong who had collaborated with the CIA were slaughtered or fled to refugee camps. Many of the Hmong refugees from the Vietnam War were relocated to the United States, primarily in Minneapolis with the second largest concentration being in the Sacramento, California area, totaling over 45,000 Hmong and over 100,000 Hmong in California. In 2015, many Hmong settled in Siskiyou County near Mount Shasta in the mountains of Northern California "because its terrain reminded them of the mountains of Laos, where the Hmong lived and grew opium and cannabis for generations."[152] Mouying Lee, a 43-year-old computer programmer from Fresno and a child of the Hmong refugee camps in Thailand, was among the first Hmong to arrive in Siskiyou County and purchased parcels which he sold to more than 300 families who set up medical cannabis farms "for the feng shui" of the mountains and to make poultices, shower rinses, broth and tea. They have encountered much persecution for their efforts though, and the local sheriff has reached out to both State and Federal authorities for assistance in combating what he claims are illegal "pot farms". In 2015 when they began creating their farms, the Siskiyou County Board of Supervisors banned outdoor cultivation of cannabis. The Siskiyou County Board of Supervisors voted, in the Fall of 2017, 5-0 to declare "a State of Emergency" caused by widespread cannabis cultivation in the county.[153] Nearby in Trinity County, over 1,000 Hmong families have moved the Hayfork/Trinity Pines area and set up medical cannabis farms.[154] The plots were generally 2 ½ acres and 99 plants are grown, one plant under the Federal Mandatory Minimum Sentencing for Cannabis. Raids and arrests have been ongoing against the Hmong cannabis growers ever since.

"When the moon gets full on the 15th, I will come to your side. In the good season of the golden autumn, let's harvest the crops together. You drive a strong bull plowing plots of terraced lands, I sit by the loom weaving twelve bolts of cloth. You take your balance and counterweights out, keeping your mind on doing business. I will stay at home sewing, making new cloths for you. Though it is not silk nor satin, hemp cloths can warm you well."[155]

Balancing Yin and Yang

"Carrying Out Practice, Sun Bu-er:
Gather the breath into the point where the spirit is frozen, and all living energy comes from the east. Don't get stuck in anything at all, and one energy will come back to the terrace. The darkness should go down the front, the light induced up the back. After a shower, a peal of thunder rumbles at the top of the mountain and the bottom of the sea.
Commentary by Chen Yingning:
The active phase is called promoting the fire of light, and its course is up the spine from the coccyx to the center of the brain. The passive phase is called converging back into darkness, and its course is down the chest into the ocean of the abdomen... thunder in the earth trembles, it rains on the summit of the mountain... dark and light alternate, everywhere producing a peal of thunder... suddenly at midnight, a peal of thunder; ten thousand doors, a thousand gates, open one after another... when the adept gathers primal energy, it thunders all night... when people know the nine flowered heaven above, all night wind and thunder shake the myriad mountains... thunder in the earth, returning... primal unified energy stored for a long time until its power is great, then emerging in action responding to situations... for women thunder is simply when in the course of the work there is energy in the lower abdomen which thrusts up to the breasts. Rain means yin energy, thunder means yang energy."[156]

"*Heaven and Earth are the Great Forge, yin and yang are the pivitos of transformation, and the unified qi (vital energy) is the great medicine. To refine the elixir, use your inner male and female, yang and yin qi, and circulate them all around the inner stars until they form the alchemical vessel. The Metal Mother (the Queen Mother of the West) resides right there, and through wondrous transformations stimulates the qi of life.*"[157]

"*Breath is the bridge which connects life to consciousness, which unites your body to your thoughts.*" - Thich Nhat Hanh

"*He who stands on tiptoe doesn't stand firm. He who rushes ahead doesn't go far. He who tries to shine dims his own light. He who defines himself can't know who he really is. He who has power over others can't empower himself. He who clings to his work will create nothing that endures. If you want to accord with the Tao, just do your job, then let go.*" Dao de Jing Ch. 24 trans. Hong Kong University

ཨོཾ་ཨཱཿཧཱུྃ་བཛྲ་གུ་རུ་པདྨ་སིདྡྷི་ཧཱུྃ༔

The Vajra Guru Mantra, which carries the entire blessing of the 12 types of teachings of the Buddha- the essence of his 84,000 dharmas:[158]

OM AH HUM
VAJRA GURU PADMA
SIDDHI HUM

"To keep on filling is not as good as stopping. Calculated sharpness cannot be kept for long. Though gold and jewels fill their house, no one can keep them. When the rich upper classes are haughty, their legacy indicts them. When one' work is accomplished honorably, to retire is the Way of heaven. Carrying vitality and consciousness, embracing them as one, can you keep from parting? Concentrating energy, making it supple, can you be like an infant? Purifying hidden perception, can you make it flawless? Loving the people, governing the nation, can you be uncontrived? As the gate of heaven opens and closes, can you be impassive? As understanding reaches everywhere, can you be innocent? Producing and developing, producing without possessing, growing without domineering: this is called mysterious power. Thirty spokes join at a hub: their use for the cart is where they are not. When the potter's wheel makes a pot, the use of the pot is precisely where there is nothing. When you open the doors and windows for a room, it is where there is nothing that they are useful to the room. Therefore, being is for benefit, nonbeing is for usefulness. Colors blind people's eyes; sounds deafen their ears; flavors spoil people's palates, the chase and the hunt craze people's minds; goods hard to obtain make people's actions harmful. Therefore, sages work for the middle and not the eyes, leaving the latter and taking the former." Dao de Ching Ch. 9- 12 trans. Thomas Cleary

Circulation of the Light and Protection of the Center

Meditation, Stage 1: Gathering the light.

"*According to the law, but without exertion, one must diligently fill oneself with light. Forgetting appearance, look within and help the true spiritual power! Ten months them embryo is under fire. After a year the washing and baths become warm.*" The Hui Ming Ching, The Book of Consciousness and Life, Ch. 3 trans. Richard Wilhelm

"*When we reverse the Light, all the Yin and Yang Breaths of Heaven and Earth coagulate. This is what we call 'refining thought,' 'purifying Breath,' or 'purifying thinking,'*" - Secret of the Golden Flower trans. F.P.

"*There is a saying: As you breathe, so the firm and yielding rub against each other, so they form the very image of Qian and Kun, opening and closing. The method of inner development which produces a divine Immortal uses man's ability to 'reflect back his brightness to light up within. His outbreath and inbreath merge together into a stage of supreme peace.*"

"*When the light is made to move in a circle, all the energies of heaven and earth, of the light and the dark, are crystallized. That is what is termed seed-like thinking, or purification of the energy, or purification of the idea. When one begins to apply this magic it is as if, in the middle of being, there were non-being... The circulation of the light is the epoch of fire.*" - Secret of the Golden Flower Ch 3 trans. Richard Wilhelm

"**The third realization is that the human mind is always searching for possessions and never feels fulfilled.**"[159]

"He who assists the ruler by Tao does not resort to arms to dominate all under Heaven by force. This thing loves to rebound. Where troops have encamped, brambles grow; After the raising of great armies a famine follows invariably. A good man merely lets it bear fruit; He does not seek to force it. He lets it bear fruit; he is not vainglorious. He lets it bear fruit; he is not boastful. He lets it bear fruit; he is not arrogant. He lets it bear fruit, out of necessity. He lets it bear fruit and does not force it. When a thing reaches its prime it becomes old. Forcing is called contrary to Tao. What is contrary to Tao expires early." Dao de Ching Ch. 30 trans. Ha Poong

Interpretation:
A solid line in between two broken lines symbolizes water, a river or stream. The two broken lines represent the depression of earth (riverbanks). The solid line in the middle represents motion. This creates the image of water flowing in a river. In addition, this kua also represents the moon. The Soul, like the river, flows from the source in the mountain to the sea, where it is dies to be transformed into clouds in the womb of the sea to be reborn as the rain in the mountains. The motivation is danger and the abyss. It is the Abysmal Gorge of the second son in motion. Water is women's wisdom and the window to the spirit world.

Right Action:
Moral, honorable, and peaceful conduct. It admonishes us that we should abstain from destroying life, from stealing, from dishonest dealings, abstinence from taking what is not given, from sexual exploitation and coercion, and that we should also help others to lead a peaceful and honorable life in the right way. It is also often taken to not eating meat from an animal that was killed specifically to feed you; as with the intention of non-harming, the literal meaning of the abstinence from the destruction of life has far-reaching implications.

Four Noble Truths

The fact of life is suffering.
The cause of suffering is desire.
The end of desire is the end of suffering.
There is a path that leads from suffering.

- **All existence is dukkha (unsatisfactory).**
- **The arising (samudaya) of dukkha is thirsty craving (tanha).**
- **The cessation (nirodha) of dukkha comes with the end of tanha.**
- **There is a path (marga) that leads from dukkha.**

It's all bullshit.
The cause of bullshit is bullshitters bullshitting.
Enough of the bullshit.
Stop bullshitting.

Four Directions and Guardians

The four cardinal points of the compass are represented by four guardians who govern the four cardinal directions and command the spirit animals of the directions who are protectors and defenders, identified by their color and symbolic representations. In traditional Chinese astronomy, the zodiacal belt is also divided into the four constellation groups corresponding to the four cardinal directions. These four, the tortoise, dragon, phoenix and tiger guard the Four Imperial Palaces, Si Yu Dian, and the Treasured Ones of the Four Corners, Si Fang Bao Ren, and are often called upon before ritual work to assume their qualities. They are reflected in the individual through the Four Majesties: "Walk like the wind, stand like the pine, sit like a bell and lie like a bow."[160] Mago's children also embody the four types of cannabis.

The limitless wuji produces the delimited youji, and this demarcation is the same as the Absolute taiji. The two opposing forces in embryonic form of the Taiji produces two manifested opposing forces named yin-yang which are called Liangyi. These two forms produce four phenomena: named lesser yin, shaoyin, greater yin, taiyin, which also refers to the Moon, lesser yang, shaoyang, and greater yang, taiyang, which also refers to the Sun. The four phenomena, Sìxiàng, act on the eight trigrams, the Bagua, eight 'eights' results in sixty-four hexagrams. - Fuxi

Xuanwu is the Black Warrior Tortoise Snake of the winter's North who hears every sound, utterance, thought and prayer, while bestowing clairaudience and being completely versed in Buddha's teachings. The tortoise stands for immutability and steadfastness, while its shell represents the vaulted heavens of the universe and its underside, the flat disk of the earth, yet also it is also a suit of armor protecting Xuanwu, the Enigmatic Dark Warrior God of the North. Du Wen Tian Wang is the Guardian of the North, the winter solstice, the energy of water and commands a legion of nature spirits while carrying his noble mushroom shaped parasol. He is patron, guardian and protector of kings, nobles, aristocrats and grants protection, shielding, stability and resilience.[161] The North is the region of Siberia, Mongolia and Manchuria, home of the Tungstic peoples and their ancient traditions of shamanism.

Xuanwu references the divinatory powers of the tortoise. The tortoise has a black back and is said to have the ability to enter the netherworld in the North to receive revelation of that which is to come. During the Shang (Yin) Dynasty Taoist Practitioners would face North when practicing divination, in the direction of Xuanwu and archaeological excavations have revealed Oracle Bones inscribed on tortoise shell in profusion from the Bronze Age Shang Dynasty in the middle and lower Yellow River Valley along with evidence of cannabis cultivation from the hemp cord impressed pottery.

Xuanwu is usually depicted as both a tortoise and a snake, often with the snake coiling around the tortoise. the Tortoise and Snake is a common symbol for longevity because the black yin tortoise and the yang snake engendered the universe through their union. Common knowledge and observation also inform us of the tortoise's notorious long lifespan. Legend has it that in the depts of the ocean there is a tortoise with one eye in the middle of its body. Once, every three thousand years, it rises to the surface of the ocean and turns over on its back so that it may see the sun.

Cannabis Ruderals is a very short plant with a thick stalk, short intermodal lengths, thin, light green leaves and almost immediate flowering time. Ruderalis grows wild in the northern regions of Eastern Europe, Russia, and Asia. A rugged plant that grows well in harsh climates with short growing seasons. This very short plant has thick stalks and stems, sparse, light green leaves and small, chunky flowers that start to flower based on its age, instead of the light and dark periods that determine flowering periods for indicas and sativas. Ruderalis has low THC content but may contain other useful cannabinoids. It, like the mushroom, is often anthropomorphized a dwarf or other "little people".

Azure Dragon of the East is azure, the color of lapis lazuli, and represents the chthonic power that supports, nurtures, develops and brings nourishment while bestowing the power of control over events. The Azure Dragon corresponds to the season spring, the element wood, and the virtue of propriety. Dragons are said to be shape shifters and may assume human form and though they may be fearsome and powerful, they are equally just, benevolent, and the bringers of wealth and good fortune. When paired with the Phoenix they represent both conflict and wedded bliss.

Chi Guo Tian Wang is the Guardian of the East, the spring equinox, the energy of wood and commands a legion of celestial musicians with his lute. He is patron, guardian and protector of arts, culture, artists, musicians and poets. His dragon supports, nurtures, develops, nourishes, and bestows the power of authority and Dong Wang Gong is the Grand Duke of the East, the personification of the divine yang.[162] The East is the region of Japan, Korea and Taiwan, of the traditions of Magoism, Muism, Shinto, Zen, Mazu and the ancient Taiwanese Indigenous Gāoshān people.

Cannabis Sativa grows tall rapidly and has a long flowering time, intoxicating flowers that stimulate the mind, and is good for producing fiber. Sativa plants thrive in the warmer equatorial climates, such as Colombia, Mexico, Thailand, and Southeast Asia. Tall, Christmas-tree shaped plants, wide at its base with a single stem at top, loosely branched with long intermodal lengths and long, thin, light green leaves. Its flowers are light, airy, and long maturing time, between 10 to 16 weeks. Noted for its "heady" effects and energizing qualities, and its qualities of enhancing creativity and productivity, and relieving depression. Sativas are also common fiber and seed producing strains with low THC and sometime high CBD concentrations, commonly referred to as Hemp.

Fenghaung is the Red Vermillion Phoenix of the South, born on the Hill of the Sun's Halo, who brings growth, advancement and innovation while bestowing the power to create, and makes small seeds grow into giant trees Fenghaung corresponds to summer, red, fire, the sun, knowledge, justice, obedience, fidelity, and the southern star constellations. Personifying the primordial forces of the heavens and the substance of the flame that lives in the heart of the sun. Lady Zhurong is the master of flying daggers and warrior chieftain. Zhurong is the God of the Southern Fire who defeated the water god Gong Gong. Zeng Chang Tian Wang is the Guardian of the South, the summer solstice, the energy of fire and commands a legion of dwarflike spirits with his sword. He is patron, protector and guardian of warriors, soldiers, teachers, professors, academics and education. His phoenix brings growth, advancement and innovation, while bestowing intelligence, cunning strategy and awareness.[163] The South is the region of Vietnam, Thailand, Laos, Cambodia, and Myanmar, the home of Satsana Phi, Theravada and Mahayana Buddhism, Đạo Mẫu, and Miao practices.

The male phoenix is named "feng" and is the yang, solar, fire bird, but the female "huang" is its feminine, yin, lunar counterpart that denotes beauty, delicacy of feeling, and peace. Feng and the Huang together symbolize everlasting love and is used as a bridal symbol to signify inseparable fellowship. The Fenghaung symbolizes a duality, the yin-yang, mutual interdependence in the universe. Fenghaung is often paired with the dragon to represent both conflict and wedded bliss, or the dragon emperor and phoenix empress found in some early artifacts. Many artifacts also show the fenghaung with a snake in its mouth.

Fenghaung has three legs, twelve tail feathers and feathers of a peacock that shine radiantly with five mystical colors - black, white, red, green and yellow. It has the face of a swallow, the forehead of a fowl, the head and comb of a pheasant, the bill of a rooster, the mouth of a parrot, the neck of a snake, the front of a swan, the body of a mandarin duck, the hinder parts of a unicorn, the stripes of a dragon, the arched back of a tortoise, tail of a fish, the legs of a crane, the wings of a swallow and carries in its bill two scrolls or a square box that contains sacred books. Fenghaung is the embodiment of the Confucian Cardinal Virtues of loyalty, honesty, decorum and justice that are inscribed upon its body that symbolizes the six celestial bodies. The head is the sky, the eyes are the sun, the back is the moon, the wings are the wind, the feet are the earth, and the tail are the planets. It is a gentle creature, alighting so gently that it crushes nothing, and eats only dewdrops, bamboo and cannabis seeds, lives in the branches of the dryandera tree, and drinks from fountains of fresh water. Fenghaung controls, and is the expression of, the harmony of the five tones of traditional Chinese music and sings the most enchanting song of any bird when appearing in times of good fortune. Fenghaung hides when there is trouble or disharmony so visions of Fenghaung are omens of great luck or peaceful and prosperous times in the future. Its qualities are expressed by its color delighting the eye, its comb expressing righteousness, its tongue speaking sincerity, its voice singing a melody, its ear enjoying music, its heart conforming to regulations, its breast containing the treasures of literature, its spurs powerful weapons against transgressors, its flight representing the capacity to leave the world and its problems behind, flying towards the sun in clear pure skies.

Cannabis Indica is a shorter, bushy plant with thick, broad dark green and purple leaves and a short flowering time, whose sticky flowers induce the classic, "body high". A subspecies of Indica is called C. afghanica, is commonly called Kush. Indica grows better in the cooler temperatures and high altitudes of the Hindu Kush mountain range and regions of Afghanistan, Pakistan, India, and Nepal. Conical to short and bushy, usually wider than it is tall, with lots of side branching, short intermodal length, short stem length and dark green to purple wide, short leaves. Its Pungent, sticky and fruity buds grow in wide, dense clusters and are heavy and fragrant. This faster growing strain usually flowers between 7-9 weeks. Noted for its heavy body effects and high THC levels, pain and stress relief and as a sleep aid.

White Tiger of the West can see every sight, act, deed, gesture and movement while bestowing clairvoyance and guarding Buddha's teachings and mankind, this the king of all animals and lord of the mountains. The White Tiger corresponds to the season fall, the color white, wind, the element metal, and the virtue righteousness and is worshiped with white jade. Guang Mu Tian Wang is the Guardian of the West, the autumn equinox, the energy of metal and commands a legion of snakes with his snake whip. He protects and defends against demons, malicious acts, temptation and evil, while granting strength and courage. His tiger sees every sight, act, deed, gesture and movement.[164] The West is the region of Tibet, the Western Steeps, India and beyond, home to the Buddha and the Indian, Tibetan, Aryan, Bactria-Margiana, Göbekli Tepe, Sumerian and Scythian cultures.

Cannabis Hybrids are a cross between various strains that can range from high seed producing, fiber producing, terpene profile, cannabinoid profile, Indica dominant, sativa dominant, auto flowering and many other variations or adaptations.[165] Hybrid strains are strains that have been bread for specific qualities or have evolved to adapt to environmental factors, or both. Not all strains are Sativa, Indica or Ruderalis. Cannabis is one of the most adaptable plants known to humankind and it has traveled, grown and evolved alongside us for thousands upon thousands of years. Between human cultivation and breading for desired qualities combined with environmental adaptation, cannabis expresses itself in thousands and thousands of varieties and expressions. It may be Sativa or Indica dominant, or they may be a mix of the two or even crossed with Ruderalis to create "auto flowering" strains that have short growing cycles that are good for indoor cultivation. Breading has been done by farmers and growers to create different types of fiber for rope and cloth, different types of seed for food and oil, various terpene and cannabinoid profiles for medicinal value, and the plant has adapted itself into hearty landrace varieties that thrive in local micro-climates. Growing seeds from the same plant won't be genetic identical, they will be like siblings, but not identical twins. Each strain is the product of mating a male and female plant. You can map out cannabis strains just like you would map out a family tree.

A verse for planting trees and plants:
"*I entrust myself to the earth,*
Earth entrusts herself to me.
I entrust myself to Buddha,
Buddha entrusts herself to me."[166]

"*The best are like water. Water benefits all things and does not compete with them. It flows to the lowest level. In this it comes near to the Way. In their dwellings, they love the earth. In their hearts, they love what is profound. In their friendship, they love humanity. In their words, they love sincerity. In government, they love peace. In business, they love ability. In their actions, they love timeliness. It is because they do not compete that there is no resentment.*" Dao de Jing Ch 8 trans. Sanderson Beck

Immortal Yellow Emperor
黄帝

The third and last sovereign, Huangdi, Haung Ti, Haung Di, or Yellow Soil, known popularly as the Yellow Emperor, was born in Shandong on the Yellow River where Chinese civilization is thought to have originated. His name Haungdi, implies that he was made of the yellow soil of the Yellow River and therefore must have been one of the first and finest of the people that Nuwa formed from the soil. He represents the center of the four cardinal directions, **humanity and the Yellow Dragon**. The Yellow Emperor, Huangdi, the Shaman King and Emperor of China lived in the Neolithic Peroid around 2704-2598 BCE. His reign as Emperor is said to have begun in 2697 BCE when he united the tribes of the Yellow River plain under a single government. The oldest oracle bones found have been dated to this peroid and there have been extensive archaeological findings of early civilzation from this era in Northern and Northeastern China.[167] The Neolithic Yangshao of the Yellow River cultivated cannabis as early as 6,000 years ago and left behind extensive archaeobotanical evidence, they also left behind many goddess sculptures.

The Yellow Emperor was known as Keeper of Bears, Son of Heaven, Yellow Deity of the Chariot Shaft, the Yellow God of the Northern Dipper, Lord Jinyun or the Yellow Lord, the last of the legendary Celestial Emperors. He gave his people the tools to create cities and civilizations, the wheel, the magnet, arithmetic, astrology, an astronomical observatory, the drum, pitch pipes, the building of houses and structures, mined bronze from Shoushan Mountain, domesticating oxen as draught animals and horses as riding animals, revealed the art of pulse measurement, manufacturing of utensils, the building of boats, wagons and carts, the pestle and mortar, bronze tripods, the creation of the calendar and compass, the development of currency, cultivation of mulberry trees and cannabis together, the breading of silkworms, silk and cannabis spinning for making clothing, caps, banners, fans and shoes, the secrets of medicine, immortality, and making gold.

Huangdi was conceived when his mother Fubao was sexually aroused while walking in the country by a lightning bolt from the Big Dipper causing a thunderclap on a clear day in the skies. Other versions relate that he was conceived of a Shenlong dragon. Fubao delivered her son after twenty-four months on the mount of Shou, Longevity, or Shou Qiu, Longevity Hill, which is today on the outskirts of the city of Qufu in Shandong Province. Huangdi was a farmer, rainmaking shaman and follower of the Dao. He visited the East sea and there met with a talking sea beast called Bai Ze who taught him the knowledge of all supernatural creatures.[168] He tamed six different special beasts: black bears, grizzly bears, foxes, panthers, lynxes and tigers. As the deity of the center, intersecting the Three Patrons and the Five Deities and the Ubiquitous God, and the Thai transmission of the Hindu god Brahma, Huangdi had four faces that could gaze upon the lands in four different directions. He was accompanied wherever he went by a procession of animals, but his totem animal was the bear and dragons pulled his chariot. He controlled lightning and thunder and was represented in the shape of the constellation of the Big Dipper. He was instructed, by both male and female teachers, in medicine and prolonging life he

learned from male teachers and magic, alchemy and sex from female teachers.[169] After being taught the Art of War by his first and primary teacher, the "Mysterious Lady of Tai Mountain," or "the Enigmatic Lady of the Ninth Heaven," who had the head of a woman and the body of a bird with wings of a phoenix, wielding a sword on one hand and a medicine gourd in the other. Haungdi was taught the secrets of the Dao by the "the Lady of Flowers and Clouds," and the Yellow Emperor urged the people to cultivate the "five grains," cannabis among them as Shennong had instructed.

"The Yellow Emperor visited the Queen Mother of the West. She instructed him in the 'art of the seven darkening' (qi mei zhi shu 七昧之術) to be avoided: eyes, ears, mouth, nose, hands, feet and heart were not to be obstructed. If only one failed, the others would be of not use in the search for the Dao. She also gave him the shape of five bodies in white jade (bai yu xiang wu shen 白玉像五軀) that was the perfect

appearance of the Yuanshi tianzun 元始天尊, *the highest deity in Daoism. She handed over to him a chart of the two powers Yin and Yang (eryi benxing tu* 二儀本形圖*), together with nineteen recipes for the pill of immortality. The Yellow Emperor thereupon ascended to a high (gao* 高*) summit, from which everything could be observed (guan* 觀; *or a place name: Gaoguan* 高觀*) where he cultivated his self, unseen by everyone, but only perceived in the shape of a multi-coloured cloud and the scent of incense. In later time the character of name of this spot was used as a term for Daoist temple, namely daoguan* 道觀*."*[170]

Haungdi had four wives. The first was Xihe, who gave birth to ten suns in the form of three-legged crows who nested in a mulberry tree. Each morning Xihe would drive a chariot across the sky pulled by one of the sun crows. Xihe computed and delineated the sun, moon, stars, celestial markers and the seasons. The ancient Chinese text the Huainanzi states that: "The sun rises up from the Bright Valley, bathes in the Pool of Xian, and rests in the Fusang Tree. This is called Dawn Light. Ascending the Fusang Tree, it thereupon commences its journey. This is called Emergent Brightness."[171] Another wife of the Yellow Emperor was Leizu or Luozu, who discovered the cultivation of silkworms to produce silk, the combining of silk and cannabis fiber to produce cloth and invented the loom. As Leizu was having tea in her garden on day under a mulberry tree a cocoon fell into her tea. Leizu had just been sampling the incense that she had grown in her garden and gazed at the cocoon unraveling in her teacup. She tried to take the cocoon from her teacup and instead was only able to grip a single strand. She walked away from the teacup with the thread in her hand and walked around in her garden, as she did, the silk thread of the cocoon unraveled and soon the garden was covered in a web of fine and sturdy silk thread. Leizu was ecstatic about her new discovery of this strong and soft thread, the perfect accompaniment to the soft and sturdy fibers of young male cannabis plants. She immediately ran to the Yellow Emperor and insisted that they immediately plant a grove of mulberry trees with cannabis plants between the rows, so that they could teach their people how to cultivate silk and cannabis fibers. She then invented sericulture and the silk loom, and taught the people how to weave fine cloth from silk and cannabis, dye the cloth, and how to create beautiful embroidery. The silkworm goddess is Cannu, Cangu, Can Gu or Can Nu, protector of silkworms, culture, mothers, children, families, healing, weaving and mulberry trees. She was whisked away to heaven in a horse skin but returned to earth in the form of a silkworm and lives in a mulberry tree. She is honored on the third day of the third month.

"The Gardner used to cultivate the fragrant herb in five colors, the tale continues, and ate their seeds for many years, until one day five colored moths gathered around the plants. The gardener collected the moths in order to get silkworms for the next generation. Eventually, when those silkworms had produced their cocoons. One night, a [spirit] woman appeared at his door calling herself his wife. She showed him how to collect the silk."[172] The fragrant herb in five colors with edible seeds is a good description cannabis and its pungently fragrant flowers with multicolored pistils and nutritious seed which was traditionally grown between the rows of mulberry trees and whose fiber was combined with silk to make fine fabrics. The excrement of the silkworms would fall to the ground and nourish the cannabis plants growing beneath, silkworm excrement being one of the best fertilizers for cannabis.[173]

The most notable and enduring contribution of Haungdi was the Huang-ti Nei Ching, "The Inner Canon of the Yellow Emperor", a text that has inspired and guided Chinese medical thought for over 2,500 years. The Inner Canon is a dialogue between Huangdi and Ch'i Po, his Minister of Health and Healing, based on the balance of yang and yin, the five phases, and the correlations found among them in human life, from family and food to climate and geography. Another text that he left behind was called "The Yellow Emperor's Classic of Using Yin Fire." A Tang era scholar tried studying the text but was unable to understand its meaning until a faerie woman appeared to him and gave him special magical grains, that after eating them, the meaning of the text revealed itself to him.[174] He also authored the "Yellow Emperor's Inner Canon," "Four Classics of the Yellow

Emperor," the "Yellow Emperor's Hidden Talisman Classic," and the "Yellow Emperor's Four Seasons Poem" which was included in the Tung Shing fortune-telling almanac. But before any of these could be written down, Haungdi had to first inspire the historian Cangjie to create the first Chinese character writing system, the Oracle bone script. The earliest Chinese writings are found on bones and were used to communicate with heaven for divinatory purposes by Neolithic shamans whose artifacts and oracle bones have been found dating from 5,000 BCE. These shamans would divine messages from nature and heaven, traveling between the worlds as messengers. Cangjie after praying and giving offerings of incense, gazed at the footprints of birds and developed symbols to exercise metaphysical control over nature and demons, by naming and identifying them and exposing their true nature, thus allowing control over the object or entity. Writing became a method by which control could be exercised over the natural and supernatural worlds.[175]

> The mulberry plant is the food upon which silkworms feed. Almost all parts of the mulberry plant have been used in Chinese Medicine since ancient times for medicinal purposes such as inflammation, coughs, colds and flues. Mulberry leaves are astringent, antibacterial and promote perspiration. The berries can be eaten raw or dried and are often made into drinks, jams, conserves, pies, tarts and puddings or can be fermented into wine or cider. The wood of the Mulberry Tree is a water-resistant hardwood that is used for joinery, lathe work, cups, barrels and snuff boxes. In Ancient China people were instructed to plant cannabis so that they will have clothes. Cannabis was grown between the mulberry trees in the groves. Near Pyongyang, the Painted Basket Tomb from 100 CE contained fragments of hemp textiles and yellow silk. Neolithic sites, dated to 1,700 BCE, containing cannabis rope, cloth and other textiles, weaving sites and burial shrouds have been found in the Hunan, Zhejiang, Hebei, Shanxi and Gansu Provinces of China. The "Shu King", dated to about 2350 B.C., says that in the province of Shantung the soil was *"whitish and rich...with silk, cannabis, lead, pine trees and strange stones..."*

Fairy Magu and the Maidens

"A fairy went riding upon a white deer, short hair, but oh, ears were long, led me on, right up great flowery hill to pluck magic mushrooms under a scarlet pennant. When we came to the house where our host was living, we gave them a box of jade all filled with drugs. When once our host had swallowed all these drugs their body grew more hale and strong, their white hair turned to shining black once more, they lengthened their years and increased their life span." [176]

In the Liao Chai Chih Yi, Strange Stories from the Liao Studio, two maidens are foraging in the Mao Shan Mountains of the Jiangsu Province, and they come across two fairy women guarding an azure bridge leading to a Jasper City. The fairy maidens invite the two maidens to cross the fairy azure bridge and were greeted with huma, Chinese hashish, as they crossed over. They entered the Jasper City and fell in love with the hostess and spent many days there, passing the days playing chess and visiting the Highest Clarity School. One day they became remembered their families left behind and returned home, where they found that seven generations had passed in their absence. In "A Plaint of Lady Wang",[177] Lady Wang is wandering in the east heavens and meets the Fairy Cannabis Maiden. They sit down and play chess, and Lady Wang was so happy that she forgot all her mortal misery and the passage of time. These two tales both illustrate the "time-distortion" and euphoric effects of cannabis rich in THC content.

"At all events the incense-burner remained the center of changes and transformations associated with worship, sacrifice, ascending perfume of sweet savor, fire, combustion, disintegration, transformation, vision, communication with spiritual beings, and assurances of immortality. Wai tan and nei tan met around the incense-burner. Might one not indeed think of it as their point of origin" [178]

These stories of Magu may connect her with early Daoist religious usages of cannabis. Cannabis is described by the oldest Chinese pharmacopeia, Shen Nong's Materia Medica, "*The best time for gathering is the 7th day of the 7th month. The seeds are gathered in the 9th month... It grows on Mount Tai.*" Magu was goddess of Shandong's sacred Mount Tai, where the seventh day of the seventh month was a day of shamanistic seance banquets in the Daoist communities. This correlates the cannabis harvest and the day of the Daoist shamanistic divination and seance. The Daoist encyclopedia Wushang Biyao, "Supreme Secret Essentials", from 570 CE states that cannabis was added into ritual censers and it is known that Daoist sages were aided by cannabis in their nightly visitations by Daoist Xians while writing the Shangqing scriptures. Daoist Alchemists also used cannabis as part of their incense preparations according to the "Wu Shang Pi Yao" or "Essentials of the Matchless Books" written in the 6th Century,[179] cannabis was added to incense burners to drive away spirits.[180]

"The censer's incense now is lit, perfuming the dharma realm, the ocean wide host of the Bodhisattvas inhales it from afar, auspicious are the clouds that gather as we now request, with hearts sincere and earnest that all Buddhas manifest. Homage to the Bodhisattvas Mahasattavas under incense cloud canopies."[181]

There are several sacred objects that Daoist priests have used throughout the centuries holding symbolic and mystical significance. Some of them show a direct connection with cannabis. The robe, often woven from hemp cloth, secured by the hempen cord gave the wearer protection and power over the energies of the universe, the hashish incense in the ornate burner, attracted the gods and carried messages to them.

"Taoist priests used a number of sacred implements during rituals, each of which held symbolic significance. Smoke from incense burners both attracted the gods and carried messages from the community to the heavens. Swords were used for exorcism and purification ceremonies, and robes worn by the priest symbolized his power over the energies of the cosmos. Scriptures and other religious documents were also considered sacred and worshiped as embodiments of the Tao."[182]

Daoism is often thought of as a religion, but there is no set guide for set daily practices or liturgical canon. To follow the way of the Dao, live according to the principle of "Te" or De, upholding the natural order, that which makes our individuality, or specialty, our unique persons and our individual and personal connection to the Dao, that manifests as the fruits moral integrity, honor, kindness, graciousness, and benevolence. As a folk religion, it has long been associated with shamanism, ancient occult practices, witchcraft, worship of ghosts and spirits, making alchemical elixirs and cultivating immortality. As a religion it is focused upon action-based worship to become worthy for the gods to impart the secret magic of the universe that bestows peace and wellbeing. The performance of ritual-theatre magical Tang-ki ceremonies to move heaven and earth, such as the "redhat," hung-tou Daoist do, hold much in common with the rituals of Yao, Miao, Na-hsi, Moso and Bon Tibetan practices, and the Ngapa or Ngawa rites of Tibetan conjurers in parts of Amdo.

Cannabis historian Chris Bennett collected the findings of researchers such as scientist and philosopher Joseph Needham, fellow of The Royal Society of London for Improving Natural Knowledge, the United Kingdom's national academy of sciences, William Emboden Fellow Linnean Society of London and Research associate Botanical Museum Harvard University and National History Museum Los Angeles, along with other academic researchers into the history of entheogenic, ritual and shamanic use of cannabis, concluded that based on the written and archaeological evidence that cannabis was used by ancient Taoist shamans, sorcerers and sages to enter into altered states of consciousness.[183] Shamanism was integral to the development of, and practices of, Taoism and cannabis was a primary ingredient in the ritual incense of Taoist sages and sorcerers. Specifically, entheogenic use of cannabis by ancient Chinese shamans and Taoists was noted by Joseph Needham, William Emboden, Harvard ethnobotanist Richard Evans Schultes, historian of religion Mircea Eliade and Dr. Ernest Abel. Cannabis is called, chu-ma, elixer of immortality in Shennong's Herbal. The Chhu Shen Wan, or Pill of Commencing Immortality, contained cannabis as a primary ingredient. The 5th Century Taoist Magicians, shu chai, combined cannabis with ginseng to see visions of the future. The 6th Century Wu Tsang Ching, the Manuel of the Five Viscera, recommends eating cannabis flowers before invoking demons. The 15th Century Chinese Pharmacopeia Rh-Ya, mentions using cannabis for the euphoric enjoyment of life and shamanistic purposes. Hemp-snake wands are used in Taoist healing and exorcism. The cannabis harvest and Taoist seance banquets are held on the same day. Taoist stories of Fairy Maidens and time- distortion infer use of cannabis, as that is one of its most notable side effects. The cannabis plant was anthropomorphized into a deity by the Taoists who resided on a mountain known for growing cannabis, the cannabis on her mountain was harvested on the same day as the Taoist Seance banquets, and there are tales of the goddess that involve hashish, cannabis wine or tincture, and time distortion. Taoist ritual incense burners were shaped like a mountain rising out of waves of water, with holes for the smoke to rise out of to engulf the mountain with a cloud of smoke. Not only have these been shown to contain cannabis residue, they also have a shape that resembles that of a cannabis cola. Textual references to cannabis also attest to the use of cannabis in the incense burners. Braziers for burning incense dated to 2.500 years ago containing concentrated amounts of THC were found at Jirzankal Cemetery in Western China in 2016 establishing cannabis as an ingredient in ancient incense.

"At all events the incense-burner remained the centre of changes and transformations associated with worship, sacrifice, ascending perfume of sweet savour, fire, combustion, disintegration, transformation, vision, communication with spiritual beings, and assurances of immortality. Wai tan and nei tan met around the incense-burner. Might one not indeed think of it as their point of origin?" [184]

Magu the Flower Maiden is manifested in the glistening trichome laden flowers of the virgin unpollinated cannabis plants, she is the shaman that imparts wisdom of the Dao, and in death she wraps herself around us with her strong and soft shroud woven from her sinews and fiber. She is both male and female, the yin and the yang, and at times she is both at once.

"'To take too much [cannabis] makes people see demons and throw themselves about like maniacs. But if one takes it over a long period of time one can communicate with the spirits and one's own body becomes light.'" - Pên Ching, 1st Century BCE quoted in Rudgley (1998).

Trichomes can be found all over the male and female plants and are particularly concentrated in the female flowers where seeds are formed. Trichomes are made up of a mixture of different chemicals, including cannabinoids and terpenes that impart the flavors and scent as well as the medical and entheogenic qualities. The outer layer is waxy and protects the terpenes and cannabinoids from oxidation and degradation. Because of the trichomes refractive quality, they are often referred to as 'crystals' and give cannabis flowers a frosty appearance. Inside of the trichome laden calyx nestles the seed. A nutrient laden powerhouse of vitamins, minerals, amino acids and essential fatty acids. It contains the optimum balance of essential fatty acids that the body needs and all the essential amino acids, being a complete protein. No other food source contains this perfect balance and ratio of essential fatty acids and amino acids except cannabis seed. Hemp seed makes an excellent meat substitute because no other single plant source contains all the essential amino acids that the human body requires, in ratios best suited for the human body, with an easily digestible protein content of 23%. 65% of the protein content in hempseed is in the form of globulin edestin, so that it can be used by the body in its raw state. Hemp seeds are not only highly digestible, but also contain a large amount of dietary fiber, many essential vitamins, antioxidants, minerals, with the optimum balance of essential fatty acids, providing the body all of the essential needs for the optimum overall health of the human body, it's ratio of Omega 6 to Omega 3 fatty acids is about

4:1 which mirrors the primitive diet people evolved on for 2.5 million years which is why it is not surprising that cannabis is a nutritious food that has often sustained entire populations in times of famine. One of the oldest recorded medicinal uses of cannabis is eating the seeds to relieve constipation. Hemp seed contains protein, omega 3, 6, and 9 fatty acids, fiber, vitamin A, vitamin B1, vitamin B2, vitamin B6, vitamin C, vitamin D, vitamin E, sodium, calcium, iron, magnesium, phosphorus, zinc, copper and niacin. An unidentified compound or compounds, from an extract of hemp seeds, has been shown to promote memory, learning, and immune function by stimulating a brain enzyme known as calcineurin. The seeds can be ground into a meal, they can be hulled and used in numerous dishes ranging from fritters to cakes, soups and breads.

"First, soak the seed in water and sow them as soon as they germinate. Soak the seed in water for about the same time required to cook two shi of rice. Then spread the soaked seeds on the bamboo bed for about three to four cun6 in thickness. Stir the seed several times and after one night they will germinate. It is best for hemp to grow after a rain, when the rain has permeated into the soil. Second, in order to avoid plant diseases and insect pests, hemp should rotate with wheat, bean, and cereals. Third, different methods should be used with different soil moistures… Disperse the sparrows for several days in order to protect the seeds that have just germinated from being eaten by them. When the seedlings have grown for some time, thin out weak ones so that there is some distance between two seedlings and good seedlings can grow well." -Essential Arts for the People[185]

Thai Cannabis Culture

Almost as early as China, Thailand also cultivated cannabis. Cord impressions on pottery from Spirit Cave, Mae Hong Son Province, dated to 4000 BC confirm that cannabis was used at this time for rope, suggesting cannabis cultivation in Thailand as early as 4000 BC. Bronze age hemp fabrics found at Ban Chiang archaeological site located in Nong Han district, Udon Thani Province, Thailand, were dated to 2100 BC.[186] The use of cannabis, known as "ganja" in Thailand, is widespread and generally tolerated in social settings and historically cannabis was a standard item on the shelves of many Thai kitchens, and widely available from local markets. The fibers of the cannabis plant have historically been used for clothing and rope in Thailand where psychoactive strains of cannabis are naturalized and widespread. The dried, ground leaves and flowers are historically used as an ingredient in kway teeow rua, or boat noodle soup, a traditional Thai dish that has been eaten in for centuries. In Thai medicine cannabis is used to stimulate the appetite, as an analgesic and sedative to control pain, to treat diarrhea and dysentery. Traditional Thai medicine and Thai massage practitioners also historically used cannabis to treat a variety of health conditions for many centuries and cannabis used in massage oils is thought to have an astringent and soothing effect on the skin.[187] Thailand became the first Southeast Asian country to legalize medical usage of cannabis in 2019. Cannabis has long been used in the manufacture of ropes, clothing and other textiles in Thailand, particularly by the Hmong tribes in the mountainous areas in the northern parts of the country. Thailand exports hemp clothing and is one of the leading suppliers of hemp since the Thai cabinet officially approved cultivation of hemp in 2009.[188] Hand woven textiles reflect a distinct cultural heritage illustrating the ancestral past through costumes, traditions and rituals. In Thailand, the colors and patterns on fabrics are not solely for beauty, they weave a philosophy and ideology intertwined with the weaving culture of Thailand that goes back to their ancestral past. Archaeological findings in Ban Chiang include pieces of cotton, silk and cannabis fibers attesting to the long tradition of weaving silk and cannabis by the Thai. As with other cultures in the area, the knowledge and skills of textile weaving was one of the required duties of a mother, she had to train her daughter to be skillful in creating beautiful patterns on a piece of cloth.[189] In mainstream Thai culture, today however, there are signs that cannabis is increasingly viewed as outdated and rustic, and that wealthy, urban Thai youth now prefer "party drugs" such as ecstasy and amphetamine.[190]

Foreigners in Thailand are advised to exercise the utmost caution if attempting to buy or consume cannabis. For possession charges, it is not even necessary to be in physical possession of an illegal narcotic. Tourist may also be targets for arrest, "just because a destination is well-known for marijuana does not mean you won't get arrested for using. Many of our drug arrest cases come from tourist areas such as Khao San Road and Koh Phangan".[191] For most of its recorded history, Thailand, as with many other nations, had no laws prohibiting cannabis use or possession. This began to change in the early 20th century as Thailand was one of the original signatories to the League of Nations International Opium Convention of 1912, Thailand, then named Siam, enacted anti-drug legislation that enabled it to receive international grants, loans and benefits. In complying with its foundation signatory status Thailand introduced its first anti-drug laws in 1922, the Narcotics Act B.E. 2465, which laid the foundation for present day drug laws in the Kingdom. As a foundation signatory, Thailand was also obligated to adhere to a USA-sponsored 1928 amendment to the original Convention that required signatories to ban the exportation of Indian hemp to countries that had prohibited its use. In 1937 Thailand's second prime minister, General Phot Phahonyothin, criminalized cannabis in Thailand by passing the country's first law specifically targeting cannabis, the Marijuana Act B.E. 2477 (1937), but penalties were light and poorly enforced. Cannabis is prohibited in Thailand under the Narcotics Act of 1979, in which it is classed as a Category 5 narcotic. in 1979 Thailand passed their own Narcotics Act, which prohibited cannabis use in all its forms. The Thai cabinet officially approved cultivation of industrial hemp in 2009, and in 2014, the Thai government has issued special permits allowing the cultivation of hemp. However, the hemp seed itself has remained illegal. In 2019 medical use of cannabis was legalized.

Thailand and the USA have a complicatedly entwined cultural and legal history. During the Vietnam War from 1955 through 1975, Thailand hosted the main bases for US soldiers serving in Vietnam and it was the primary destination for soldiers on leave. At any given time during the Vietnam War, there were more US soldiers in Thailand than in Vietnam and about 80% of U.S. airstrikes in Vietnam were led from bases located in Thailand. It was these American solders that introduced Thai cannabis and Thai Sticks to American cities and suburbs. The U.S. government opened its first DEA office in Bangkok in 1963 and continues to be one of the agency's main allocations of personnel.[192]

Thai Landrace Cannabis Strains
Thai is a pure sativa landrace native to the tropical jungles of Thailand well-known for its speedy, cerebral high. Thai landraces are sativa strains, resulting in tall and stalky plants that can grow to incredible size with heavy buds, are often very prone to hermaphroditism and have some of the longest flowering times known in cannabis, up to twenty weeks sometimes. The buds can become so heavy that the plants will bend over and grow along the ground sometimes, because cannabis is like the Dao, it bends, yields and adapts to its environment and circumstances. The sharp smell of Thai cannabis is very distinctive earthy-sweet, lemony-citrusy smell and taste, primarily fruit and citrus with a distinct diesel undertone. Thai cannabis can be very effective for depression, stress, pain and fatigue. Thai's strong Sativa effects and its appealing flavor profile have made it a valuable strain for crossbreeding and has been used to produce popular hybrids like Haze and AK-47. Wild Thailand, a pure strain from the Ko Chang archipelago in Thailand, has THC levels that are among the highest in the world, the result of continual interbreeding using the best examples of this Thai Ko Chang lineage over many generations. It is one of Thailand's most productive strains and has a relatively short flowering cycle for a pure Thai Sativa. Chocolate Thai is another entirely Sativa landrace that has a very distinct terpene profile, giving it its chocolate flavor. Chocolate Thai seeds are dark, often black, tiny, and spherical. A dark plant, it has long and slim leaves growing in an asymmetrical fashion. The strain has been used in several hybrids in an attempt to replicate its particular flavor and effects. Thai Sticks can refer to both a landrace strain and a method of curing and packaging. The heavy trichome laden flowers and sometimes leaves are tied with a red hemp string, called Rasta Hair, onto the stalk of the plant or a bamboo skewer, sometimes they are then dipped into hash oil or opium, and then dried and cured on the sticks. The strain Thai Stick was often cured in this manner and also Chocolate Thai. It became very popular in the United States during the Vietnam war.

Bongs
Our modern word "bong", may come from the Tia word "baung", meaning a cylindrical wooden tube, pipe or container cut from a bamboo stem. It may however have come however from Africa, as some of the oldest pipes were found in Ethiopia and African tribes such as the "Sons of Cannabis" used bong-like pipes in their communal cannabis smoking rituals, in Kenya there is a tribe called the "Bong'om" and there is a "Bong Country, Liberia" named after "Mount

Bong".¹⁹³ In any case, for centuries the Hmong of Northern Thailand and Laos have used bamboo bongs. In Thailand in 1968-1969 American soldiers during the Tet Offensive could get a grocery bag full cannabis for ten dollars and cooled the hot smoke the way the native tribes did, with a bamboo baung, or bong. In the 1970's when soldiers returned from military bases in Thailand the brough a love of cannabis and bongs back with them. An article in the Marijuana Review in 1971 mentions the word "bong". A glassblower, Bob Snodgras, developed a technique called fuming using gold and silver to put colors on borosilicate glass is swirls and patterns and applied this to making glass bongs. He toured the country with the Grateful Dead in the early 1970s and the popularity of the glass bong spread across the globe. A Russian discovery in 2013 claimed to have uncovered Scythian tribal chiefs used gold bongs 2400 years ago to smoke cannabis and opium due to the traces of THC found inside them, but the artifacts more resembled goblets for consuming the legendary Soma. The Manchurian Empress Dowager Cixi who ruled China after the Opium Wars and ushered in the modernization of China, was buried with three bongs it has been claimed also. However, though she may have used a bamboo pipe with a clay bowl for opium smoking, it was not a bong. Dowager Cixi was also fond of smoking tobacco in a waterpipe and it is said she was buried with three, but they were waterpipes and not tubular bongs. The Manchurians were a shamanistic culture who revered Abka Hehe, the Sky Woman, eternal mother of the universe who created Banamu Hehe the Earth Mother and Ulden Hehe the Light Mother.¹⁹⁴ Like other Siberian shamanic peoples they practiced drumming and inducing trance states but through the ages incorporated Daoism and Buddhism into their practices.

Mindfulness

"The mind is like a river, with many thoughts and feelings flowing along. From time to time, it is helpful to recite a gatha, a short verse, to remind us what is going on. When we focus our mind on a gatha, the gatha is our mind at that moment. The gatha fills our mind for a half a second, or ten seconds, or one minute, and then we may have another gatha a little further downstream." [195]

Jana Drakka was a Soto Zen Priest with a San Francisco street ministry she called "Zando Without Walls". Jana developed "Harm Reduction Meditation", while working with homeless, disenfranchised and substance addicted people teaching in shelters, hospices and low-income hotels to offer the possibility of peace of mind to all without exception. She used a variation of zazen sitting meditation, in community gardens, what she called "cup-of-coffee meditation" or "looking-at-the-trees meditation," to focus attention on something other than one's own thoughts, "just be right here in this moment and realize that thoughts are all barriers to perceiving reality. That's it. Right there. Not beating yourself up because of your past failures…. putting people in the situation where they begin to see it for themselves… This is nirvana right here. Right here in this moment, with this breath. And we also talk a lot about the preciousness of breath. Because, you know, when we stop to look down upon ourselves, and treat ourselves badly, we don't really think there's anything much precious going on… This breath is your last breath… The next one is always a gift. People can get down with that. And it doesn't matter who you think the gift came from, or where it came from, the fact is that every single one of us gets a precious gift very often."[196] The meditations would be ten minutes long so that they corresponded to the amount of time that a craving usually lasts to illustrate that cravings could be overridden and a since of accomplishment is achieved. Harm Reduction is reducing the harm that one does to oneself and the motto is: "Any small change is a success." Jana embraced medical cannabis as a tool for harm reduction along with mindfulness meditation. Rather than the use of a substance, instead the focus is on the harm associated with the use of the substance and ways to reduce the harmful effects or find substitutions such as cannabis, with less harmful effects.[197] Cannabis provides many benefits to meditation including pain relief to help one sit still without pain while amplifying the experience of "being present and mindful". In 2012 Amanda Reiman, with the Drug Policy Alliance and SPARC Medical Cannabis Dispensary, did a study utilizing Jana Drakka's Harm Reduction Meditation combined with Cannabis, treating a group of methamphetamine addicts. The study found that Cannabis assisted in mindfulness and calmed the internal "craving voice", while reducing use of methamphetamine and alcohol.[198]

Mindfulness is the practice of maintaining a nonjudgmental state of heightened awareness of one's thoughts, emotions, or experiences on a moment-to-moment basis. In short, paying attention right now. Cannabis can aid in mindfulness meditation and other meditation practices as it decreases muscular tension which improves the ability to relax, it enhances sensory perception by heightening awareness of and ability to concentrate on sensation, it expands breathing increasing parasympathetic nervous system activity precipitating a feeling of relaxation, it expands the alveoli of the lung increasing oxygen intake that stimulates the sympathetic nervous system, it aids in letting go of stress and distractions by improving mood which is often described as a sense of bliss or euphoria, and increases sense of contentment, tranquility, and wellbeing. Cannabis and mindfulness have been successfully used together to treat PTSD, depression, anxiety, muscle and spinal pain, to make it through the day-in, day-out struggle of disability, to help be productive, focused, creative, and motivated, to help transition from one activity to another, and, to just plain stop and smell the roses. The attitude you have going into is the most important aspect, the intention, to aid in that you can create a nice atmosphere, being mindful of what you are doing, and make it your own personal ritual.

"We constantly worry, relive arguments and conversations, dwell on old problems – or on the positive side, we play with mental trivia, hope and dream of the future, or happily remember the past; and because of this internal dialogue, we miss out on experiencing the full depth and immediacy of everything else that happens to us and around us... the time-dilation effects of becoming very mindful... are exactly the same as those you'll often experience when you're deeply high. Cannabis enhances mindfulness to some degree..."[199]

"Here's a ritual we share in our Harm Reduction Meditation Groups that you might like to try:
We sit quietly then silently chant loving kindness, beginning with ourselves, then sending it out to anyone we know who is in need, then to all beings.
May I Be Happy.
May I live in Peace.
May I live in Good Health.
May All Beings Be Happy."[200]

Circulation of the Light and Making the Breathing Rhythmical

"According to the law, but without exertion, one must diligently fill oneself with light. Forgetting appearance, look within and help the true spiritual power! Ten months then embryo is under fire. After a year the washing and baths become warm." The Hui Ming Ching, The Book of Consciousness and Life, Ch. 4 trans. Richard Wilhelm

"Breathing comes from the heart. What comes out of the heart is breath. As soon as the heart stirs, there develops breath-energy. Breath-energy is originally transformed activity of the heart. When our ideas go very fast they imperceptibly pass into fantasies which are always accompanied by the drawing of a breath, because this inner and outer breathing hands together like tone and echo. Daily we draw innumerable breaths and have an equal number of fantasies. And thus the clarity of the spirit ebbs away as wood dries out and ashes die." - Secret of the Golden Flower Ch 4 trans. Richard Wilhelm

"Without going out of your door You can know all things on Earth. Without looking out of your window. You could know the ways of Heaven. The farther one travels, the less one knows, the less one really knows. Arrive without travelling, see all without looking, do all without doing." Dao de Ching Ch. 47 trans. George Harrison (The Inner Light, Beatles 1968)

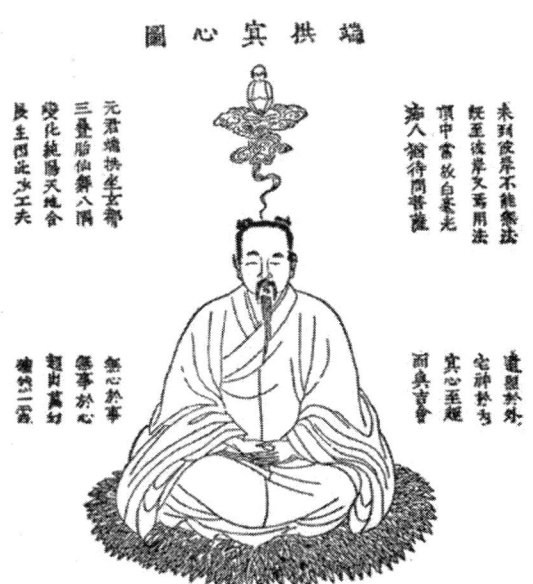

Meditation, Stage 3: Separation of the spirit-body for independent existence.

"The fourth realization is the awareness of the extent to which laziness is an obstacle to practice."[201]

"All men know that beauty and ugliness are correlatives, as are skill and clumsiness; one implies and suggests the other. So also existence and non-existence pose the one the other; so also is it with ease and difficulty, length and shortness; height and lowness. Also Musick exists through harmony of opposites; time and space depend upon contraposition. By the use of this method, the sage can fulfil his will without action, and utter his word without speech. All things arise without diffidence; they grow, and none interferes; they change according to their natural order, without lust of result. The work is accomplished; yet continueth in its orbit, without goal. This work is done unconsciously; this is why its energy is indefatigable." – Dao de Ching Ch. 2 trans. Alister Crowley

Interpretation:
Two solid lines on top a broken line symbolize wind, the energy of the heavens and sky, the invisible breath of the spirit and the visible movement of smoke and clouds. The broken line represents earth. The wind cannot be seen, but it can be seen moving the treetops and felt caressing the skin. The motivation is to be soft and penetrating. The image is grass and wind; the wind does not harm the rooted grass. It is the experience of sensuality and experiencing the five senses. It is the Gentle Ground, the first daughter, the gentle entrance.

Right Livelihood: One should abstain from making one's living through a profession that brings harm to others, instead it should be honorable, blameless, and innocent of harm to others. If what we are doing is for a good cause and the work is done with earnest effort without attachment or desire for the result or reward, it produces goodness. Right livelihood, right speech and right action produce ethical and moral conduct that promotes a harmonious life.

Wu Xing – Five Phases

The five relative directions are those of left, right, above, below and center, or front, back, left, right and middle. They are also the houses and residences of water (north), wood (east), fire (south), metal (west) and the center is the house of earth, and each is represented by a resident emperor, a celestial of wealth, and a demon. The Five Celestials of Wealth that are invoked for prosperity and before ritual, often the four cardinal directions and the five relative directions are invoked also. In motion the five relative directions manifest as the five dynamic moving phases of wood, fire, earth, metal, and water called Wu Xing, the five basic transformations of energy into mater. The five phases are expressed in human relations as the five virtues of love, righteousness, propriety, wisdom and faith.[202]

Light and shade are fundamental aspects of yin and yang, their kanji represent the banks of a river in the shade and in the sun, or that of a hill. This was applied to the human body alchemically and the inner was the yin and the outer the yang, with specific organs being either yin or yang. Yin and yang generate wu hsing, the five elemental energies or phases of fire, earth, metal, water and wood. These five phases of yin and yang and are reflected in the tales of the Five Deities of the Dao that correspond to the five phases of creation, the five constellations rotating around the celestial pole, the five planets, the five sacred mountains and five directions of space, and the five Dragon Gods which represent their mounts, that is to say the material and chthonic forms and forces they preside over.

Wu Xing are not a whole, but rather how Qi is expressed by the yin and yang as they move, change and shift through their interactions and relations as they form the Ba Gua trigrams. Qi gives rise to the five tastes which display themselves as the five colors and manifest as the five sounds. Qi comes in six forms that must be kept in homeostasis, yin, yang, wind, rain, dark and light. The five phases are aspects of the cycle of changes, linked by relationships of generation and destruction, yang and yin. Blue water is created and fortified by white metal, which is created and fortified by yellow earth, created and fortified by red fire, created and fortified by green wood, which in turn is created and fortified by blue water. The green wood yields to and is subdued by white metal, which yields to and is subdued by red fire, which yields to and is subdued by blue water, which yields to and is subdued by yellow earth, which yields to and is subdued by green wood. Green wood burns and creates red fire, red fire leaves ash and produces yellow earth, yellow earth contains ore which produces white metal, white metal melts as ice and produces blue water, blue water nourishes plant life and creates green wood, green wood destroys yellow earth by drawing strength from it, white metal chops down green wood, red fire melts white metal, blue water puts out red fire, yellow earth pollutes blue water. Wu Xing are the foundation of Traditional Chinese Medicine, social and political cycles, metaphysical cycles of the universe, inner cultivation, alchemy, divination, fortune telling and feng shui. Wood, fire, earth, metal and water represent the phases that all creation and destruction in the universe follow illustrated by metaphysical chemistry that explains how the five phases interact with each other and how they strengthen or attenuate each other's energy and potency.[203]

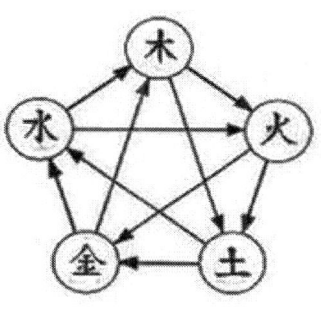

"By the transformation of yang and its union with yin, the five elemental energies of wood, fire, metal and water arise, each with its own specific nature according to its share of yin and yang... the five elemental energies combine and recombine in countless ways to create manifest existence. All things contain all five elemental energies in various proportions... the five elemental energies permeate every realm of nature and function ceaselessly on all three levels of human existence- body, energy and mind, the three treasures of life."[204]

1. wood: astringent/concentrating, sour, liver/gallbladder, nervous system, tears, anger, windy
2. fire: drying/purging, bitter, heart/small intestine, blood/endocrine, sweat, joy, hot
3. earth: nourishing/digestive, sweet, spleen/stomach, digestion/lymph, saliva, worry, damp
4. metal: stimulating, pungent, lungs/large intestine, respiration, mucus, anxiety/grief, dry
5. water: softening/diuretic/laxative, salty, kidney/bladder, urinary, urine, fear/fright, cold

These are reflected in the five virtues: uprightness, manners, knowledge, trust and piety; the five blessings of long life: wealth, peace, virtue and fame; and we revere the five animals that sacrifice themselves for our food: fish, fowl, sheep, pig and cow, and all food express one of the five tastes of pungent, sweet, sour, bitter and astringent. Of course, our world is experienced and viewed by the five senses of sight, touch, taste, smell and hearing.

The five precepts are:

1- the universe is regulated by order
2- mankind is basically good
3- people do wrong due to lack of knowledge or lack of good moral example
4- government must lead by good moral example
5- development is inward through self-observation and analysis and outward by self-sufficiency and conscientiousness

Five Basic Laws of Chinese Medicine:

1. All events and phenomena have two complementary polar aspects, called yin and yang, and this polarity is the basis of all organic structures and their functions.
2. Every yin-yang system contains myriad constituent subsystems and is also contained within myriad yin-yang supersystems.
3. Yin and Yang mutually give rise to one another and are functionally dependent on one another. Their activities are always relative and their qualities complementary.
4. Yin and Yang naturally balance and regulate each other. Their relative balance determines the equilibrium, stability, and functional viability of the whole human energy system and each of its organic subsystems.
5. Yin and Yang are transmutable and mutually transform into each other. Their transformations initiate all creation, growth, change and decline

Five Dragons

The Chinese Dragon is a symbol of benevolence, wisdom and protection. Coiling and uncoiling, retreating and advancing, illustrating wu-wei, effortless action, the heart of the Dao. The I-Ching was said to have been transmitted to Fu Xi, first emperor of China, by a celestial dragon that emerged from the Yellow River. Mount Tai, the sacred mountain of Ma Gu and the Daoist Xians, is located at the mouth of the Yellow River. Magu and her Korean counterpart, Mago, are both associated with dragons in their mythologies and symbolism, a connection that can also be in the mythologies of Vietnam and Japan. Dragons are associated with the Three Sovereigns who ride upon dragons or are associated with them as are other deities and immortals. The primary association of the dragon in global mythology is that of primordial wisdom, arcane knowledge, the primal chaotic origins and the blending of fire and water mediated by air.

There are five main types of Chinese dragon:
Celestial Dragons guard the abodes of the gods.
Spiritual Dragons rule wind and rain and can cause flooding.
Earth Dragons cleanse the rivers and deepen the oceans.
Treasure-Guarding Dragons protect precious metals and stones.
Imperial Dragons with five claws instead of the usual four.

Chinese or Korean Imperial Dragons have five toes on each foot, Indonesian dragons have four toes, Japanese dragons have three toes and Vietnamese dragons can have from three to five toes. Interestingly, cannabis leaves can have three, five, seven or nine blades on each leaf, five and seven being the most common.

The five immortal Dragon-kings are spirits of the waters, beneficent beings that produce rain and represent the fecundating principle in nature and the roaring of hurricanes and raging of typhoons. They can be seen flying in the heavens above the clouds with a serpentine tail. The Dragon-King is the personification and essence of yang. The five Dragon Kings manifest as an archetypical function: the celestial dragon guards and supports the mansions of the gods; the divine dragon, causes the winds to blow and produces rain for the benefit of mankind; the earth-dragon, marks out the courses of rivers and streams; the dragon of the hidden treasures, watches over the wealth concealed from mortals. From these great dragons were born the great emperors of ancient times.

Five Dakinis

Dakinis are female celestial beings evoking the movement of energy in space, śūnyatā, the insubstantiality of all phenomena and the pure potentiality for all possible manifestations. The Dakini is the embodiment of wisdom which when combined with skillful means gives rise to enlightened compassion. The word Dakini can have many meanings and translations ranging from an honorific term for the wife of a guru or lama to demonic witch or enlightened consort.[205] Dakinis are called space-goer, sky dweller, celestial woman, cloud fairy, cloud rider, sky dancer, emanations of Enlightened Mind, holding the bodhisattva commitment, or the feminine principle of wisdom that manifests in female form to benefit beings. The dakini manifests as one of the Three Roots: a guru who transmits the Vajrayana teachings; a yidam, a meditational deity such as Vajrayogini who is depicted as a red goddess with white adornments standing on one leg like an amanita muscaria mushroom; or a protector with special power and responsibility to protect the integrity of oral transmissions. The lama's mind should embody the inseparability of emptiness and wisdom becoming the absolute dakini. In meditation, dakinis are visualized, identified with, internalized and invoked.

- Buddha Dakini (white)
- Vajra Dakini (blue)
- Padma Dakini (red)
- Ratna Dakini (yellow)
- Karma Dakini (green)

The Buddha (Sangye) dakini, knowledge holder of the evolved self is bluish white, smiling, content and long-lived. She confers longevity and rebirth in the dakini paradise. Her iconography associates her with psilocybin mushrooms.

The Vajra (Dorje), thunderbolt dakini is fair, flushed and radiant. She has special marks such as 5 white moles at her brow. Her iconography identifies her with the amanita muscaria mushroom. She is compassionate, pure, virtuous devout, and will prevent all who beseech her from allowing their consciousness to descend into ignorance and lower vibrational realms where demons and fear dwell.

The Lotus (Padma) lotus dakini, knowledge holder of the Dao, is stocky with oily, pink skin, talkative and lusty. She controls gods, demons, men and closes the doors to rebirth in lower realms. Her iconography is obvious identifying her with the lotus and perhaps in her hidden aspect as the blue lotus or lily.

The Jewel (Ratna) dakini, life sustaining knowledge holder, is tall, slim, golden-skinned with white hair sings and dances. She grants wealth, success in life and closes the doors out the realms of hell. Her iconography associates her with the golden elixir.

The Activity (Karma) dakini, earth abiding knowledge holder, is white and radiant, smiling, respectful, trustworthy, and generous. She grants worldly success and rebirth as a human. Her iconography associates her with with the luminous pearl.

Five Buddhist Precepts for Living a Wise Life:
* Abstain from killing living beings.
* Abstain from stealing or taking what is not given.
* Abstain from lies and speaking falsely.
* Abstain from coercive sexuality or engaging in sexual conduct that is harmful.
* Abstain from the use intoxicants to the point of heedlessness or that removes the sense of attention or awareness.[206] When consciousness is freed of ignorance, the precept of non-intoxication is practiced.[207] If an intoxicant causes harm to oneself or another, it should not be used.

Five Bhikkhus
"*The Bodhisatta went in search of a better system and came to a settlement of five bhikkhus in the jungle of Uruvela… they revered him, their junior as their master… he ate each day one hemp grain only, seeking to cross the ocean of birth and death to arrive at the shore of deliverance.*"[208] This practice of the Buddha led to the revealing of the Four Nobel Truths and the Eightfold Path to Knowledge.[209]

"*A good traveller leaves no tracks. A good speaker is without flaw or disgrace. A good accountant needs no counting tokens. A good door has no bolt but can't be opened. A good binding has no rope but can't be loosened. Thus, the sage always rescues people, so no one is abandoned. The sage always preserves things, so nothing is abandoned. This is called innate wisdom. So, a good person is a teacher of a bad one, and a bad person is a lesson for a good one. If no respect for the teacher, then no care for the lesson. Even with wisdom there is great confusion. This is called the essence of mystery.*" Dao de Jing Ch 27 trans. Jeff Pepper and Xiao Hui Wang

Magu and the Peach

Magu's father, Ma Qiu, breed horses and Magu made her livelihood by sewing and weaving fabrics and cloth from cannabis. She would rise early in the morning and retire late in the evening, busy spinning delicate hemp and silk thread into fine fabrics. One day, as Magu was leaving the Weaver Girls Lover's Festival on the 7th day of the 7th month, to return home, a woman stopped her and gave her a beautiful Peach. As Magu hurried home to share the peach with her father, an old woman in yellow cloths collapsed on the street. People stood around her concerned, but no one offered her aid. Magu rushed over to the old woman and offered her the peach to eat. The old woman took a bite of the peach and was revived. She asked Magu if she had some porridge, as that may restore her strength. Magu said yes and rushed home to prepare some cannabis seed porridge for the old woman. When her father learned what his daughter was doing, he became angry and said that she could not cook porridge for a stranger, then locked her in the house. Once Magu was sure her father was asleep, she filled a bowl with cannabis seed porridge and snuck out of the house, hurrying back to the spot where the old woman had collapsed. The old woman in yellow was gone, but a peach stone was there where the old woman had been laying on the ground. In a dream that night the old woman thanked Magu and told her "that the peach had given her life". In the morning Magu planted the peach stone which she now knew had magical powers. Within a year, it had grown into a large peach tree that flowered after a few months and produced big red peaches. Magu picked the peaches and gave them to poor, old people who were filled for days and cured of minor ailments. Her gift of peaches was called "MaGu Xian Shou" or "Magu offers life".

Japanese Goddess Taima Mako Asa Amaterasu

"Cannabis was the most important substance for prehistoric people in Japan, they wore clothes made from its fibers and they used it for bow strings and fishing lines."[210]

In Japan Ma is Maku or Mako, and cannabis is Ōnusa, taima, seima or asa. Pottery relics, from the prehistoric Jamon period of Japan, found in the Ja Fukui Prefecture, contained cannabis seeds and scraps of woven cannabis fibers dated to around 3,000 BCE and recently there were discovered prehistoric cannabis seeds on the Japanese Honshu Island. Its usage can be found throughout Shinto ritual practice and Japanese history, industry, and art.

"In Kojiki (the Record of Ancient Matters) the story relates: After creating the country the primal pair consulted together saying, 'We have now produced the great eight island country, with the mountains, rivers, herbs and trees. Why should we not produce someone who shall be lord of the Universe.' This first pair then begat the founding goddess-figure, Amaterasu Omi kami (Sun Goddess). She is enshrined at the holiest of place, the Ise Jinja (shrine) along with the ancient sacred mirror Ameratsu gave to her grandson when he descended from above to reign over the eight-island kingdom. At that shrine on the Ise peninsula, the special prayer given for the founding Goddess of Japan is called Taima. Further, hemp, salt and rice are the sacred staples that are used as part of all the rites at the shrine (Yamada). Indeed hemp and mulberry fiber, and clot, and paper made from them, as well as salt, sake, and rice are offered to the gods at the Shinto shrines."[211]

In Japan the Goddess manifests as the archaic ancestor of all races, Amaterasu, the Sun Goddess of the Japanese imperial family, goddess of rice and cannabis. There are five taima [cannabis] ceremonies conducted each year at the Shinto shrines in her honor, where the rope for the bells is made of cannabis fiber as are the curtains of the shrine and the garments of the priests. In the enthronement ritual of the Japanese emperor, a ritual cloth, called aratae, the cloth of the gods, woven from cannabis fibers by four maidens.[212] In Shinto ceremonies cannabis leaves are burned as an "invitation to the spirits" and in ceremonial purification rites for driving away evil spirits.

Amaterasu Ōmikami, Great Divinity Illuminating Heaven, in a challenge against her brother, Susano-o, god of the storm and sea, enraged him by winning the challenge, and he went into a fit of rage against the goddess. He destroyed the rice and hemp fields that she had planted, threw a flayed pony into her loom where she was weaving hemp garments for the gods, and reeked havoc across the land disrupting the cannabis harvest festivals and killing one of her attendants. Filled with fear, embarrassment and anger, Amaterasu retreated into Ama-no-Iwato, the Heavenly Rock Cave and blocked its entrance with a large bolder, returning to her chthonic dragon serpent primal nature. With the Light of Heaven gone, the earth was plunged into darkness and chaos descended upon the land. The gods and Kami begged her to come out of the cave, to no avail. Omoikane, the god of wisdom began preparations for rituals to appease the goddess and lure her out of the cave so that sunlight and life could return to the land. The gods made an alter outside of her cave with a five hundred-branched sakaki tree (Cleyera japonica) adorned with a sacred eight-fold mirror (Yata-no-kagami), a necklace of sacred jewels (Yasaka-no-magatama) and sacred strips of white and blue-green nigitae cloth made of mulberry and hemp. Offerings of incense and sacrifices were made for her, and then the goddess Amenouzume (Ama-no-Uzeme) jumped up upon an upturned tub and began to dance ecstatically in a trance, baring her breasts and dropping her skirt as she danced, invoking the creative, protective and nurturing nature of women. The eight hundred assembled gods roared with laughter and cried that there is a deity greater than Amaterasu. Her curiosity getting the better of her now, Amaterasu moved the bolder aside slowly to peek outside. When her brilliance shone out from behind the rock, the cocks saw her light and began to crow, the Magatama jewels glittered, and the mirror hanging on the tree reflected her light. She saw her own reflection in the mirror and thought to herself that there must be someone or something equal to herself illuminating the world. As she opened the door a little wider to see who it was, the deity Ama no Tajikara-wo no Kami, who was waiting behind the door, pulled Amaterasu out of the cave and quickly threw a shimenawa, a sacred hemp rope, before the entrance to prevent her return to hiding. Ever since, she has been honored in the Taima (cannabis) ceremonies held five times a year, with the winter solstice ceremony remembering her coming out of the cave.

Cannabis fiber was highly regarded among the Japanese and was central in everyday life and legends. Cannabis was the primary material for clothes, bedding, mats and nets. Clothes made of cannabis fiber were especially worn during formal and religious ceremonies because of traditional association of purity with cannabis in Japan.[213] As recently as 1945, Japanese Buddhist priests in San Francisco would annually honor the ancestors by dancing with burning flowering cannabis stalks with which they would carve "elaborate geometric patterns with flaming trails", engulfing the participants in the intoxicating smoke.²¹⁴ In the traditional Taimatsu matsuri fire festivals of the Fall, large columnar bundles of cannabis plants are ritually burned in an open field to ensure a bountiful harvest.²¹⁵

Once upon a time in Ancient Japan there were two weaver women that lived next door to each other. They were both fine weavers of hemp cloth, one was fast but wove course material, the other slow, but wove fine hemp fabric. Market time was a festive occasion, and the weaver women would make dresses special for the occasion. The quick working weaver woman made herself a plain hemp dress in ample time for the market, but the slow weaver woman did not have her dress finished when market day came. The only part of the dress that was finished were two unbleached white strands of cloth which she wore around her neck. Knowing that she had to go to the market to sell her fabrics, she persuaded her husband to carry her to the market in a large jar so only her neck and head would be visible and no one would know that she had no dress on inside of the jar. Her husband agreed and carried her to the market in a jar upon his back. On the way to the market, the woman in the jar saw her neighbor and started making fun of her plain dress. The neighbor replied and to her saying that at least she was clothed. "Break the jar!" she exclaimed loudly, "There is a naked woman inside the jar!". The husband of the slow weaving woman became so surprised that he dropped the jar, which broke, revealing his naked wife, clothed only in hemp strands around her neck. The naked weaver woman was so ashamed that she stood naked before everyone at the market, so she buried herself in the earth hoping no one would see her. When she emerged from the earth, she had transformed into a silkworm with two rings of white around its neck, and climbed into a mulberry tree.

*"The prayer given at the Ise Jingu, which is the shrine to Amaterasu, the founding god of the Imperial family, is called taima, or marijuana. Hemp and rice are two sacred things which are part and parcel of the rites conducted at Ise Jingu."*²¹⁶

Japanese Cannabis Culture

"Japanese culture not only stands out from the all the others for having placed cannabis in the irreplaceable, vital, sacred and ritualistic category, but rather since the very origins of Japanese civilization, cannabis has been associated with the incarnation of the divinity itself, being a symbol of purity... Both the Divine Emperor and hemp remain the chief symbols of protection in this country. Cannabis is planted in gardens and temples across the nation in order to protect the country from evil. And, once its life cycle is over, the fibers are made sacred by turning them into clothes for the Emperor and priests... Japan must literally have been "divested of its protective thread", a celestial thread that united "the spiritual world above" to "the Earth below" for it to have been possible for it to have been attacked so brutally with the atomic bomb in 1945. Beyond this metaphysical vision, which cannabis has always represented not only in its industrial or traditional aspect, but also and above all as a mystical vehicle with the gods... The Cannabis Control Act (in Japanese, Taima Hirishimari Hô), the first Japanese law to restrict the cultivation and possession of cannabis, was passed in 1948 when Japan was not a sovereign country but still occupied by the United States, under the supreme command of General MacArthur. The Japanese word 'taima' (cannabis) refers not only to the more traditional, pragmatic use of the plant, rather than its medicinal or psychotropic uses. It was the founding goddess and literally means "tall hemp", to differentiate it from other shorter hemp-like plants... astute Japanese negotiators managed to save industrial hemp from the soldiers, through the granting of special permits issued in Japan, allowing for the subsistence of thousands of traditional hemp farmers and basic supplies for the country... set against the splendid backdrop of the past, with its emphasis on beauty, delicacy, quality but also time rusticity and strength, all incarnated in hemp, as a symbol of its rustic and cultural idiosyncrasy. With their infinite patience, the Japanese have used the plant to create paper and fabrics, which are really exquisite, unparalleled, true masterpieces of Japanese culture. Their use in ancient times goes back to the Japanese Neolithic period, known as the "rope-patterned" or Jomon Period in Japanese, which flourished between 10,000 BC and 300 BC. Hemp was used above all for food, to make rope and baskets, in a hunter-gatherer evolutionary context."[217]

The original religion of Japan was Shinto (Shen-dao), "the way of the Kami" or Spirits. The Kami are anything that inspire awe or reverence and express themselves in many different manifestations including the spirits of the sun or moon, wind, mountains, rivers, seas, trees, rocks, animals or as guardians of locals, towns or villages and tribal clans. They can even be Buddhist deities, evil spirits or souls of the dead. It is probable that during the Jamon period of Japan from 5,000 to 300 BCE, and at its height in 1000 BCE, cannabis was an important part of culture and religion. Cannabis was revered for its cleansing abilities and Shinto priests would wave bundles of cannabis leaves to welcome benevolent spirits and repel evil spirits and influences. This use of cannabis as a religiously important plant ally continues to the present day in the thick ceremonial ropes woven from cannabis fibers displayed at Shinto shrines and Shinto priestly wands decorated with strips of the gold-colored rind of cannabis stalks and in the early Twentieth Century travelers in Japan would leave small offerings of cannabis leaves at roadside Shinto shrines to ensure safe journeys and families burned bundles of cannabis in their doorways to welcome back the spirits of the dead during festivals and rituals for the ancestors. Shinto worships the vertical dimension of the heavenly realm with the attainment of purity being central and ancestor worship, shamanism and cannabis were at one time paramount to its practice. Cannabis was used in religious rituals to strengthen the union between couples, to drive off evil spirits and to bring happiness in marriages.

Rock art on Kyushu Island from the Jomon Period have been found illustrating some of the earliest examples of art. The rock paintings depict individuals alongside symbols that look like modern representations of cannabis leaves surrounded by a sunlike aura that could suggest the connection between the sun goddess and cannabis in Shinto.[218] Although there are archaeological artifacts containing remnants of cannabis, it is commonly believed that cannabis was introduced to Japan from Korea around 500-600 CE at the latest, when Buddhism was introduced to Japan by Korean monks. But even before that, in 300 BCE papermaking, rice cultivation and Cangjie writing were introduced to Japan, and cannabis was used for papermaking in the region at the time. Paper was made from cannabis, mulberry and hemp rags, as in Korea, and cannabis and mulberry were both used in the worship of the gods.[219] Until the mid-Twentieth century ban, cannabis was cultivated all over Japan, particularly in Tohoku and Hokkaido, and was frequently mentioned in literature, such as the "Manyoshu," Japan's oldest collection of poems, the book of woodblock prints "Wakoku Hyakujo" of the Edo Period as well as the "Floating World" erotic prints, and paintings of the Edo Period,[220] and in haiku poetry key words describe the stages of cannabis cultivation and denoted the season when the poem is set. In the feudal times of the Samurai the vassals were encouraged the vassals to grow cannabis and it was prized for its fiber. The Samurai iron helmet, kabuto, was fitted inside with hemp covered in silk, the shoulder, sleeve and thigh protectors were made from hemp impregnated with persimmon juice to make it waterproof, silk and deer leather on which iron plates were stitched with hemp twine. The erotic art of rope binding, Shibari, descended from the Samurai practices of binding, also employing hemp ropes.

It was in Shinto religion and folk healing, however, that the use of cannabis was most prevalent. Shinto belief holds that cannabis is a symbol of purity, and since evil and purity cannot exist side by side, cannabis is used in purification and exorcism.[221] While tiama means cannabis, it also refers to Shinto hemp paper offerings. Shinto religion has many ritual items that are made from cannabis. The shimenawa rope is hung across the torii, the entrance to Shinto temples that represents the transition from the mundane to the sacred. The shimenawa rope purifies all who pass beneath it, and shime, white paper streamers made of hemp are suspended from it, mark off the sacred space and protect the objects of worship. There is also a thick tapered hemp rope, the suzunawa bell rope, which is placed in front of Shinto altars, pulled to bestow blessings of good fortune.[222] The gohei are wooden wands to which are attached two shide, white or golden zig-zag hemp paper streamers. The gohei sit upon the altar and are the descendants of the original hemp cloth that was hung upon the sakaki tree for the goddess Amaterasu and may be inhabited by a Kami.[223] The haraenusa, or onusa wand, is made of wood with multiple shime suspended from it and often embellished with golden hemp fiber strips. The haraenusa is used for ritual purification to cleanse, bless, exorcise or sanctify a person or object and is waved or shaken over the person or object being purified. It is both a sacrificial offering to the Kami and a messenger. The purity of the shime attract the Kami, and they enter the haraenusa causing it to shake. The haraenusa acts as a conduit for the Kami to enter the person or object, the cannabis serving as a pathway for the Kami and spirits to travel to and fro, as in Hmong and Korean shamanism. The haraenusa is placed in the hands of the person or upon the object and the Kami is invoked. The Kami travel along the cannabis path into the person or object, or the evil spirit is exorcised and leaves the person or object.[224]

"The Asanoha (Hemp Leaf) pattern is a popular traditional pattern often seen on Japanese kimono. Though often people forget about this today, the regular geometric pattern represents overlapping hemp leaves. Because hemp was known for its rapid growth, the pattern was often used for clothes of newborn children. The wives of merchants would also often wear it. It was believed to bring good fortune to the wearer."[225]

In 1948 after defeat in World War II and occupied by United States military forces, the Cannabis Control Act was passed in Japan which bans the import, export, cultivation and purchase of cannabis and Article Four of the Act expressly forbids the use of cannabis for medical purposes. Cannabis-based cures were available from Japanese drug stores to treat insomnia and relieve pain until the ban by the Cannabis Control Act. The growing of hemp was still permitted as a cottage industry only, requiring stringent and difficult conditions to obtain a license. Emperor Hirohito died in 1989 and his son Akihito was crowned during a special ceremony in which he had to wear a traditional gown made from hemp. A number of farmers in the region Shikoku gave the new emperor a present of illegally planted hemp with which to make the garment. In gratitude they received a license to grow hemp on a small scale for the making of rope, paper and the clothing for the imperial family.[226]

Although medical use of cannabis is no longer legal, it once held an important place in Japanese traditional medicine, called Kampo. Cannabis was known as masho, mashinin, kaminin or taimanin and was used for the spleen, stomach, and intestines, and given to those recovering from an illness. It was said to heal five ailments and seven types of injuries.[227]

Japan still has very stringent drugs laws but there are efforts to restore cannabis to its traditional place of respect and honor in Japanese culture. Saya Takagi of Shinto Kaikaku, the New Renaissance Party proposed "lifting the ban on research [into cannabis] to see what the truth is." In 2016 there was the Kyoto Hemp Forum held at the Kyoto International Conference Center, the same location where the 1997 Kyoto Protocol was signed as a part of the UN Framework Convention on Climate Change to regulate the emission of greenhouse gases. The Forum was held to discuss sustainability, the climate emergency, and the need for the ban on the cultivation of industrial hemp to be lifted internationally. Among the speakers and attendees was Akie Abe, a fervent advocate of hemp and wife of then Japanese Prime Minister Shinzo Abe. Akie Abe has stated, "Hemp is a plant all of whose parts can be used effectively… While [hemp] is not yet permitted in Japan, I think it can be put to great practical use for medical purposes as well."[228] Ms. Abe said in an interview that she would like to revive Japan's tradition of growing hemp and stated that "I've even considered myself to apply for a permit to grow hemp." The article included a photo of the former first lady at a legal hemp farm in western Japan posing for the photo in the middle of the cannabis plants.[229] Junichi Takayasu was inspired by tales of ninjas-in-training starting a crop of cannabis and jumping over it each day as it grew. It grew rapidly and as it grew taller the ninja would be forced to leap higher and higher over it, and thus develop their leg muscles and superior jumping abilities. Years later Junichi Takayasu is one of Japan's leading experts on cannabis and the curator of Taima Hakubutsukan, the only museum in Japan dedicated to cannabis. He opened it in 2001 in the town of Nasu, Tochigi Prefecture, approximately 160 km north of Tokyo, with the mission is to teach people about the history of cannabis in Japan and it sponsors monthly workshops to teach people about weaving cannabis fibers. According to Takayasu, the earliest evidence of cannabis in Japan dates to the Jomon Period (10,000-200 B.C.), with pottery relics recovered in Fukui Prefecture containing seeds and scraps of woven cannabis fibers. Takayasu says. "Cannabis has been at the very heart of Japanese culture for thousands of years… Cannabis was the most important substance for prehistoric people in Japan. They wore clothes made from its fibers and they used it for bow strings and fishing lines." [230]

"In traditional Okinawa, women took care of affairs dealing with the spiritual world, the kami and ancestors, while the men took care of world affairs. Finally, in the household, while the man wore the pants in the everyday world, the women wore the spiritual pants and took care of religious rituals and other matters relating to the ancestors and the kami." – Nuru, Official Priestess of the Kami[231]

An old Japanese legend tells of a young maiden from a simple family that had a secret lover. One night just before her lover departed, she fastened a hemp thread to his clothing as he kissed her goodbye. She then followed him tracing the thread until she arrived at the Temple of Miva, Beautiful Harmony, and remained there with her divine consort.[232]

Seven Fragrant Tastes Powder
(from the Edo Period)

Mix together:
Dried Orange
Lemon and Yuzu peel
Ground long chili pepper-
(Capsicum annuuum var longum)
Ground Japanese Sansho pepper-
(zanthoxylum piperitum)
Ground Ginger
Poppy Seeds
Black Sesame Seed
White Sesame Seed
Hulled Cannabis Seed
Roasted & Cracked Cannabis Seed
Nori Seaweed
Dried Cannabis Leaves
Crushed Cannabis Flowers
Shiso-
(Chinese Basil, Perilla frutescens var. crispa)
Sea Salt
Raw Sugar

Sprinkle over food to taste.

Invocation

Invocations, or dharani, are used to cultivate Qi energy. Invocations are believed to exorcize the body and mind of toxins, impurities, evils and malignant energies, while inviting spiritual beings and energies to raise power and vitality. Inner deities are invoked as administrators of the palaces of the body, that is, 39 deities that govern various body organs, parts and systems. Invoking the inner deities assists with purification and cultivation of Qi while cleansing it of metaphysical toxins and prolonging life.[233] Invocations may be passed from teacher to student, it is passed down through family traditions, it is a traditional mantra or invocation, or it is a self-crafted mantra or invocation that resonates deeply and personally with the individual. Whatever the source, it must be profound and make one feel empowered and bigger than oneself. Mantras are phrases in sacred languages whose utterance, or meditation upon, amplify connection to a specific deity and activate altered states of consciousness wherein contact with deity is more accessible.[234] Invocations, incantations and mantras are uttered over and over to establish a connection with the higher states of consciousness and higher beings. The more often they are repeated, the stronger the connection to the higher entities and it becomes easier and quicker to reach the higher states of consciousness. The use of sacred languages intensifies the power of the invocation due to the collective energy of the ages infused into it and by speaking it aloud, or focusing singularly upon it in the imagination, specify intentions and focus the energies. The elements that an invocation should include are invoking a metaphor, acknowledging a higher purpose, calling forth divine blessing, and should be stated in an affirmative language.[235] Control of the breath and channeling of the Qi by breath control, is a vital and indispensable component of invocation. Various methods may be used, but the goal is to collect and channel Qi. Invocations may be closed with the utterance: Ji ji lu ling, it is so ordered.[236]

Kai Gaung

Statues and images of deity that are placed upon the altar need to first be properly consecrated through Kai Gaung, to "open their light." The eyes are smudged with cinnabar or red ink, and often other body parts as well, sometimes then blindfolded and the blindfold removed at the end of the ritual to allow the deity to see through the eyes of its likeness. Sometimes the ritual is reserved and contemplative, other times accompanied with music and drumming.[237]

Deities of Prosperity

 The character for deity can mean God, deity, supreme, emperor, or imperial, it could also be interpretated as a pictograph of a plant calyx. Early oracle bone inscriptions from 1600- 1050 BC have been found with this character, assumed to be invocatory in nature. It is also found in combine with shang, implying the supreme deity or god of the Shang Dynasty which has been identified as the highest deity in Chinese Folk Religions and also within Chinese Christianity. The character basically represents or invokes the divine.[238]

Cai Shen, Zao Gong Ming, god of Wealth and Prosperity. The Daoist and folk god is invoked for wealth, prosperity and success.[239] Cai Shen has many manifestations and is known by many names varying from tribe, tradition, religion, region and country. Cai Shen, the Daoist god of wealth and prosperity was incarnated at one time in the body of Zhao Gong Ming, who was born the poorest of the poor and had a black dog who could not bark and a hen that could not lay eggs. He would beg for food every day and then go home and give the food to his dog and hen, with never any left for himself. One night, after fasting for days on end, the heavens opened to him and the immortals appeared to him. He begged them that he would never again be poor or hungry. The gates closed and he fell into a deep sleep. When he awoke, every time his dog barked a silver nugget fell out of its mouth, and every time his hen laid an egg, it was a gold ingot. He was now a wealthy and prosperous man and he used his abundance to help the needy and poor. He then commissioned eight shamans to craft joss paper made from the silver and gold, from his dog and hen who were in fact a black tiger and a phoenix and offer them to the ancestors and gods daily. It is he who selected the Four Treasures and with Cai Shen at the center, they form the Five Celestials of Wealth.[240]

Bu Dai, or Hoti the Laughing Buddha with his hemp (cloth) sack, is patron of psychics, shamans, diviners, and fortune tellers. He is the jovial, eccentric and deeply compassionate god of fortune, wealth and prosperity. Rubbing his belly is believed to bring luck and dispel misfortune.[241]

Mo Li Zhi Tian, Marisheten, Dou Mu, Marici, Mother of the Dig Dipper, the Heavenly Healer who commands all fates and fortunes.

Mistakes During the Circulation of the Light

"Outside the body there is a body called the Buddha image. The thought which is powerful, the absence of thoughts, is Bodhi. The thousand-petal lotus flower opens, transformed through breath-energy. Because of the crystallization of the spirit, a hundred-fold splendor shines forth."- The Hui Ming Ching, The Book of Consciousness and Life, Ch. 5 trans. Richard Wilhelm

"One must be careful that, quite automatically, heart and energy are coordinated. Only then can a state of quietness be attained. During this quiet state the right conditions and the right space must be provided. One must not sit down [to meditate] in the midst of frivolous. That is to say, the mind must be free of vain preoccupations. All entanglements must be put aside; one must be detached and independent. Nor must the thoughts be concentrated upon the right procedure. This danger arises if too much trouble is taken. I do not mean that no trouble is to be taken, but the correct way lies in keeping equal distance between being and not being. If one can attain purposelessness through purpose, then the thing has been grasped... Now one can let oneself go, detached and without confusion, in an independent way."- Secret of the Golden Flower Ch 5 trans. Richard Wilhelm

"A willful doer cannot, as I see it, win the world. The world cannot be willfully manipulated or controlled. One who tries to manipulate it will destroy it. One who tries to control it will lose it. The wise does nothing to manipulate or control, and will therefore, neither destroy nor lose. For there are forever subtle changes in the world. People walk either in front or behind. They are either inhaling or exhaling, either strengthening or weakening, and doing either good or harm. That is why the wise will never desire too much." Dao de Jing Ch 29 trans. Yi Wu

"Heaviness is the basis of lightness. Stillness is the standard of activity. Thus the Master travels all day without ever leaving her wagon. Even though she has much to see, she is at peace in her indifference. Why should the lord of a thousand chariots be amused at the foolishness of the world? If you abandon yourself to foolishness, you lose touch with your beginnings. If you let yourself become distracted, you will lose the basis of your power." Dao de Jing Ch 26 trans. J.H. McDonald

"The fifth realization is the awareness that ignorance is the cause of the endless round of birth and death."[242]

"Using the right lawfulness to govern the country. Using unexpectancy to conduct the battle. Using disengagement to take over the world. How do I know this is so? Thus. The more prohibitions there are in the world, the poorer people will be. The more destructive weapons people have, the more chaotic the nation will become. The more know-how people have, the more bizarre things will appear. The more rules and demands that flourish, the more thefts there will be. Therefore the sage says: When I am inactive, people transform themselves. When I abide in stillness, people organize themselves lawfully. When I am disengaged, people enrich themselves. When I choose nondesire, people remain simple." Dao de Ching Ch. 57 trans. Tao Huang

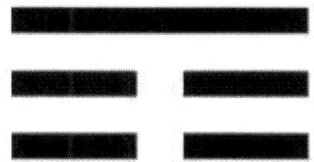

Interpretation:
A solid line on top of two broken lines symbolize a mountain. The solid line represents elevation, and the bottom two broken lines represent earth. The image is a mountain elevated above the earth; the motivation is keeping still. Only in the tranquility of silence, of deep sleep or illness, can your body talk to you about its motivations. It is the Keeping Still, bound, resting, stand-still, and the completion of the third son.

Right effort- (Samma vayama) is preventing the arising of unwholesome states, and the generation of wholesome states, including indriya-samvara, guarding the sense-doors, or restraint of the sense faculties, the energetic will to prevent evil and unwholesome states of mind from arising and to get rid of such states that have already arisen and also to produce or cause to arise, good, and wholesome states of mind that have not yet arisen, and to develop and bring to perfection the good and wholesome states of mind already present, cultivating these wholesome thoughts, and rooting out unwholesome ones by emphasizing self-awareness over action. The excess or deficiency of yin or yang manifests as these unwholesome states and are brought back into balance by focusing upon its opposite, manifested and represented by the internalization of deity.

Smooth Lucky Number Six

Going with the flow
六六大顺

Six Classical Arts:
- Etiquette
- Music
- Archery
- Riding
- Writing
- Mathematics.

Six Sense Organs and Objects:
- Eye and Vision
- Ear and Hearing
- Nose and Olfaction
- Tongue and Taste
- Skin and Touch
- Mind and Thought

Six Buddhist Deities:
- Vajradhara
- Maitreya
- Mahakala
- Mahavairocana and Marichi
- Tara
- Avalokitesvara Guanyin

Six Kinfolks:
- father
- mother
- brother
- sister
- wife
- children

Six Activities:
- walking
- standing still
- sitting
- eating
- lying down
- speaking

Six Aspects of Deity
- emptiness
- syllable
- sound
- form
- mudra
- attributes

Six Fortunes
- The power of mastering the will.
- The marks and signs of the Buddha Body.
- The wealth of immeasurable things.
- The perfect fame.
- The wisdom of knowing things as they are.
- The perfect diligence of accomplishing the benefit of all sentient beings.

Six Harmonies of the Sangha
- Physical harmony of the same work.
- Verbal harmony of the same silence.
- Mental harmony of the same tolerance.
- Ethical harmony of the same practice.
- Ideological harmony of the same understanding.
- Material harmony of the same equality of benefits.

Six Points of Equanimity
- I have suffered as have all sentient beings. My suffering has helped and benefited others, and their suffering has helped and benefited me.
- The help and benefit of all sentient beings was greater for me than their harm to me and all I have, and need depends on others.
- Death is definite and its time is uncertain, therefore wanting to harm or seeking revenge on another makes no sense.
- All sentient beings are equal in wanting happiness and not wanting suffering.
- Since all sentient beings want happiness, it is unjust to help only some of one's choosing and discrimination, when all need help.
- All sentient beings hope for help so one should not be biased in the treatment of them.

Six Perfections
- perfect charity (generosity, dana)
- perfect observation of the precepts (ethos, discipline, sila)
- perfect perseverance (patience, endurance, ksanti)
- perfect energy (zeal, effort, progress, virya)
- perfect meditation (concentration)
- perfect wisdom (prajna)

Six Fruits of the Path
- the psychic power of the heavenly eye - divine sight
- the psychic power of the heavenly ear - divine hearing
- psychic power with regard to past lives - knowledge of all forms of previous existences of self and others
- psychic power with regard to the minds- knowledge of the minds of all beings
- the spiritually based psychic powers - power to appear at will in any place and to have absolute freedom of movement
- the psychic power of the extinction of outflows - insight into the ending of birth and death, possession of deliverance of mind through wisdom after having understood and realized it.

Six Realms
- Hell realm- Hell-beings wracked by torture and characterized by aggression, the passionate intensity of hatred and fear, the cold cruelty of hardheartedness and apathy.
- Preta realm- Hungry ghosts characterized by great craving, eternal starvation, greed and jealousy.
- Animal realm- Animals and livestock, characterized by ignorance and servitude, prejudice and complacency, their behavior follows instinct without deliberation, and they avoid discomfort or anything unfamiliar. Connected to the human real through the dreams and the astral.
- Human realm- Humans exist in a material world, and the mind activities are always connected with the principles of matter, limited by the body and sense organs, but most are blinded and consumed by desires.
- Asura realm- Faries, Demigods, Devas, Angels, Immortals their powers bind them to the world of suffering because their pleasure is greatest, so too is their misery. Can be reached from the human realm through the dreams and astral.
- God realm – Archetypes, Gods, Celestials, Bodhisattvas, reached through meditation, ritual, sacrifice and devotions.

Six Bardos

The term Bardo refers to an "in-between" or "intermediate" state, that is, a division of time between two transition points. There are three bardo states that occur between birth and death and three that occur between death and birth. The Bardos of birth are the bardos of life, dream and meditation. The bardos of the after-life are the bardos of death, luminosity and karma. In Tibet, the Bardo Thodol, popularly known as the Tibetan Book of the Dead, is viewed as a manual for guiding the soul on its journey at death. In the West, there are variant approaches to Buddhism that differ greatly from eastern traditions. In the 1800's in Paris and Vienna, Buddhist and Taoist teachings were studied and combined with the accompanying hashish, opium, psychology and Theosophy. Later these same systems were studied by researchers such as Aldous Huxley who combined his studies in Chinese mysticism and psychedelic explorations with mushrooms, peyote and LSD, and Aleister Crowley who combined his study of Taoist and Buddhist mysticism with his experiments with mescaline, hashish, cocaine, heroin, nitrous oxide, ether and other substances. In this way they were not dissimilar from the ancient Taoist alchemists that employed cannabis, opium, datura, mushrooms and other substances to create the elixir of life. In the 1950's the popularity of Buddhism increased amongst the "Beats," who once again merged Buddhist philosophy and psychoactive sacramental substances such as cannabis, hashish, heroin and methamphetamine. This Western Buddhism grew with spokespeople like Alan Watts, Allen Ginsberg, Jack Kornfield and Jack Kerouac, at centers like the Tassajara San Francisco Zen Center and the Maui Zendo where the psychedelic experience and Buddhism converged like they did in the Psychedelic trip guide: "The Psychedelic Experience, A Manuel based on the Tibetan Book of the Dead" by Harvard professors Ralph Mentzer, Timothy Leary and Richard Albert. While many in the Buddhist community may have disagreed or not approved, both then and now, nonetheless the fact remains that Entheogenic Buddhism is a very real and present thing and there has been research done that suggests that it is in fact a return to a much older and ancient Buddhist tradition that has been forgotten and obscured through the passage of time. One thing that has come from all of this is the established fact that the Tibetan Book of the Dead is in fact an excellent guide for the ego death experience that happens after the ingestion of entheogens. Used as a tool for the entheogenic experience it can be interpreted as a map of the psychic states of consciousness progressively encountered when ingesting a powerful entheogenic substance. It is a map of the visionary initiation experience of the death of the ego, the transcendence of the personality into other realms of consciousness and how to avoid the limiting process of the ego.

The Bardo of Death is the bardo that commences at the moment of death when the outer and inner signs reveal the onset of death, just before the physical death, and continues through the dissolution or transmutation of the Mahabhuta the elements of mater, until the external and internal breath has completed, and the luminosity of the dharmakaya, the dharma body, dawns. This is the bardo of the Hell Realm, where the five elements dissolve, the realm of pleasure and pain, of creating and destroying, the realm of death and rebirth found through the yoga of inner heat in which we experience the 'clear light' followed by unconsciousness, usually lasting approximately three days.

The Luminous Bardo, is the bardo of the dharmakaya luminosity of the true nature which commences after the final 'inner breath' and the prana or Qi, leaves the body. This is the realm of spontaneously manifesting visions both visual and auditory, based on remaining karmas, intense aversions and desires, that can inspire profound peace and pristine awareness, inner equanimity, experience transcendent realms of being, or trapped in full delusion. 'When terrifying hallucinations of hungry ghosts appear do not cling to them, let them pass. When beautiful visions of celestial wonders appear, do not cling to them, let them pass.

The Karmic Bardo, is the bardo of becoming or transmigration, the process of becoming or being reborn. This bardo begins the moment the bardo body is created and continues until the inner-breath begins in the transmigrating form determined by the "karmic seeds" within the storehouse of consciousness. Generally, this lasts for forty-nine days and recall of the bardos and past lives vanishes leaving a state of naked mind-body.

The Natural Bardo, is the bardo of birth and life the natural bardo of this life begins when a connection with a new birth is first made and continues until the conditions that lead to death manifest and mindstream, the moment-to-moment continuum of consciousness, leaves our body.

The Dream Bardo, is the bardo of the dream state. The Bardo of Dreaming is connected with, and reflects the habitual patterns we experience in the Natural

Bardo. Through the dream body the animal realm and the Asura realms can be contacted. Dream Yoga can integrate the dream state into sadhana.

The Meditation Bardo, or Samadhi Bardo, is the bardo generally only experienced by meditators or through spontaneous experiences where one experiences a state of recognition or no distraction. The Celestial realm of the gods may be accessed through the Samadhi Bardo.

> *The mind is a mirror.*
> *Grasping nothing- refusing nothing.*
> *Receiving but letting go.*
> *Like wild geese flying over a lake*
> *casting a reflection of their image unknowingly*
>   *that the lake has no desire to retain.*
>   -Allan Watts

"In the Age of Gold, the people were not conscious of their rulers; in the Age of Silver, they loved them, with songs; in the Age of Brass, they feared them; in the Age of Iron, they despised them. As the rulers lost confidence, so also did the people lose confidence in them. How hesitating did they seem, the Lords of the Age of Gold, speaking with deliberation, aware of the weight of their word! Thus they accomplished all things with success; and the people deemed their well-being to be the natural course of events. When men abandoned the Way of the Tao, benevolence and justice became necessary. Then also was need of wisdom and cunning, and all fell into illusion. When harmony ceased to prevail in the six spheres it was needful to govern them by manifesting Sons. When the kingdoms and races became confused, loyal ministers had to appear. If we forgot our statesmanship and our wisdom, it would be an hundred times better for the people. If we forgot our benevolence and our justice, they would become again like sons, folk of good will. If we forget our machines and our business, there would be no knavery. These new methods despised the olden Way, inventing fine names to disguise their baneness. But simplicity in the doing of the will of every man would put an end to vain ambitions and desires. To forget learning is to end trouble. The smallest difference in words, such as "yes" and "yea", can make endless controversy for the scholar. Fearful indeed is death, since all men fear it; but the abyss of questionings, shoreless and bottomless, is worse! Consider the profane man, how he preeneth, as if at feast, or gazing upon Spring from a tower! But as for me, I am as one who yawneth, without any trace of desire. I am like a babe before its first smile. I appear sad and forlorn, like a man homeless. The profane man hath his need filled, ay, and more also. For me, I seem to have lost all I had. My mind is as it were stupefied; it hath no definite shape. The profane man looketh lively and keen-witted; I alone appear blank in my mind. They seem eagerly critical; I appear careless and without perception. I seem to be as one adrift upon the sea, with {24} no thought of an harbor. The profane have each one his definite course of action; I alone appear useless and uncomprehending, like a man from the border. Yea, thus I differ from all other men: but my jewel is the All-Mother!" Dao de Jing Ch 17- 20 trans. Alister Crowley

Six Root Verses of the Bardo Thodol:

Kyema! Dawning upon me is the bardo:
Chikhai:
Now that it is clear that you are dying, abandon cravings and attachments clearly remembering and holding in the forefront of your mind the teachings you have received in this life. Merge with the space of the uncreated, it is time to leave this transiant body of illusion.
Chönyi:
In the bardo of dharmata abandon all fear and terror recognizing that all that appears are merely projections of thought-forms at this crucial crossroads. Don not fear or cling to the beautiful or terrifying visions projected by the mind.
Sidpa:
Now you realize you have to let go of everything in the bardo of becoming, so hold one single point of intention in your mind continuously directing you intention there with a positive outlook. Closing the entrance to the womb, to reverse samsara and nirvana, delaying the return to Earth-Life as long as possible, concentrating on pure energy and love, to cast off jealousy while meditating on the Guru with his consort.
Kyenay:
In the Bardo of Life I will abandon laziness for there is no time to waste,
and enter, undistracted, the path of study, reflection and meditation, taking the path of appearance-mind to actualize the three kayas, [dharmakaya- the truth body made of the nature body and the wisdom body being the embodiment of wisdom, sambhogakaya- sensual body of perfect enjoyment of the primordial nature of the great emptiness, and nirmanakaya- the emanation body].
Milam:
Now that you are drifting off to sleep, abandon the careless sleeping like an ignorant corpse. Control and transform your dreams in luminosity. Do not be like unconscious animals, but learn to maintain the same awareness and mindfulness of the waking state.
Samten:
Now that Dhyana is dawning, abandon the crowd of accumulated distractions, illusions and confusion and rest in the middle place without cravings or distraction. Remain with single pointed concentration, motionless and not tossed and swayed by emotions.

Zen, Hashish and the Psychedelic Experience

*"The case of Zen is especially pertinent here, for it pivots on an enlightenment experience- satori or kensho- which some (but not all) Zennists say resembles LSD. Alike or different, the point is that Zen recognizes that unless the experience is joined to discipline, it will come to naught. Even Buddha had to sit... without jo riki, the particular power developed through zazen (seated meditation), the vision of oneness attained in enlightenment... in time becomes clouded and eventually fades into a pleasant memory..."*²⁴³

*"There is no difference in principal between sharpening perception with an external instrument, such as a microscope, and sharpening it with an internal instrument such as one of these three drugs [mescalin (the active ingredient of the peyote cactus), lysergic acid diethyl-amide (a modified ergot alkaloid), and psilocybin (a derivative of the mushroom psilocybe mexicana)]. If they are an affront to the dignity of the mind, the microscope is an affront to the dignity of the eye and the telephone to dignity of the ear... I can find no essential difference between the experiences induced, under favorable conditions, by these chemicals and the states of cosmic consciousness... of mysticism..."*²⁴⁴

*"What is Imprinting?... It is very rapid learning that takes place... at a certain early stage of development... Certain alkaloid molecules posses the power of dramatically suspending the familiar, learned structural aspects of the nervous system; Consciousness is suddenly released from its conditioned patterning and flung into a flashing loom of unlearned imagery... The psychedelic drugs may not only suspend old imprinted patterns, they may also provide the possibility of the 'death-rebirth' experience... Reimprinting means that during the psychedelic session the subject's nervous system is in a state of disorganized flux closely analogous to that of infancy. The planned, voluntary release of fixed perceptual patterns and the temporary opening of fluid, boundaryless awareness suggests the hope of controlled, self-controlled reimprinting... visionary experiences are, I submit, the key to behavior change- drug induced satori. In three hours under the right circumstances the cortex can be cleared.... There are many methods for for expanding consciousness... Physical trauma can do it. Electric shock. Extreme fatigue."*²⁴⁵

*"But I have no doubts. Let the investigator study his own brain on the lines I have laid down, possibly in the first place with the aid of hashish or some better physical expedient to overcome the dull skepticism which is begotten of idleness upon ignorance."*²⁴⁶

"*The partial becomes complete; the crooked, straight; the empty, full; the worn out, new. He whose (desires) are few gets them; he whose (desires) are many goes astray. Therefore the sage holds in his embrace the one thing (of humility), and manifests it to all the world. He is free from self- display, and therefore he shines; from self-assertion, and therefore he is distinguished; from self-boasting, and therefore his merit is acknowledged; from self-complacency, and therefore he acquires superiority. It is because he is thus free from striving that therefore no one in the world is able to strive with him. That saying of the ancients that 'the partial becomes complete' was not vainly spoken: - all real completion is comprehended under it.*" Dao de Jing Ch 22 trans. James Legge

"*I myself have experimented with five of the principal psychedelics… as William James tried nitrous oxide, to see if they could help me in identifying what might be called the 'essential' or 'active' ingredients of the mystical experience… the classical literature on mysticism is vague, not only in describing the experience, but also in showing rational connections between the experience itself and the various traditional methods recommended to induce it-fasting, concentration, breathing exercises, prayers, incantations, and dances…. In the course of two experiments I was amazed and somewhat embarrassed to find myself going through states of consciousness that corresponded precisely with every description of major mystical experiences that I had ever read. Furthermore, they exceeded both in depth and in a peculiar quality of unexpectedness the three 'natural and spontaneous' experiences of this kind that had happened to me in previous years… I found that LSD-25 and cannabis suited my purposes best. Of these two, the latter---cannabis… proved to be the better… Almost invariably, my experiments with psychedelics have had four dominant characteristics… The first characteristic is a slowing down of time, a concentration in the present… The second characteristic I will call awareness of polarity. This is the vivid realization that states, things, and events that we ordinarily call opposite are interdependent, like back and front, or the poles of a magnet. By polar awareness one sees that things which are explicitly different are implicitly one… The third characteristic, arising from the second, is awareness of relativity… The fourth characteristic is awareness of eternal energy, often in the form of intense white light, which seems to be both the current in your nerves and that mysterious e which equals mc^2. This may sound like megalomania or delusion of grandeur-but one sees quite clearly that all existence is a single energy, and that this energy is one's own being. Of course there is death as well as life, because energy is a pulsation, and just as waves must have both crests and troughs, the experience of existing must go on and off.*" – Alan Watts, California Law Review, Vol. 56, No. 1, January 1968

Om Mani Padme Hum

Six Auspicious Syllables that form the innermost heart of the bodhisattva Avalokiteshvara and summarize all the teachings of the Buddhas. Used by Tibetan, Mongolian and Chinese Buddhists and Chinese Taoist alike.

"It is beneficial to recite the mantra om mani padme hum, but while you are doing it, you should be thinking of its meaning, for the meaning of the six syllables is great and vast. The first, om, is composed of three letters, a, u, and m. These symbolize the practitioner's impure body, speech and mind; they also symbolize the pure exalted body, speech and mind of a Buddha… The path is indicated by the next four syllables. Mani, meaning jewel, symbolizes… the altruistic mind of enlightenment is capable of removing the poverty or difficulties of cyclic existence… The two syllables, padme, meaning lotus, symbolize wisdom. Just as a lotus grows forth from mud but is not sullied by the faults of mud…. There is wisdom in realizing impermanence, wisdom in realizing that persons are empty of being self-sufficient or substantially existent, wisdom realizing the emptiness of duality… the main one of all these is the wisdom realizing emptiness. Purity must be achieved by an indivisible unity of method and wisdom, symbolized by the final syllable hum, which indicates indivisibility… Thus, the six syllables, om mani padme hum, means that in dependence on the practice of a path that is an indivisible union of method and wisdom, you can transform your impure body, speech, and mind into the pure exalted body, speech, and mind of a Buddha… As Maitreya says in his Sublime Continuum of the Great Vehicle (uttaratantra, rgyud bla ma), all beings naturally have the Buddha-nature in their own continuum. We have within us the seed of purity, the matrix-of-One-Gone-Thus, that is to be transformed and fully developed into Buddhahood."[247] – His Holiness the Fourteenth Dalai Lama Tenzin Gyatso

The basic English translation of Om mani padme hum is "Om Jewel in the Lotus Hum" or "Praise to the Jewel in the Lotus." But on a deeper level, the mantra crates a harmonious vibration in each of the six realms of existence.

Om purifies bliss and pride (realm of the gods)
Ma purifies jealousy and need for entertainment (realm of the jealous gods)
Ni purifies passion and desire (human realm)
Pad purifies ignorance and prejudice (animal realm)
Me purifies poverty and possessiveness (realm of the hungry ghosts)
Hum purifies aggression and hatred (hell realm)

"*The mantra Om Mani Pädme Hum is easy to say yet quite powerful, because it contains the essence of the entire teaching. When you say the first syllable Om it is blessed to help you achieve perfection in the practice of generosity, Ma helps perfect the practice of pure ethics, and Ni helps achieve perfection in the practice of tolerance and patience. Pä, the fourth syllable, helps to achieve perfection of perseverance, Me helps achieve perfection in the practice of concentration, and the final sixth syllable Hum helps achieve perfection in the practice of wisdom. So, in this way recitation of the mantra helps achieve perfection in the six practices from generosity to wisdom. The path of these six perfections is the path walked by all the Buddhas of the three times. What could then be more meaningful than to say the mantra and accomplish the six perfections?*" – His Holiness Lama Dilgo Khyentse Rinpoche

Magu's Magic Cannabis Wine

Magu opened a wine shop in the market and began to produce cannabis wine. One day an old man came in and ask for some of her wine. He told Magu that he had traveled from far away to try this wine that he has heard so many remarkable things about, but in his travels there, he had used all his money and he had no money left to pay her for the wine. Magu replied that she was honored that he had traveled so far just for her wine and gave him a glass to drink and a bottle to take with him. After drinking the wine, the old man told Magu that the wine was even more wonderful than he had been told. He presented Magu with "the Book of the Plain Girl," and esoteric manual of Daoist secrets for women. Magu read and practiced the exercises within the book until she had mastered the arts revealed within its pages. After many years, the old man returned to Magu's wine shop and said to Magu: "You have not aged a day since I last saw you. I see that you have read the book that I left with you." Magu presented the old man with a glass of her cannabis wine and a bottle for him to take on his journey, but the old man replied: "Magu, to steal the Dao without studying with a teacher is like having wings but being unable to fly." With that, he took Magu by the hand and they flew upon a cloud to the Heavenly Grotto of Taishan Mountain, were even today, devotees of Magu make a pilgrimage up the sacred mountain asking Magu for health and longevity while tossing cannabis seeds off its summit which is called, the Head of Pan Gu the creator. The slopes of Mt. Taishan are heavily laden with feral cannabis growing in response to the prayers of the pilgrims.

This simple story reveals deep alchemical secrets. The wine of Magu was made from an alchemical process. The peaches of immortality that she grew in her garden were fermented with mung beans and kombucha or other microbial or fungal cultures into wine, the wine was then distilled into a pure spirit. This alchemically refined spirit of the peach was then mixed with dried and gently roasted cannabis flowers. This was then left to commingle the essences for three moons. The cannabis wine is then strained off and bottled. The sage, saw that Magu has mastered the arts of physical alchemy, the arts of physical transmutation: smelting metal into tools and vessels, sand into glass, clay into vessels, plants into food, clothing or medicines and extracting the quintessence out of substances and the alchemical art of transforming fruits and grains into pure spirits. The book that he gave her contained instructions on taking these arts and turning them inward to perfect the quintessence of the self. When he returned, he saw that Magu had indeed internalized the practices and they joined together like Fuzi and Nawu blending the yin and yang to return to the source.

The cannabis plant, the Tree of Life, also blends together the yin and the yang, serving as a bridge to return to the source. Its flowers reach up to the Heavenly Realms and its root delve deep into the underworld. It brings the power of the heavens down to manifest in the physical by absorbing the energies of the heavens through photosynthesis and concentrating them in its trichomes. Through its roots it absorbs nutrients released through the alchemical process of decay and purification in the underworld to be reborn in the flowers and leaves and glistening trichomes. Cannabis, like humans, stand, grow, and flourish between the heavens and the earth and draw their nourishment and substance from them both. Standing between the two worlds and drawing in the power and lifeforce of each, cannabis mediates between the two and can reveal the powers and secrets of both to those that listen. The cannabis plant is the embodiment of compassion and charity. Its gives itself to nourish, sooth and heal, and to help in practical and pragmatic ways.

In 1070 AD, a Song Dynasty text, "Illustrated Classic of Materia Medica" by Tu Jing Ben Cao quoted a previous herbal titled "Formulas Within a Small Box" by Qie Zhong Fang, giving a formula for severe pain that inhibited movement: "'…the preparation method specifies that the seeds of cannabis are soaked in water, then the sediment is collected from the bottom of the water, stir-fried until aromatic in a silver vessel, and ground into a fine white powder; this is then boiled with alcohol and taken internally on an empty stomach. By 10 servings the suffering must be alleviated; its effect cannot be surpassed.' This prescription was repeated in many later texts under the name 'cannabis seed wine,' da ma ren jiu, under entries for the achenes, however it differs strikingly from other preparations of the achenes because it is used for severe pain. If the achenes were soaked in water with the bracts intact, it is possible that the preparation method described would yield cannabinoids, as broken resin glands from the bracts would sink in water; when this sediment was stir-fried, THC acids would be decarboxylated into bioavailable THC, which would then be efficiently extracted when boiled with alcohol, as in the original preparation."[248]

"There was another aspect of Japhy that amazed me: his tremendous and tender since if charity. He was always giving things, always practicing what the Buddhist call the Paramita of Dana, the perfection of charity…. [he said] 'you don't realize it's a privilege to practice giving presents to others.' …Sometimes his gifts were old beat up things but they had the charm of usefulness and sadness of his giving." – Jack Kerouac, The Dharma Bums

"When a good man hears the word of the way, he hurries to put it into practice. When the average man hears the word of the way he takes from it what he wants to hear. When a worthless man hears the word of the way he makes fun of it. It would no longer be the way if he did not laugh at it. That is what these maxims express: the bright way is dark, the way that progresses recedes, the smooth way is rough, the highest virtue is like a ravine, true candor seems sullied, the amplest virtue narrow, the firmest virtue shaky, absolute sincerity seems suspicious. A great square has no corners, a great vase takes long to perfect, great music spares notes, the great image has no form, the Tao is too great to have a name, the one that completes all it undertakes." Dao de Jing Ch. 41

Laos and Cambodian Cannabis Culture

Laos and Cambodia are nestled between Vietnam and Thailand, bordered by China and Burma to the north. The early settlers of Laos migrated from the Yangtze River area of China into Laos and Northern Thailand in the first century BCE of the last millennium, and a large-scale migration took place from the seventh through the thirteenth centuries CE, with the peak concentration between the eight and tenth centuries CE and the "Land of One Million Elephants" was established in the fourteenth century CE. Theravada Buddhism was introduced at the same time and is still the largest religion in Laos, although throughout the centuries it has been mingled with tribal folk, shamanistic and animistic beliefs and practices known as sasna phi, "religion of the spirits," like the Japanese Shinto. The indigenous tribal people of Cambodia are spread throughout the region in Thailand, Laos and Vietnam. There are archaeological remains of stone age cave dwellers dated to 5,000 BCE and by 1,000 BCE they had established Bronze Age settlements. Their religion is still a shamanistic based animism as it was when dwelling in caves. Although each tribal Folk Religion is individual and unique, they also share many practices in common. According to the tribespeople in a Non-Governmental Organization Forum on Cambodia 2006 "We have indigenous blood (our parents and grandparents are indigenous), we live communally, we respect spirits and have ceremonies for the village spirit every year, we call (pray) for help and have ceremonies to compensate when the spirits help, we have ceremonies to call up 'araks' (a spirit called up to find out why someone is sick), we practice or have a history of practicing rotational agriculture, we hold sacrifices when we farm, we have village leaders (chahsrok), and we have burial forests." While Hinduism and Buddhism were both introduced early on in the history of Cambodia, the indigenous religions maintained their influence and became integrated with the foreign religions. By the second century AD, Cambodia was a major trading center, and artifacts originating from Rome, India and China have been found. Hinduism and Buddhism were introduced and a syncretic form of Hinduism, with Buddha a member of its pantheon, emerged blended with the indigenous tribal shamanism. In the ninth century the Khmer Empire was established with its central capital, Anghor, in the heart of Cambodia. Theravada Buddhism, a tolerant, non-prescriptive religion that does not require belief in a supreme being, but instead requiring each individual take full responsibility for his own actions and omissions, became the state religion. Today Theravada Buddhism is still the largest religion in the country. But what was developed in the Khmer period that lasted until the Fourteenth Century was a synchronistic blend of Tribal

Shamanism, Hinduism and Buddhism. After the fall of the Khmer Empire, Cambodia became a part of neighboring Siam, now Thailand, and in the Nineteenth Century became a colony of France. Following the Geneva Treaty, in 1954 Cambodia gained its independence. Today there is Cambodian Buddhism that combines Brahmanism, Buddhism, spirit mediums, animism and shamanism. What is common to these religious expressions is cannabis. Hinduism was the parent of Buddhism, and cannabis is sacred to both Vishnu and Shiva as well as many other Hindu gods and goddesses and essential in the worship of Shiva. Cannabis has grown since the earliest times in the region and its cultivation spread alongside the cultivation of rice. In Laos cannabis is used by shamans to heal possessed people.[249] Cannabis appears again and again in shamanistic cultures, and illustrates animism: the plant is truly the physical expression of the spirit of the plant, in that it provides protection from the elements in the form of clothing, fuel, canvas for shelter and spiritual protection by the burning of the leaves and flowers, it provides blessings in the form of nutrition, medicine and soothing of the spirit, if reverence and respect is shone to the plant and its spirit, then the plant will bestow its blessings in return. The plant is a living sentient being just like you or me, and from that starting point a relationship can be established.

Laos is one of southeast Asia's poorest countries and the most bombed country in history. Laos has been involved with opium production since its time as a French Colony. By the 1930s, opium had become an important cash crop for the Hmong who have traditionally grown opium in small quantities for medicinal and ritual purposes, and some other Lao Sung groups being encouraged to grow it by the French administration of Indochina that financed its covert operations with the drug trade. After the French pulled out of Laos, the CIA had simply replaced the French, to finance similar operations. "During the 40 years of the cold war, from the late 1940s to this year, the CIA pursued a policy that I call radical pragmatism. Their mission was to stop communism and in pursuit of that mission they would ally with anyone and do anything to fight communism. During the long years of the cold war the CIA mounted major covert guerilla operations along the Soviet-Chinese border. The CIA recruited as allies people we now call drug lords for their operation against communist China in northeastern Burma in 1950, then from 1965 to 1975 during the Vietnam war their operation in northern Laos, and throughout the decade of the 1980s, the Afghan operation against Soviet forces in Afghanistan."[250] While cannabis is illegal in Laos a cannabis culture still exists. Cannabis is widely available in Laos despite its illegal status and cannabis grows wild along the rivers in the south of

Laos. In 1961 Cambodia entered into the Single Convention on Narcotics treaty making cannabis illegal, but it was not enforced locally. In 1965 United States air raids on Cambodia began and escalated until in 1970 troops were sent into Cambodia and remained there until 1973. After the withdrawal of the United States troops, the Khmer Rouge came into power in 1975 and Cambodia's cities were emptied, its economy was militarized, its Buddhist religion and folk culture were outlawed, and more than one million of its eight million people were starved and massacred. The Vietnamese Army defeated the Khmer Rouge in 1979 and controlled the country for the next ten years. In 1992 Cambodia was placed under the United Nations Transitional Authority and cannabis was again banned, but again the ban was not enforced locally. In 1996, the new government passed its first law on drugs, succumbing to pressure from the United States to withhold much needed aid, declaring cannabis illegal but allowing Cambodians to grow a small number of plants for medicinal or cooking purposes. In 2009, the United Nations Office on Drugs and Crime stated that cannabis production and cultivation had "ceased to be a major concern" in Cambodia. Cannabis is illegal and public usage is punishable by 12 months in jail, and in cases of trafficking a mandatory death penalty can be applied.

"Vientiane is exceptional, but inconvenient. The brothels are cleaner than hotels, marijuana is cheaper than a cold glass of beer. Opium is a restful drug, the perfect thing for geriatrics, but the chromatic snooze it induces corrects fatigue; after an evening of it the last thing you want to do is sleep again." [251]

In the Laos tourist area of Vang Vieng, cannabis is openly sold by bars as cannabis flowers or as infused "happy pizza" and some restaurants even have a "happy" menu" where customers can get a variety of infused foods, sometimes along with "magic" goods containing psychedelic mushrooms. The entire town has become a backpackers' bazaar catering to the estimated 170,000 who arrive every year to enjoy a jumble of restaurants, bars, internet cafés, pancake stalls, travel agents' cheap guesthouses, "happy" pizzas and "magic" shakes or teas laden with cannabis, opium and mushrooms. Cannabis has been traditionally grown in Cambodia and is a common ingredient in food and a traditional ingredient in Khmer noodle soup. Many "Happy" restaurants located in Phnom Penh, Siem Reap and Sihanoukville publicly offer food cooked with cannabis, or as a side garnish and cannabis is openly sold in markets and bars. Many villages grow local strains and bribe the police to create a "Green Light District." [252] Cannabis is not intensively farmed but instead grown in small plots around houses.

"Marijuana grows very easily on the fields by the river. The farmers can just scatter the seeds and let it grow; they don't need to take care of it. Old men smoke it, and young people see it as an 'old man's habit.' Also, some people have the custom of eating it in chicken soup in the morning. But this is a very small amount, and the Ministry of Health does not see any problem with this."[253]

In Cambodia cannabis leaves are a commonly used in soups, curries, fish fritters and other dishes and have been for centuries.[254] Iindividuals infected with malaria were traditionally treated with cannabis, the smoke from one kilogram of male and female plants was inhaled twice daily until the fever has passed.[255] In Cambodia leaves are used fresh in curries, soup, and fritters with fish paste for the flavor and medicinal qualities. Textile use was limited but there were extensive medical uses for pain relief, facilitating contractions during difficult childbirths, cholera, dysentery, anorexia, loss of memory, asthma, coughing, dizziness, convulsions, intestinal parasites, paralysis and much more.[256] In 2015 a local Cambodian farmer said: "Here, ganja is just like in Jamaica, because we don't grow much, maybe 10 to 15 plants [the authorities] let us grow it." He went on to say that police had never requested bribes from him, and he grew a few plants in his vegetable garden at home year-round, he and his neighbors grew an annual crop in the Cardamom Mountains saying, "In the nighttime in the mountains, with the dew, it helps the plant grow a lot of buds." Cannabis is still an accepted part of life in the community and is used for chicken soup seasoning, topical skin rash ointment, anti-nausea tonic, anti-headache tincture, cow medicine and recreational intoxicant. "It's ancient medicine," the farmer maintained.[257]

"Ganga came from India or the Himalayan region to Cambodia, which was Hindu from the first to the fourteenth centuries, and there may be no other people which know how to use the plant in so many ways as the Khmer." - Stefan Haag[258]

Six Mystical Steps to the Six Subtle Dharma Doors
(Based on the teachings of T'ien-t'ai master Chih-I and Yin Shih Tzu.)

counting, following, resting, visualization, returning, clarifying

1. Counting (shu) the breath so that it is the only focus and becomes even and rhythmic.

2. Following (sui) the breath going in and out, focused solely upon the breath until breath and mind become one.

3. Stopping (chih) everything and focusing on the tip of the nose until awareness of all else falls away.

4. Seeing (kuan) by turning back the light of the mind upon itself and visualizing the breath coming in and going out of the body as a brilliant light.

5. Returning (huan) to dissolve the duality between the mind that contemplates the breath and the breath that is contemplated understanding that the mind like the breath rises and falls in a rhythmic manner so to do thoughts, but these are not the true mind which is empty and returns us to the original meditation of the Buddha.

6. Refining (ching) by clearing the mind of all thought keep your mind like still water, with all random thinking and discrimination stopped so as to observe the true mind.

"*The great Tao flows everywhere. All things are born from it, yet it doesn't create them. It pours itself into its work, yet it makes no claim. It nourishes infinite worlds, yet it doesn't hold on to them. Since it is merged with all things and hidden in their hearts, it can be called humble. Since all things vanish into it and it alone endures, it can be called great. It isn't aware of its greatness; thus it is truly great.*" Dao de Ching Ch 34 trans. Stephen Mitchell

Confirmatory Experiences During the Circulation of the Light

"Every separate thought takes shape and becomes visible in color and form. The total spiritual power unfolds its traces and transforms itself into emptiness. Going out into being and going into non-being, one completes the miraculous Tao. All separate shapes appear as bodies, united with a true source." - The Hui Ming Ching, The Book of Consciousness and Life, Ch. 6 trans. Richard Wilhelm

"If, when there is quiet, the spirit has continuously and uninterruptedly a sense of great joy as if intoxicated or freshly bathed, it is a sign that the light-principle is harmonious in the whole body; then the Golden Flower begins to bud. When, furthermore, all openings are quiet, and the silver moon stands in the middle of heaven, and one has the feeling that this great earth is a world of light and brightness, that is a sign that the body of the heart opens itself to clarity. It is a sign that the Golden Flower is opening..." - Secret of the Golden Flower Ch 6 trans. Richard Wilhelm

"The sixth realization is the awareness that poverty creates hatred and anger, which creates a vicious cycle of negative thoughts and activity."[259]

"Sunrise doesn't last all morning. A cloudburst doesn't last all day. Seems my love is up and has left you with no warning. It's not always going to be this grey. All things must pass. All things must pass away. Sunset doesn't last all evening. A mind can blow those clouds away. After all this, my love is up and must be leaving. It's not always going to be this grey. All things must pass. All things must pass away. All things must pass. None of life's strings can last. So, I must be on my way. And face another day. Now the darkness only stays the night-time. In the morning it will fade away. Daylight is good at arriving at the right time. It's not always going to be this grey. All things must pass. All things must pass away. All things must pass. All things must pass away." Dao de Jing Ch 23 trans. George Harrison (All Things Must Pass 1970 Apple Records)

Interpretation:
A broken line between two solid lines symbolize fire. The two solid lines indicate the movement of fire. The broken line is the center of the fire which is still. In addition, this kua also represents the Sun and the intellect. Thinking links sense data with words, following the will or motivations and impulses. Thinking, like burning wood has a beginning and end, therefore do not think beyond the solution of the problem. The motivation is to attain clarity unattached to thought. It is the clinging, radiance of the second daughter, the adaptable light-giving, dependence.

Right Effort: Cultivating wholesome internal states such as generosity, diligence, insight, wisdom, equanimity, compassion and lovingkindness, while renouncing wholesome internal states such as greed, hatred, and delusion, even in their subtlest forms of sloth, torpor, restlessness, remorse, and doubt.

Queen Mother of the West

Xiwang Mu, Xi Wangmu, Xi Wang Mu, Spirit Grandmother of the West, Queen Mother of the West, Perfected Marvel of the Western Florescence, Ultimate Worthy of the Cavernous Darkness, Golden Mother of the Tortoise Pedestal, the Golden Mother of the Jade Pool, known as the Golden Mother in Taiwan, Seiōbo in Japan, Seowangmo in Korea, and Tây Vương Mẫu in Vietnam. Xi Wangmu predates Daoism and represents the divine yin, the archetype of the Great Mother Goddess and all women who attain the Dao are her under her protection and guidance. Xi Wangmu, in times before memories, patched the sky with five gems to restore the balance of the five forces of the five elements when her people had lost coherence and were on the brink of destruction. The first historical mention of the Queen Mother is written upon oracle bones dated to 1300 BCE. Of the Queen Mother it was said, "No one knows her beginning; no one knows her end." The chthonic goddess, Golden Mother of the West, is the archetypical ancient shaman, the village wise woman who later became the Daoist Immortal, a Xian. Her name Mu indicates she is the ancestor of all shamans, the shape-shifting masters of wind and rain who ride upon dragons and beat the sacred drum. Her reign dates back to the Stone Age cave dwellers as the embodiment of the village elders, female tiger shamans in charge of life, death and immortality.

The Queen Mother of the West lives in her palace of Jade on the Isles of P'eng-lai in the Lake of Gems hidden within the Kunlun Mountains with her companions the hare, the tortoise, the three eyed crow and the three-legged toad with five Jade Fairy Maids attending her, and bluebirds as her messengers. She rides upon a white crane, and grows the peaches of immortality in her celestial garden that enable shamans to travel back and forth between the three worlds.[260] It is also said that the Queen Mother of the West lives upon the Mountain Kunlun that rests upon the back of the Jade Tortoise, the grindstone base of the World Pillar around which the earth turns, and the shamans once flew up and down between the three worlds of the Heavens, Earth and Underworld. This pillar of the Queen Mother reaches up into the Heavens to the Five Shards Constellation, the womb point of the universe from whence the universe was born and around which all the stars and constellations revolve. Kunlun was a hollow, or cavernous mountain that housed Grotto Caves of the immortals and fairies, located directly under the Pole Star. There are over seventy volcanic cones in the Western Kunlun Mountains and the last known eruption in the volcanic group was in 1951. The Kunlun Mountains run east from Tajikistan along the northwest border of the Tibetan Plateau, where cannabis is believed to have originated, to the Qinghai Province in the east. From the Kunlun Mountains flow the Black Jade River and the White Jade River into the Taklamakan Desert and the Bayan Har Mountains, a southern branch of the Kunlun Mountains, form the watershed between the catchment basins of China's two longest rivers, the Yangtze River and the Yellow River.

Xiwang Mu has the fangs of a tiger and the tail of a leopard, a dark fearsome goddess with teeth of a tiger who can bring havoc, chaos and destruction when displeased but also the goddess of longevity, immortality, and magic, who wields the powers of creation and destruction. To her left stands the dragon of the east, to her right the tiger of the west, the yang and yin, sun and moon. At her feet are two hares that pound the elixir of immortality, like the Soma of the people in the lands to the west. She is the mistress of the spinning wheel of rebirth, weaving fine strands of cannabis and silk into lives and experiences. She guards the herb of immortality and determines those to whom she would bequeath the peaches of immortality. Her consorts were the Jade Emperor, Dongwanggong 東王公, King Duke of the East, Mugong, 木公 the Duke of the Woods and Yi the Archer, Hòuyì 后羿. She is the patron deity of shamans, nuns, singing girls, widows, unmarried women, and the patron deity of all women, outcasts and outsiders. She is revered not only throughout China's history, but also in Korea where there is a mountain named for her, in Japan during the Tanabata festival, and also by the modern Compassion Society in Taiwan.[261] She is the great Primordial Ruler, progenitor of all shamans, magic and healing, the guardian of the gates to live, death and rebirth.

"The Tigress first learns from her mother how to survive. She then has three paths in which to begin her hunt. No matter which path she walks, the Green Dragon is her prey. She gathers the essences of the dragon and tiger. When the essences fuse, the spirit embryo manifests. The spirit embryo carries her to the Heavenly Abode where Wang Mu happily bestows the Peach of Immortality upon her new daughter." – The White Tigress Manual[262]

Trees are the natural altars of the Dao and are constantly filtrating impurities out of the air releasing it as fresh oxygen. Peach trees according to Feng Shui hold the sacred properties of five types of holy trees. The peach represents youth, marriage, wealth, longevity and are a symbol of the female genitals. In China peaches were regarded as the source of the ambrosia of life which gives gods their immortality, in the magic peach garden in the west, where the gods were reborn. 'Peach Blossom' meant a virgin in Taoist symbolism, while the fruit stood for a mature woman whose juices were essential to men's health. China's patron saint of longevity Shou Lou was an old man with a high bulging forehead, bursting with "yin juice" he had absorbed and sent up to his head through sexual coupling with many women. To reveal his mystical secret, Shou Lou always held up a peach with one of his fingers stuck into its cleft.

"The holding of her two breasts represents the two female attendants offering the peach of immortality. The taking of her orgasmic fluids represents eating the peach of immortality." – The White Tigress Manual

The ancient Chinese believed the peach possessed more vitality than any other tree because their blossoms appear before leaves sprout. The purifying nature of the tree itself, is in its fruit and can be eaten to purify the internal organs of the body. Peaches are rich in phytochemicals called phenols that act as antioxidants and also contain protein, Vitamins A ,C, E, K, plus niacin, potassium, iron, magnesium, copper and selenium. Peaches are said to have a diuretic effect which helps cleanse the kidneys and bladder and also antimicrobial properties. Linalool, d-limonene and α-terpineol are the dominant terpenic compounds in peaches. The peach-tree wood (t'ao-fu) was said to ward off evil, and demons, so was used to construct ritual instruments. When a Daoist priest performs an exorcism, or banishing, they sometimes use a seven-star sword made from the wood of a peach tree. When early rulers of China visited their territories, they were preceded by shamans armed with peach rods to protect them. On New Year's Eve, local magistrates would cut peach wood branches and place them over their doors to protect against evil. Peachwood was also used for the earliest known door gods and peach-wood bows strung with hemp cord were used to shoot arrows in every direction to dispel evil. Peach-wood seals or figurines guarded gates and doors. Carved peach kernels, tao ren, which contain strychnine, were used to make talismans to aid in incantation and invocation. Peach-wood slips or carved pits were amulets for protection, longevity and health. Peach kernels are a common ingredient used in traditional Chinese medicine to dispel blood stasis, counter inflammation and reduce allergies.

"The facts of life are common sense.... Everyone recognizes that the clouds and mist are the Yin-juices of the earth and that Jade is the Yang-essence of the Heavenly Dragon... I am called the Peach of Immortality because I bear the sweetest fruits of the earth and bestow lasting transcendence. The tortoise, unicorn, phoenix and dragon are all creatures with counterparts within the human body. All are called Ling, which means transcendental. The tortoise enjoys this earth without haste, and as a result, lives for a very long time; the unicorn is much loved by women, and though rarely found, his horn is always hard; the phoenix is born from the ashes of earth and rises constantly; the dragon, though originally resting in the bowels of the earth hides in the heavens. In ancient times I, Hsuan-nu, made magic drums for the Yellow Emperor and helped him to slay the monster of Time." – The Yellow Emperor; quoted in Sexual Secrets, Douglas & Slinger p. 159

Magu's Long Fingernails

Lord Wang Yuan would visit on the "seventh day of the seventh month" for the feast of the Cowherd and Weaver Girl lovers' festival. The immortal Blue Lad, summoned all the fairies and immortals to witness the blossoming of Magu's flowers, saying that Magu's jade stamens have opened and are whiskers, like threads of ice, with golden grain sewn on top.[263] When Lord Wang and his celestial entourage arrived, he invoked Magu to join their celebration saying, "It has been a long time since you were in the human realm." Magu's invisible messenger replied, "Maid Ma bows and says: 'Without our realizing it, more than five hundred years have passed since our last meeting!'" After she apologized that she would be delayed with the Queen of the West at Penglai Mountain, Ma arrived four hours and twenty minutes later. She appeared in a cloud as a beautiful young maiden. Her gown had a pattern of colors so bright that they dazzled the eyes, but it was not woven; it shimmered and was indescribable appearing as if it was not of this world.[264] When Magu was introduced to the women present, she transformed some rice into pearls as a trick to avoid the unclean influences of a recent childbirth that one of the women had. Then Wang presented Cai's family with a strong liquor from "the celestial kitchens" and warned that it was "unfit for drinking by ordinary people." Even after diluting the liquor with water, everyone became intoxicated and wanted more.

"There is a goddess named Ma Gu. She is very youthful and pretty. She looks like an 18-year-old girl, but in fact, she has lived for thousands of years. Because Ma Gu has such longevity, if one accepts an offering from her, they will also be youthful, beautiful, healthy and alive forever." - Way of Infinite Harmony, Ma Guang Wei

During the feast Magu said to Wang Yuan: "Canghai Sangtian, things have changed a lot. Since I got the Tao to accept his destiny, I have personally seen the East China Sea turned into mulberry field three times. I just came to Penglai and saw that the seawater was half as shallow as in the previous period. It has become land!" Wang Yuan also sighed. "Yeah, the saints say that the sea is falling. Soon, dust will rise there again."

Magu's fingernails resembled bird claws. When Cai Jing noticed them at the feast, he thought to himself, "My back itches. Wouldn't it be great if I could get her to scratch my back with those nails?" Cai Jing became obsessed with the idea of how wonderful it would be to have his back scratched by her long nails. Lord Wang knew what Cai was thinking in his heart, so he ordered him bound with hemp cords and whipped, chiding, "Maid Ma is a Xian. How dare you think that her nails could scratch your back!" The snake whip lashing Cai's back was the only thing that was seen, no one was seen wielding it as he was lashed with the hemp whip and Magu said to Cai, "My whippings are not given without cause." Then all knew whose invisible hand wielded the knotted hemp whip and the phrase "as delightful as being scratched by Magu," became an expression of sexual delight. When the dinner was over Lord Wang Yuan and Magu climbed his coach and ascended to Heaven. The famous Tang Dynasty Daoist calligrapher Yan Zhengqing visited Mt Magu and inscribed the Magu Shan Xiantan Ji, the "Record of the Mountain Platform where Magu Ascended to Immortality." Because of this Magu is the protector of honor, women, prostitutes, brides, and marriage. Drawings of Magu are often given as birthday presents, or to married couples on important anniversaries. From this episode come the classic expression "Magu saobei" (姑搔背)Magu scratches [my] back" meaning that things are going as imagined, and also the saying: Canghai sangtian (滄海桑田) "blue ocean [turns to] mulberry fields" meaning "great changes over the course of time."[265] In the novel "Journey to the West" Xi You Ji, Ma Gu attended the peach banquet held by the Queen Mother of the West, for which she brewed a special wine made of cannabis. She gave this to the Queen Mother, and the image of this scene has become renowned as "Ma Gu Offers Longevity," Ma Gu Xian Shou. Followers use the words "Ma Gu Xian Shou" as a statement of faith, and believe hearing these words gets one closer to knowing the Self and attaining the Dao. It is also therefore often said as a mantra by devotees.

"*There is no greater sin than desire, no greater curse than discontent, no greater misfortune than wanting something for oneself. Therefore, he who knows that enough is enough will always have enough.*" Dao de Ching Ch. 46 trans. Gia-fu Feng and Jane English

Myths are to be interpreted on many levels. On the surface, they are cute stories that we tell our children usually with some moral lesson, but myths always have deeper, more esoteric meanings. In this tale, Magu's fingernails invoke an image of the prehistoric bird shamans of old. Ma Gu was associated with the sparrow, sometimes called the cannabis bird, due to its fondness of eating cannabis seeds. The sparrow was also considered the most sensuous of all birds. This illustrates both the psychoactive, entheogenic and aphrodisiac properties of cannabis, but the tale also teaches of the topical applications of cannabis. Cannabis does literally "scratch the itch" and has been used for millennium for a wide range of skin problems from eczema to cuts and burns.

"There I saw Master Wang and made him salutation, and I asked him about the balance made by unifying essence. He said: 'The Way can only be received; it cannot be given. Small, it has no content; great, it has no bounds. Keep your soul from confusion, and it will come naturally. Unify the essences and control the spirit; Preserve them inside you in the midnight hour. Await in emptiness, before even inaction. All other things proceed from this: This is The Door to Power... Sweet odours and rich savours mingle in the wild abundance: but the flowers and the fragrance come from within my breast. The ravishing sweetness reaches far and wide; it fills all my frame within and is wafted abroad outside. In spirit and substance truly to be trusted, though I dwell unseen and obscure, my frame can yet be bright... The two Masters held zithers and tuned them in harmony, so I sang the Ch'ing Shang air to their playing. In genital ease I took my enjoyment, sucked all the vapors of the air, and freely soared aloft... Where is it that people do not age? Where do giants live? Where is the nine branched weed? Where is the flower of the Great Hemp?... Now take up rich and fragrant flower offerings... Flourish the drumsticks and beat the drums! The singing begins softly to a slow solemn measure; then as pipes and zithers join in, the singing grows shriller. Now the priestesses come, splendid in their gorgeous apparel. And all the hall is filled with a penetrating fragrance. The five sounds mingle in a rich harmony; and the god is merry and takes his pleasure... Flying aloft, he soars serenely, riding the pure vapour, guiding yin and yang. Speedily, lord, I will go with you, conducting High God on his way to Chiu Kang. My cloud coat hangs in billowing folds; my jade girdle pendants dangle low; a yin and a yang, a yin and a yang. None of the common folk know what I am doing. I have plucked the glistening flower of the Holy Hemp to give to one who lives far away.'"[266]

Quan Yin

觀音

Avalokiteshvara Bodhisattva is the embodiment of great compassion. He has vowed to free all sentient beings from suffering. One of his manifestations is the goddess Quan Yin, also spelled Kwan Yin, Kuanyin and Guanyin, she is the Goddess of Mercy, the Maternal Goddess, the Protectress of Children, the Enlightened World Savior, the Observer of All Sounds, in Sanskrit, Padma-pâni, or Born of the Lotus, and in Vajrayana Buddhism she is manifested as Tara. In Tibet she is Chenrézik, in Nepal she is Seto Machindranath, in Japan she is Kannon, in Korea Gwan-eum, in Thailand she is Phra Mae Kuan Im, in Vietnam she is Quán Thế Âm and to the Hmong she is known as Kab Yeeb. Quan Yin is a transgender Buddha who was originally a man who became a bodhisattva and changed into a woman so all, including women, could receive her teachings and help. Quan Yin vowed not to return to nirvana until all beings achieved Buddhahood also. Peace, mercy, sacrifice and compassion are the keynotes of her expressions. No other figure in the Chinese pantheon appears in a greater variety of images, of which there are said to be thousands of different incarnations or manifestations all over China and Indochina. She has been revered throughout the region for at least the past 500 years, not only in Buddhism, but she also revered in Daoism, Confucianism, Shinto, Cao Dai and ethnic tribal folk religions.

Born on the Fragrant Mountain, the goddess of mercy, the "one who hears the cries of the world" in the Lotus Sutra, an embodiment of compassion that has occupied a central place in Buddhist teaching and practice in a variety of forms. Guanyin is usually depicted as a barefoot, tall, slender, graceful woman dressed in beautiful, white flowing robes, with a white hood gracefully draped over the top of the head, sometimes with one or both breasts exposed and infrequently entirely naked, but always an appearance that embraces the qualities of compassion and motherly love. She is frequently depicted as riding a mythological animal known as the Hou, which somewhat resembles a Buddhist lion, and symbolizes the divine supremacy exercised by Guanyin over the forces of nature, and sometimes a dragon, sea turtle, elephant or other animal, but other times she is perched upon the crescent moon, but it is her raft of salvation that brings all to the shores of safety. Her bare feet are the consistent quality and the fact that they are obviously unbound. Often her image is carved in jade, frequently flanked by two acolytes, to her right a barefoot, shirtless youth with his hands clasped in prayer known as Shan-ts'ai, the Golden Youth, and on her left a maid demurely holding her hands together inside her sleeves known as Lung-nü, the Jade Maiden.

She is a feminine presence, serene, arms outstretched, and eyes open, at times she holds a willow branch, symbolizing her resilience, bending in the face of the fiercest storms without being broken and to heal people's illnesses or bring fulfillment to their requests. She may hold a vase with water holding the dew of compassion to remove suffering, purifying the defilements of our body, speech and mind, lengthening life and cleansing of people's sins or illnesses. Other times she may hold a lotus flower to represent the flowering and unfolding of the mind, soul, and spirit. Guanyin's right hand often points downward, with the palm facing outward, the posture of granting a wish, a typical image in China and Taiwan. Guanyin may be shown either in a standing or in a sitting position and often on top of her crown there is an image of a buddha. She may be depicted with a thousand arms and hands, each with an open eye in its center, her constant awareness of suffering and a symbol of her aspiration to reach out to any being in any form to help them, but most of all so that she may key an eye on the needs of the children of the world. The Lotus Sutra lists thirty-two typical forms in which Guanyin may appear and Sino-Japanese Buddhist art depicts thirty-three different appearances of the bodhisattva. Worshiped especially by women, this goddess comforts the troubled, the sick, the lost, and the unfortunate, she is the protector of seafarers, farmers and travelers, she cares for souls in the underworld, and is invoked during burial rituals to free the soul of the deceased. One can invoke Guanyin's assistance by simply calling out her name, making her very approachable and common in household alters.

The bodhisattva Guanyin appears unconditionally for all who invoke her sincerely, bestowing mercy, redemption, help and alleviating pain and suffering. Namo Guanshiyin pusa. Na mo Guanshiyin Pusa. Namo Avalokiteshvaraya. Namo amitofuo guanshying pusa. "I invoke the venerable Kuan Yin to show mercy on me from my own bad karma and to alleviate my pain and suffering." The Heart Sutra is also used to invoke Kuan Yin. Gate Gate Paragate, Parasamgate Bodhi Svaha. Om mani padme hum.[267]

The dharani of Quan Yin should be recited 108 times after bathing in the morning to raise the vibrations of the practitioner so that they are noticed by the heavenly spirits and advert physical suffering, harm and disease, guard from malevolent spirits and bad intentions, while empowering and bringing abundance and prosperity to the practitioner.[268]

While she is not exoterically associated with cannabis, Guanyin and cannabis have a very intimate relationship. The relationship is not held within their form or function, but in their effects and results. Guanyin answers the petitions of all those who call upon her, healing their bodies, hearts, minds, souls and spirit. So too, does cannabis heal the sickness of the body, the lifts the heaviness of the heart and spirit. On a physical level, cannabis is the embodiment of the Middle Path, it is an antidote to the extreme swings of the body, it does not stimulate, it does not depress, it does both at the same time, thus balancing the entire system. Cannabis causes more expansive breathing that increases parasympathetic nervous system activity precipitating a feeling of relaxation. At the same time, cannabis expands the alveoli of the lung, resulting in increased oxygen intake that stimulates the sympathetic nervous system and increases the heart rate. The brain in turn receives blood that is more oxygenated and due to the relaxation of the parasympathetic nervous system dilating the capillaries, and the feeling of being relaxed yet alert may be what is referred to a "being stoned".[269] Beyond this physical action though, there is a spiritual action as well. Cannabis helps to open the heart to compassion and the mind to understanding. It aids in uniting the mind and the heart, by aiding in letting go of thoughts and relaxing into the body. It is an aid to mindful awareness and meditation, called by some a portal to inner stillness. Cannabis is a modulator in difficult emotional times and on entheogenic journeys, where it aids and smoothing our difficult patched so that the journey can continue, and it helps to guide on safely back home after a difficult or long journey of the spirit. Cannabis can act as a sensory enhancer, emotional reliever, pain modulator, mood elevator, boundary dissolver and time stretcher,[270] thus, being the perfect flower for the goddess of mercy and compassion. When medical cannabis was legalized in California, it was done under the "Compassionate Use Act", underscoring the relationship between cannabis and compassion. The medical dispensaries provided a model and a beacon of compassion for those suffering and made sure that they had access to the sacred and holy herb of the goddess of compassion and mercy.

Prajñāpāramitāhṛdaya Sūtra / ཤེས་རབ་ཀྱི་ཕ་རོལ་ཏུ་ཕྱིན་པའི་སྙིང་པོ་ / 般若波羅蜜多心經
The Heart Sutra: Heart of the Transcendent Perfection of Wisdom

Avalokitesvara Bodhisattva immersed in union with Prajnaparamita illuminated the five skandhas- the gestalts, and perceived they were all sunyata, dynamic transient patterns existing only in the present moment, and thus attained deliverance from all suffering.

Sariputra, form is not different from sunyata, and sunyata is not different from form, form is sunyata and sunyata is form. So too are feelings (vedanā), perceptions (saṃjñā), thinking (saṃskāra), and consciousness.

Sariputra, all dharmas are marked with sunyata, they are not created or destroyed, they are not tainted or pure, do not increase or decrease. Therefore, in sunyata: bodily feelings, perceptions, thinking and consciousness are not separate self-entities. There is no eye, ear, nose, tongue, body or mind. There are no sights, sounds, scents, tastes, sensations or dharma. There is no field of vision and there is no realm of thoughts. There is no ignorance nor elimination of ignorance, and no Dao, no wisdom and also no attainment. Whoever can see this no longer needs anything to attain.

Bodhisattvas through the reliance on Prajnaparamita, their minds without delusions and since they have no delusions, they have no fear. Since they have no need for daydreams and wishful thinking, they experience Nirvana.

All Buddhas of the three periods of time attain Anuttarasamyaksambodhi through reliance on Prajnaparamita. Therefore, one should know the Prajnaparamita as the great spell, the spell of great knowledge, the utmost spell, the unequalled spell, allayer of all suffering, it is genuine and not false.

The perfection of wisdom is declared with the Prajnaparamita mantra –
Chant: Gate Gate Paragate Parasamgate Bodhisvaha!
(Go, go, go beyond, go totally beyond, be rooted in the ground of enlightenment!)

གཏེ་གཏེ་པཱ་ར་གཏེ་པཱ་ར་སོ་གཏེ་བོ་དྷི་སྭཱ་ཧཱ

Vietnamese Cannabis Culture

Cannabis is called day, lanh or gai in Vietnamese and was likely first used for twisting cord, followed by tying nets and finally weaving fabric for clothes. Throughout the region of Vietnam, Laos, Cambodia, and the Yunnan Province in southwest China there is a tradition of cannabis cultivation and many of the minority ethnic groups continue to use cannabis for medicine, fiber and food. The area now known as Vietnam has been inhabited since Palaeolithic times and by 1200 B.C., rice was cultivated and bronze was being cast in the Ma River and Red River plains by the Dong Son culture. Imprints of hemp cloth on artefacts from the Bronze Age were recovered from the Hong and Ma river deltas of northern Vietnam, along with trapa used for beating cannabis to make cloth.[271] Stone and earthenware vases and pottery with cord imprints found at the prehistoric site of Go Trung in Thanh Hoa, Vietnam are additional evidence for the use of cannabis since 4000 BC.[272] The "Nan Fang Shu Mu Tzang" written in the 6th century AD describes cannabis cultivation and use as the main material for making cloth.[273] The belief in good and evil spirits, or animism, antedated all organized faiths in Vietnam and permeated the society, especially in the rural areas and in the highlands. Nearly every house, office, and business in Vietnam has a small altar which is used to commune with ancestors. Offering of "ghost money," paper replicas of gifts and offerings, originally made of hemp paper, are burnt so that the spirits of the gifts can ascend to heaven for the ancestors to use.

In the first century BC, the Chinese Han Dynasty conquered the people of the Red River Delta and ruled for 1000 years influencing Vietnamese literature, language, and culture by introducing Mahayana Buddhism, Taoism and Confucianism. In Vietnamese Taoism there are three souls and seven spirits called three hồn and seven phách. These are the physical soul, the mental soul and the central or celestial soul, which are surrounded by seven protective spirit layers that kep the souls in place and protected throughout life. When these protective spirit layers fade and die out, the three souls are released. First the celestial soul merges with the Universal Qi, the mental soul sinks into the ground and when the last of the seven spirit layers is gone, there is nothing left to hold the physical soul any longer and it sinks into the ground to merge with the mental soul. There they exist as one in a twilight dimension between the yin and yang until it is reincarnated into either the yin or yang realm.

During the first century AD, Indian merchants voyaging to China established Hindu outposts enroute, one of which was on the southern coast of Vietnam that grew into a city state with trading partners as far away as Europe while the Hindu Kingdom of Champa was spreading into the centre of Vietnam from the west. Theravada Buddhism was introduced through these contacts. At its height, the Cham ruled over most of the southern half of Vietnam, with its base around what is now Da Nang. The UNESCO World Heritage site of My Son, a large complex of richly adorned sacred brick towers and temples, was the spiritual heart of the entire Cham Empire. Ruled by divine kings, the Cham worshipped Shiva[274] and other Hindu deities. Shiva is associated with cannabis, a herb that was sacred to the god and that the god was frequently intoxicated with.

One important feature of the religious attitude of the Vietnamese is its lack religious fanaticism or religious warfare and its attitude of tolerance. The predominant religious belief of the common Vietnamese is primarily a synthesis of animism, Taoism, Buddhism and Confucianism which have been coexisting peacefully for centuries in Vietnam. This attitude of tolerance could be from the influence of Confucian teachings. Confucius and his student Mencius were both raised by their mothers in single parent homes, as were many of their successors.[275] According to Confucius, there are four rules which must be followed to achieve perfection. First, one must be interested in e everything which exists, and second, be able to penetrate the secret, inner essence of things. The third requirement is clear thinking, and the fourth is a pure heart. Confucianism teaches that poverty is less to be feared than injustice, since the latter engenders hatred and jealousy.

This religious inheritance from China of Confucianism, Daoism and Buddhism, have coalesced with ancient Vietnamese animism to form a single entity – 'tam giao' – the 'triple religion'.[276] "Cao Daism began in 1919 as an indigenous Vietnamese religion composed of "spiritism" or "spirit mediums" and a "Ouija-board" type device called corbeille a bec (beaked-bag). It sought to form a synthesis of the fundamental doctrines of Daoism, Confucianism, Buddhism, Christianity and a Roman Catholic type church organization. It was formed in an attempt to create a universally acceptable religion in an area of the world where there is an intermingling of many religious beliefs often found in the same individual. But equally, the animistic tribal beliefs are still strong among many tribes. In Vietnam the principle of communal autonomy is as important as religious tolerance. It can be summarized as the customs of the village take precedence over the laws of the government, the administration of the village is handled by a council elected by the people. The ancient Vietnamese society was divided into four loosely defined classes of farmers, artisans, merchants and scholars and none was a prisoner of his class at birth.

Today Vietnam has the richest and most complex ethnic make-up in the whole of Southeast Asia. Ethnic minority groups with members numbering upwards of 500,000 include the Tay, Thai, H'mong, Muong, Hoa, Dao and Nung, while Kinh (or Viet) people make up about 88% of the population. The vast majority of Vietnam's minorities live in the hilly regions of the Northern part, down the Truong Son mountain range, and in the Central Highlands.[277] Despite their different origins, languages, dialects and hugely varied traditional dress, there are a number of similarities among the highland groups' matriarchal customs, animist beliefs, weaving and cultivating cannabis.[278] One suc tribe, the Black Lolo, live in small villages in a remote area of Caobang and remain strongly connected to their ancestral past. The Black Lolo are one of the few groups that continue to use the bronze drums of the ancient cannabis cultivating ancestors[279] They are played during funeral rites when the ancient creation myth is enacted. Two kettledrums, embodying the female and male principles of Yin and Yang face each other, representing the brother and sister that floated in kettledrums during the time of the great flood. When the flood subsided, the two married and begat a family became the genesis of the Black Lolo people. Through the sound of the kettledrum, the deceased's spirit would be able to find its way back to the place of the ancestors. These rare ancestral drums are so valued that they are buried in a secret place and only taken out for use during funeral rites.[280]

In Vietnamese mythology, spirits and 'fairies' are everywhere and often living among human beings. All phenomena and forces in the universe were controlled by spirits and that the souls of the dead were instrumental in determining an individual's fate. If propitiated, they provided the living with protection; if ignored, they induced misfortune. The Vietnamese people themselves were born from Au Co, a faerie maiden that married Lac Long Quan, son of the dragon king of the lands under the sea, and a mountain goddess. He was given the land of Lac Viet, or Vietnam by his parents. Au Co laid one hundred eggs and these eggs hatched and became the Lac people. Lac Long Quan taught the people tidal irrigation of rice fields through a system of canals and dikes, called Lac fields. The Lac cultivated rice and cannabis, becoming renowned for their weaving of hemp fabrics. This ancient Vietnamese society was matrilineal and without class, there were no masters nor slaves. The relation between its people was a system of extended family sustained over centuries where they called each other by the role in the family, such as grandfather and grandmother, father and mother, uncle and aunt, brother and sister, even when they didn't belong to the same line of blood. Many of the mountain tribes still observe Matriarchal traditions such as the Cho Ro, the Dao, and the E De where women are the heads of their families, the children take the family name of the mother, the right of inheritance is reserved only for daughters, and the husband comes to live at his wife's house after marriage. The Tho traditionally cultivate cannabis and weave hemp fabrics, they too, follow Matriarchal practices and have an animistic world view worshiping innumerable genies and spirits.[281] Another group of skilled fabric weavers are called Ma. They too have matriarchal practices and believe in the existence of spirits in the river, the mountains, and the rice and cannabis fields.

Core concepts found in Vietnamese culture include:
- Harmony
- Humility
- Honour
- Resilience
- Filial piety
- Perseverance
- Stoicism
- Modesty

The Vietnam War, or the Second Indochina War, started with conflicts in 1955 that erupted in Laos, Cambodia and Vietnam when the United States began providing military support following the French withdrawal in the aftermath of the First Indochina War. By 1963, then President John F Kennedy, had provided South Vietnam with 16,000 military advisers. In 1964 the United States deployed combat units to Vietnam and deployed 184,000 troops to the area. The extreme violence of the Vietnam War left many of the American soldiers with Post Traumatic Stress Disorder and the readily available cannabis growing in the area allowed many soldiers a form of psychological decompression to help them deal with the horrors of war. The area was traditionally a region that grew opium and cannabis as primary crops and these habits were not only adopted by many soldiers, but also imported back to the United States when their tours of duty were over. By 1968 it was estimated that 25% of the troops stationed in Southeast Asia during the Vietnam Ware smoked cannabis regularly, by 1970 heroin addiction among soldiers had reached epidemic proportions. In 1971 more than 16,000 soldiers had been discharged from service in Vietnam for drug abuse. During this time an interesting cannabis ritual emerged, it was called "Blowing a Shotgun." Originally it was a soldier's rite popularized in a 1970 film clip that showed a group of solders performing the ritual. A shotgun would be taken out and then the shells pumped out to empty the chambers of the rifle.

Then a pipe filled with cannabis was lit, and once burning well, it was reversed and the smoking bowl was placed in the mouth and the stem of the pipe placed in the open chamber of the gun. Blowing hard on the bowl of the pipe, the smoke is forced down the barrel of the shotgun where it is inhaled by a soldier on the other end of the shotgun by placing the end of the barrel in his mouth and inhaling deeply. Once back in the United States, the practice lost its martial aspects and evolved into an intimate method of sharing the breath of sacred smoke by placing a burning joint in one's mouth backwards and blowing on it while another inhales the smoke coming from the end of the joint.

Today in Vietnam cannabis is illegal both for recreational and medicinal use. Drug laws in Vietnam are extremely strict, including execution. That said, cannabis is common in Vietnam nonetheless. Da Nang has a reputation for numerous pubs and bars where cannabis is openly sold and smoked, Saigon has "Party Hostels" and Hanoi you can find both it is rumored. Nowadays in Vietnam, there are still a few large factories producing specialty products from hemp fiber, but virtually nothing remains of the thriving hemp cultivation and production that was some of the finest in the world from the Fourteenth through the Nineteenth Centuries.[282] It should be stressed that even though cannabis may be available in Vietnam, it is illegal and penalties can be as severe as years in a forced labor camp or even execution.

"When the gentleman is at home he values the left; When using weapons he values the right. Therefore we say, weapons are instruments of ill omen; If you have no choice but to use them, it is best to be dignified and reverent. Never see them as things of beauty. To see them as things of beauty is to delight in the taking of life. And if you delight in killing, you will not achieve your aim in the world. Therefore, in auspicious affairs we honor the left; while in matters of mourning we honor the right. As a result, [when they go into battle] the lieutenant general stands on the left, While the supreme general stands on the right. This means they act as they would at a funeral rite. Therefore, when large numbers of people are killed, stand before them in grief and sorrow. When the battle is won, then act as you would at a funeral rite." Dao de Jing Ch 31 trans. Robert G. Henricks

The Magu Mantra

In 1116 AD, Emperor Hui Zong, of the Song Dynasty, gave Magu the title of Immortal Xu Miao, the Infinite Harmony. Emperor Hui Zong was unparalleled among Chinese Emperors in his artistic talents and achievements, he was a Daoist painter, poet, musician and calligrapher, he wrote the famous, "Treatise on Tea", describing in detail the performance and meaning of the tea ceremony. He also invented the "Slender Gold" (瘦金體) style of calligraphy and crackled glaze porcelain ceramic technique. That he should honour Ma Gu is of no surprise as it was from her body, the cannabis plant, that the paper was made from; and her spirit, the intoxicating incense of her flowers, was the inspiration for the art that was imprinted upon the hemp paper. Remains of Song Dynasty statuary made with hemp cordage have been excavated near Chin-Ch'eng in Shanxi Province.[283]

For thousands of years devotees have been reciting Magu's mantra as part of their meditation practices. Her Holiness's mantra is:

Magu Xian Shou
麻姑獻壽
Magu Offers Longevity

The mantra was created when Magu gave the Queen Mother of the West wine she had made resulting in the Queen Mother saying this mantra for the first time. Devotees will typically count their mantras using malas of 18, 27, 54 or 108 beads. Malas can be made from a vast array of different materials ranging from simple wood to rare and exotic crystals and precious stones. The most highly prized by Maguists, however, are those made with lotus seeds strung on hemp cord. Lotus seeds are prized by devotees due to the dream Magu's father had the night before She was born. Devotees will often begin and end a meditation session with Om and use Ma Gu Xian Shou for the bulk of the session.

The Living Manner of the Circulation of the Light

"The shapes formed by the spirit-fire are only empty colors and forms. The light of human nature [hsing] shines back on the primordial, the true. The imprint of the heart floats in space; untarnished, the moonlight shines. The boat of life has reached the shore; bright shines the sunlight."- The Hui Ming Ching, The Book of Consciousness and Life, Ch. 7 trans. Richard Wilhelm

Meditation, Stage 4: The centre in the midst of the conditions.

"When occupations come to us, we must accept them; when things come to us, we must understand them from the ground up. If the occupations are properly handled by correct thoughts, the light is not scattered by outside things, but circulates according to its own law."- Secret of the Golden Flower Ch 7 trans. Richard Wilhelm

"*Essence (jing), Breath (qi), and Spirit (shen) affect one another. When they follow the course, they form the human being; when they invert the course, they generate the Elixir. What is the meaning of 'following the course?' 'The One generates the Two, the Two generate the Three, the Three generate the ten thousand things.' Therefore Emptiness transmutes itself into Spirit, Spirit transmutes itself into Breath, Breath transmutes itself into Essence, Essence transmutes itself into form, and form becomes the human being. What is the meaning of 'inverting the course?' The ten thousand things hold the Three, the Three return to the Two, the Two return to the One. Those who know this Way look after their Spirit and guard their corporeal form. They nourish the corporeal form to refine the Essence, accumulate the Essence to transmute it into Breath, refine the Breath to merge it with Spirit, and refine the Spirit to revert to Emptiness. Then the Golden Elixir is achieved.*"[284]

"How to keep body and mind one?
    Be like a child.
    Be aware of breathing, soft and pliant.
    To see the transcendent Dao, have a pure mind…
    Don't say no.
    To receive heaven's blessing,
    Be empty like a mother's womb.
Give birth and let go."[285]

"The seventh realization is that the five categories of desire lead to difficulties."[286]

"*Those who of old got to be whole: Heaven through its wholeness is pure; earth through its wholeness is steady; spirit through its wholeness is potent; the valley through its wholeness flows with rivers; ten thousand things through their wholeness live; rulers through their wholeness have authority. Their wholeness makes them what they are. Without what makes it pure, heaven would disintegrate; without what steadies it, earth would crack apart; without what makes it potent, spirit would fail; without what fills it, the valley would run dry; without what quickens them, ten thousand things would die; without what authorizes them, rulers would fail. The root of the noble is in the common, the high stands on what is below. Princes and kings call themselves orphans, widowers, beggars, to get themselves rooted in the dirt. A multiplicity of riches is poverty. Jade is praised as precious, but its strength is being stone. Return is how the way moves. Weakness is how the way works. Heaven and earth and the ten thousand things are born of being. Being is born of nothing.*" Dao de Ching Ch. 39- 40, Trans. Ursula Le Guin

Interpretation: A broken line on top of two solid lines symbolize marsh, valley or lake. The top broken line is water, and the bottom two solid lines is sky. If we are looking down at a body of water anywhere on earth, we will see the reflected sky below the water surface. The image is the clear lake which you can look through. The motivation is serenity and feeling, empathy, compassion. It is the Joyous, Open, tranquil devotion and pleasure of the third daughter.

Right Mindfulness- bare naked attention- aware, mindful, and attentive, being conscious of one's surroundings and actions both internally and externally including the activities of the body, sensations or feelings, the mind, ideas, thoughts and conceptions.

The Valley Spirit

The deathless Valley Spirit is called the Enigmatic Mother. The womb of the Enigmatic Mother is the foundation of heaven and earth. Lingering like gossamer thread she remains inexhaustible. Dao de Jing Ch. 6

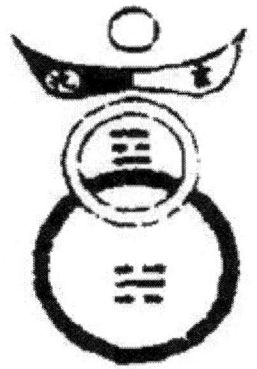

Chart of the Enigmatic Mother

Li ☲ Yang containing True Yin
Kan ☵ Yin containing True Yang

- Gather the solid line from the center in the position of Kan ☵
- Transmute by projection the innermost Yin in the palace of Li ☲."

Valley of Empty Non-Being — Root of Heaven and Earth
Mystery and then again Mystery — Gate of All Wonders

"In general, what is most essential at the beginning is a matter of mind and breathing resting on each other. This means that the mind rests on the breathing and the breathing rests on the mind. What is most important in this is harmony. Harmony is in balance; balance is in harmony. Are they one or two? The union of balance and harmony is called the go-between... The reality behind all of these sayings is spirit and energy being together, which means mind and breathing being together. Spirit is essence, energy is life... The joining of the two into one is a reversion of the two modes- yin and yang- back into one totality. This is called the twin cultivation of essence and life. The twin cultivation of essence and life is a matter of keeping the mind and breathing together, not letting them separate even for a moment. Therefore, an ancient alchemist said that 'firing the medicine to produce the elixir' means driving energy by spirit, thereby attaining the Dao... Earth the receptive is associated with the southwest: it is known as 'the region where the medicine is produced,' 'the land of primordial nondifferentiation,' and 'the opening of the Mysterious Female.'" [287]

"Sweep clear the ocean of birth and death, stay firm by the door of total mastery. The ocean of birth and death is people's thoughts. Random thoughts come from nowhere in an instant, occurring and passing away, impossible to stop altogether. The occurring of a thought is a birth, the passing away of a thought is death. In the space of a single day, we are born and die a thousand times; so transmigration is right in front of us- no need to wait till we die to experience it. But if we want to sweep clear those thoughts, that is easier said than done. There is a method to unify thought, which is to stay firm by the door of total mastery. The door of total mastery is what the Old Master called the door to the Mysterious Female, and what later Daoist's called the opening to the Mysterious Pass. Zhan Boduan said, 'This opening is not an ordinary opening. It is made of creativity and receptivity joining together. This is called the lair of spirit and energy. In it are the essences of desire and reason.' Put simply, it is just one yin and one yang, one spirit and one energy, that is all; if you can get yin and yang to combine, spirit and energy to mass together, then the substance of the Mysterious Female will be established." [288]

The low ground represented by the "Valley Spirit," or "Water Spirit," as it is known in other texts, is the place where water collects. Through absorbing the "water spirit," plants, trees and other living things flourish and grow. This low ground, these "valleys," are considered to be nearer to the Dao than the hills; and in the whole of creation, it is the negative, passive," female" element alone that has access to the Dao, which can be mirrored in a still pool. Daoist meditation cultivates this stillness, transmuting the essences of the body so the heart and spirit can return to emptiness.

"You should teach people to first learn to steady the mind. When the mind is steady, energy stays; when energy stays, spirit is complete, and when spirit is complete the body is firm. Do this continuously yet with the utmost subtlety; use it endlessly, and you will see its effect. The Valley Spirit, undying, merges with your real source." [289]

The Eightfold Path:

Right Virtue- Belief- Ethos
Right Intention- Thoughts
Right Speech
Right Action
Right Livelihood/Works
Right Effort- Exertion
Mindfulness- Remembrance
Concentration- Focus- Meditation

- *Get your head on straight. .*
- *Observe your thoughts.*
- *Be Mindful of your speech.*
- *Get free of desire, it's a roller-coaster, that's just an objective observation.*
- *Get to work, do everything by doing nothing and leaving nothing undone.*
- *Live your life in such a way to become free of attachment.*
- *Remember- Be Here Now.*
- *Calmly maintain your center.*

According to the Buddha, an individual's fate in this existence is determined by what he has done in his previous existence due to the law of Karma, or cause and effect. One was born into this world to suffer due to craving for wealth, fame, and power that necessarily brings about frustration and disappointment. In order to be free from suffering, one must suppress craving by not being attached to this worldly appearance and live according to the Eightfold Path. This is the core of Buddhist teaching: right views, right thought, right conduct, right speech, right livelihood, right effort, right mindfulness and right meditation.

In the Kalama Sutra the Buddha states: "*Do not go upon what has been acquired by repeated hearing: nor upon tradition; nor upon rumor; nor upon what is in a scripture; nor upon surmise; nor upon an axiom; nor upon specious reasoning; nor upon a bias towards a notion that has been pondered over; nor upon another's seeming ability; nor upon the consideration that this monk is our teacher. Only when you yourselves know- these things are good; these things are not blamable; these things are praised by the wise; undertaken and observed, these things lead to benefit and happiness- should you abide in them.*"

Ba Gua – Eight Trigrams

The Three pure ones, Heaven, Earth and Humanity harnessed yin and yang through the permutations of trinary yin and yang lines, yin represented by a broken line and yang represented by a solid line, combined in trinities to form eight gua or trigrams, expressing the fundamental building blocks of existence known as Ba Gua, the cornerstone of Daoist metaphysical and cosmological theory and practice.[290]

He Tu – Earlier Heaven
There are two sequences of Ba Gua, the Fu Xi, Earlier Heaven and the King Wen, Later Heaven. The Fu Xi sequence is named after its creator, Fuxi and is based upon a numerical sequence known as He Tu, the River Pattern, or map, that represents the spiral dance of creation expressed in physical laws of nature like the Fibonacci Spiral and the law of opposites expressed by the yin and yang. The Fu Xi illustrates how physical nature governs the metaphysical realm and the interaction between the two. It is often used on mirrors to neutralize atrophic or malignant Qi energy and to align natural Qi energy in an environment. Fuwi observed the He Tu pattern on the back of his horse when it emerged from the Yellow River and documented it with dark and light connected dots, paired, yin and yang, to form a spiral pattern with a numerical sequence moving from lower to higher representing the creation of the heavens, earth, humanity. He Tu illustrates creation pushing out from a central point, expanding outward into an expanding and dynamic universe.[291] From the He Tu, Fuxi conceived the Earlier Heaven sequence.

Lo Shu – Later Heaven
The King Wen is based on the Lo Shu magic square of nine cells which led to the arrangement of the Ba Gua into the I Ching. The King Wen sequence illustrates how the metaphysical realm governs the earthly realm and the interaction between the two. It is often used to harness the energies of the heavens and earth to create change in the universe. The Lo Shu dates back to the prehistoric shamans of the Xian Dynasty when a turtle emerged from a flooding river with the Lo Shu square imprinted upon its shell, where the numbers one through nine are positioned on a nine celled grid so that the sum of fifteen is reached in every direction, because fifteen is the sum of the three pure ones multiplied by the five phases, the number of the Dao.[292]

Eight Ritual Offerings

- pure water for the deity to drink
- water for the deity to wash with
- scented oil for the deity to be anointed with
- flowers
- incense
- lamps or candles
- food
- music

Eight Ritual Items

- Mala
- Bell and Dorje
- Varaja
- Drum
- Lamp
- Cup and Bowl
- Snake Wand, Whip or Staff
- Incense Burner

Eight Ritual Steps

- Creating and Defining Sacred Space
- Purifying and Exorcising the space with cannabis or snake whip
- The Offering of Incense
- The Sacrament of the Wine of the Immortals
- Invocation of the Four Guardians
- Invocation of Magu
- Invocation of the Immortals
- Invocation of the Gods of Medicine and Ancestors

Eight Immortals

The Eight Immortals of the Bamboo Grove, Pa Hsien or Baxian, the eight Xian, Immortals, faeries, genii, or transcendents. The character Hsien is composed of the characters for man and mountain, being the men who dwelled in the mountains. There were eight famous Immortals, corresponding to the eight trigrams of the I-Ching and the Eightfold Path of the Buddha and are said by some to have resided in the eight caves named the Baxiandong Caves of Taiwan or on a group of five islands in the Bohai Sea, which includes Penglai Mountain-Island. The Eight Immortals are considered to be signs of prosperity and longevity. They were said to know the secrets of nature and to represent all people of the world: male, female, the old, the young, the rich, the noble, the poor, and the humble. They are often contacted through shamanistic ritual, seances or mediums. Each Immortal's power can be transferred to a power tool (法器) that can bestow life or destroy evil. Together, these eight tools are called the "Covert Eight Immortals" (暗八仙).

The names of The Eight Immortals vary from place to place and there were also Eight Genii of the Wine-cup, Eight Immortals who Indulged in Wine, or the Eight Drunken Faeries of the Wine Cup, scholars known for their love of alcoholic beverages. They were the originators of Zui Quan, Drunken Fist Martial art practiced by both Daoist and Buddhist Shaolin traditions.

"Accepting life and death as a single flow, they take neither seriously and make the best of all they meet. Their happy attitude, their playful way of being, is characteristic of the popular image of the immortal today."[293]

Zhongli Quan, Concentrated Distance of Han, was an military officer who retired to a hermit's life in the Yangjiao mountains. The Five Heroes taught him how to turn copper into silver. He then became an alchemist and producing silver to give to the poor. One day a wall of his house collapsed revealing a jade box containing the secrets of immortality, he suddenly heard strange music of an unearthly order and the stone house was illuminated with bright clouds of rain-bow hue. Erelong, a heavenly crane, came and whisked him to the land of the immortals. He makes his appearance whenever there is a message from the heavens to be conveyed to the mortal world, sometimes accompanied by a tiger. He is depicted as a scantly clad bearded fat man with a bare belly carrying a feather-fan in his hands which could be employed as a magic weapon against his adversaries, used to deflect negative Qi or evil, and has the power to bring the dead back to life. His fan is the symbol of delicacy of feeling. He also carries a peach of immortality and has the Elixir of Life, the power of transmutation and symbol of longevity. Patron of military officers, alchemists, the poor, magicians and practitioners of the sacred arts. He is the archetypal man, the first alchemist, and he embodies the eightfold noble path of right views and the trigram qian, heaven.

Zhang Guolao, Archer Fruit Old, lives in seclusion on mount Zhong Tiao. Depicted as an old man, riding a white donkey backwards, covering over one hundred miles a day, and at the end of his journey, he would fold up his donkey like a piece of paper and store him in his wallet. When he was ready to travel again he would sprinkle water on his wallet and the Donkey would reappear. He carries "fish drum" a bamboo tube drum with two drumsticks to beat it which he carries inside the drum. The drum represents old age and is a symbol of longevity. He is often shown with peaches or phoenix feathers, and accompanied by a three legged toad. His magickal gifts bring happy marriages, numerous offspring, and fertility to elderly couples. Zhang Guo Lao is the Patron Saint of magic, necromancy, wine-making, magicians, occultists and is invoked to amplify magical workings.[294] He is the archetypal elder, fortune teller, and the embodiment of the noble path of right intention and the trigram Dui, lake.

Lu Dongbin, Lu Cave Visitor, travelled the country killing dragons, ridding the world of evil, and preventing catastrophes for four hundred years. He performed ten arduous tasks and learned of magic and the secrets of immortality from a faerie, he was given a sword known as Chan yao kuai, the Devil-slaying sabre, with the power of invisibility, by a fire dragon, and a fly-whisk, called yun chou, the cloud sweeper, that enabled him to walk on clouds. A fly whisk is also a symbol for the Buddhist admonition 'Do not Kill,' for magic and leadership. There is a monastery known as Chih Nan Kung, southwest of Taipei, where the Goddess of Mercy, Guan Yin was associated with Master Lu as divinities of equal standing. Master Lu Dongbin was also known for his scholarship and is the patron of scholars and barbers is also worshipped by the sick and scholars who credit him with writing the Kong kuo ge, a table or code of morality and is the god of Ink-makers. He is the archetypal Noble Leader, spiritual guide, and embodiment of the noble path of right speech and the trigram Kan, water.

Han Xiangxi, Han of the Xiang River, could grow plants in a small handful of earth and became immortal by climbing into the peach trees of Immortality and falling to the ground. His flute is a symbol of delusive pleasure and harmony that attracted the birds and soothe wild animals, while having the power to make flowers grow and blossom immediately. He carries a bamboo basket with peaches of immortality and is clothed in plants and rags as he wanders through town begging for handouts and singing loudly while clanging a bamboo clapper and acting intoxicated. He was considered crazy by many as he sees no value in money, giving away any he was given and able to predict the future. He is the patron of musicians Patron Saint of Gardeners, Florists and Musicians, and the archetypal starving poor artist, Philosopher, and the embodiment of the noble path of right action and the trigram Xun, wind.

Li Tieguai, Iron-Crutch Li, was a handsome healthy man and a personal friend of Lao Tzu, who taught him the esoteric scriptures essential to achieving divinity as a fairy. One day, he made a spiritual excursion to the heavens to see Lao Tzu, but when he astral projected his spirit out of his body his disciples thought he was dead and had his body cremated in a simple Daoist ceremony. Returning from his spiritual excursion to see Lao Tzu, he could not find his body, so he entered the first body he found, the body of a beggar dying of cold and hunger with a leg paralyzed from frostbite. His eyes did not fit the beggar's head properly and give the impression of Hollow Eyes (hence he is also called Kong Mu). He sprinkled water on his bamboo cane and it turned it into his iron walking crutch. He is the dispenser of the sacred medicines, and carries a pilgrims double gourd fill with the life preserving nectar of the gods across his shoulders. He is often represented standing on a crab or accompanied by a deer and a fu bat often flutters nearby which means happiness is nearby. Patron of pharmacists, doctors, physicians, chiropractors, healers, herbalists, path-workers, dreamers and especially the down-trodden, destitute and poor. He is called on in times of desperation and suffering. He is the archetype of humility and astral travel, while being the embodiment of the noble path of right livelihood and the trigram Li, fire.

Cao Guojiu, Imperial Brother-in-law Cao, met Han of the Xiang River and Lu Cave Visitor and they inquired of him what is was that he was doing walking around dressed in formal court dress, holding a ruyi sceptre and carrying a jade tablet while playing a paiban, a Chinese percussion instrument sometimes referred to as castanets. Cao Guojiu replied he was "Looking for the Way" and they asked "Which way and where?" Cao Guojiu responded by pointing to his heart and saying "The heart is heaven and heaven is the Way." He is the patron of theatre, actors and nobility the archetypal Royal Uncle, the hermetic tradition and the embodiment of integrity, the noble path of right effort and the trigram zhen, thunder.

Lan Caihe, Blue Gather Gentle, was a young boy that travelled the empire busking from town to town, dressed in a blue dress with a black wooden belt, with one shoe off and one shoe on, carrying a fruit basket while playing the flute and paiban. When she sang, her breath was a shining mist, singing of the short and fleeting lives of mortals. All of the tips she would receive she would throw out on the sidewalk for the neighbourhood children to scurry and collect. One day she was got drunk in an inn and disappeared into a cloud leaving her shoe, blue dress, black wooden belt and castanets behind. She is the patron of transvestites, transexuals, transgender, LGBQ people, the indignant, singers, buskers, beggars, wanders, musicians, actors and the poor. She is the archetypal youth and unencumbered life, and the embodiment of the noble path of right mindfulness and the trigram Gen, mountain.

"Musicians who pander to the tastes of the leisure class are o different than dogs who wag their tails in the presence of their masters.- ***Lan Cai He****"* [295]

He Ziangu, the Female Celestial Being, moved to the Mother of Pearl Mountains where she was taught the secrets of the Dao and given a powdered stone that bestows immortality. She then founded the Morning Cloud lineage of the Complete Perfection Daoist sect. She rides upon the phoenix, feng haung, an omen of prosperity, and plays the sheng, a musical instrument made of reed pipes or rides upon clouds eating mother of pearl and moonbeams. She carries with her a lotus, a symbol of compassion and longevity, which opens the heart, heals the sick and cures illness.[296] She is the patron of woman and gives assistance in housekeeping, and also patron of fortune tellers and diviners. As the Goddess of Destiny she responds to the queries of literates and officials on their futures and destinies. He Ziangu is the archetypal woman, representing the of cultivation of Qi, purity and self-sacrifice, and is the embodiment of the noble path of right concentration, the fixing of the mind on a single point, and the trigram Kun, earth.

Mazu
媽祖

Mazu, Matsu, Ma Su, Ma Tsu, Tein Hou, or Má-chó· in the Taiwanese language, the Empress of Heaven, Maternal Ancestor, the Heavenly Grandmother of Luminous Grace, was a shaman that could foretell a person's good and ill luck and aid sailors at sea navigating troubled waters. Mazu is the Mother Ancestor, protector of seafarers and sea merchants living in the coastal areas of China, Japan, Singapore, Malaysia, Thailand, Hong Kong and Taiwan and the Chinese diaspora as far as Honolulu and San Francisco who pay homage to Mazu, the savior dressed in red, that provides protection to sailors, fisherman, and travelers. Statues of the goddess usually depict her with black skin, a beaded veil and a red cape. Today she has a following of more than 100 million people across the globe and Mazuism is practiced in about 5000 Mazu temples across the globe, 2000 of which are located in Taiwan whose population of more than 23 million people has around 17 million Taiwanese Mazu believers. Mazu is perhaps the ultimate synchronistic Chinese goddess exhibiting a synergistic blend of religions with an entourage effect. As a Buddhist she manifests the compassion of Guanyin, as a Daoist, she is uniquely versed in the way of the Dao and ascended to heaven like the immortals, attesting to the fact that if she could do it, others can too. To the followers of Confucius, she exemplifies the familial bond by rescuing her brothers at sea and to the tribal folk religion she is the sea goddess invoked by the female shamans; she has withstood time as not only an emblem of Asian seafarers but an emblem of each primary Chinese religion. She is believed to have been born on the 23rd day of the third month in the Chinese lunar calendar, which corresponds to a different date each year in the western calendar but is around the end of April or start of May. Celebrations for her birthday in Taiwan are numerous and vary hugely in scale, and are spread around a month or two before and after this date.

As a sea goddess, Mazu is intimately connected with cannabis since boats depend upon hemp ropes and rigging, as well as canvas for sails, hence the prefix Ma in the name Mazu. Early Post-Glacial fishing sites and Neolithic sites in Taiwan revealed pottery with hemp cord impressions dated to around 5,000 BCE and a 10,000-year-old Neolithic site at Yuan-shan in Taiwan revealed pottery with hempen cord marks covering the surface, and a stone beater used to pound hemp,[297] showing that cannabis was cultivated in Taiwan in the earliest of times.

Mazu lived in a small fishing village on Meizhou Island in the Taiwan Straights, part of Fujian's Putian County in the late 10th century which has now been declared a UNESCO Heritage site of Culture. Mazu was born after her mother prayed to Quan Yin for a son. Quan Yin appeared to the mother and gave her a magical pill. When she awoke, the pill was still in her hand and so she swallowed it. The pill was the Jade Woman of Marvelous Deeds that Laojun pulled from her place in the Dig Dipper constellation and concentrated into the red pill that Mazu's mother swallowed so that she could be incarnated to protect those at sea and bestow compassion to any who call upon her. At birth, Mazu shot from her mother at birth in the form of a fragrant flash of red light and as Mazu was born, she did not cry at all, as she grew, she became known as the "Silent One" or "Silent Girl", because she was always quiet and contemplative. When Mazu was four she visited a temple dedicated to Quan Yin and became entranced while gazing at the image of the Bodhisattva and received the power to foresee the future by the goddess. That was when her parents knew that Mazu was indeed an incarnation of Quan Yin. By the age of eight Mazu had mastered the Confucian Classics, by eleven the Buddhist Sutras, by thirteen she has mastered the Daoist Esoteric Arts and could spirit travel and divine the future. She began swimming at fifteen, becoming quickly an adept and powerful swimmer and then started guiding fishing boats safely ashore in times of storms and danger while dressed in a red hemp garment. At the age of sixteen a Daoist Immortal gave Mazu an amulet and two tablets that she used to heal, exorcize demons, advert disasters, forecast the weather, and bring rain in times of drought. One legend tells of Mazu being given a bronze disc from a sea creature that bestowed upon her magic powers. Mazu could travel across the sea with a hempen mat and encouraged the people to conquer nature and defeat evil making her much loved and esteemed by the people.

From the age of sixteen, Mazu watched over the oceans and protected the sailors and fishermen of her village. One day she went in a boat to the middle of the sea. The Dragon Kings of the four seas came with their sea tribes and greeted her. She implored them to not bring storms to her island and to protect the people that made their livings upon the seas. The Dragon Kings all agreed and every year since then, several days before and after Mazu's birthday, the 23rd day of the 3rd lunar month, the sea tribes gather to celebrate her birthday and the fishermen refrain from catching or harming the fish and sea creatures during this time and instead spend their time in celebrations at Mazu's Temple.[298] During those days of celebration, many fishes and other animals come to Meizhou Island to lay eggs and Mazu's birthday serves as a fishing ban to facilitate the reproduction of sea creatures, and promote the harmony between people and nature.

Mazu is guarded by two demons, Qianliyan (千里眼), Eyes That Can See One Thousand Miles, red-faced with two horns, whose eyes were two rubies, and Shunfenger (順風耳), Ears That Can Hear the Wind, green with one horn, whose eyes were two yellow sapphires. Both Qianliyan and Shunfenger had asked for Mazu's hand in marriage. Mazu agreed, under the condition that they defeat her in combat. During combat she blew sand into their eyes with her magic red hemp scarf and easily subdued them with her martial arts skills. Qianliyan and Shunfenger vowed to serve as her guardians and to never leave Mazu's side. Together they are "all eyes and ears," Qianlinyan's all-seeing eyes keep a lookout on the weather on the horizon and sailors in need of the sea goddess's assistance. Shunfenger's all-hearing ears listen for sounds of distress on the open waters and cries for help. One day, Mazu sat before her loom weaving cannabis threads with incense burning on her mantle next to the icons of her two guardians, Qianliyan and Shunfenger. Her brothers had gone fishing and as she was weaving, she fell into a trance and saw that her brothers were in danger. A typhoon descended on Mazu's brothers and their wooden fishing boat was tossed about on the waves as they were thrown from it. In her trance she reached out to her brothers to pull them safely to shore, but her mother awoke her, not knowing what her daughter was doing, and Mazu's hold on her eldest brother slipped and he was lost to the sea. News of Mazu's remarkable abilities spread rapidly through the village.

At the age of twenty-eight Mazu was engaged in an arranged marriage. Instead of accepting her fate, she went on a hunger strike and left the village. Mazu climbed to the peak of the highest mountain on the island and sat in meditation until she had actualized the Dao. On the ninth day of the ninth month in the lunar calendar, from the highest peak of the mountain, Mazu dove into the ocean. As she hit the water, her body transformed into a pure beam of celestial light that ascended to Heaven leaving behind a bright rainbow stretching across the sky. After her death, the people of her village erected a temple for her and being freed from the constraints of her body, she began to appear more and more frequently to sailors and her reputation grew and multiplied. Soon she was known throughout the region. As her fame grew, she absorbed the attributes of the local goddesses and became the patron not only of sailors and pirates, but also of childbirth and mothers.

"Most Mazu temples are positioned so the main door faces the sea, so that the goddess can watch over the people there. Villagers have originally found a washed rotten root fluoresced at night in a beach, but they did not know the reason. A villager took the root home, but it was found to return to the beach the next day. The villager had a dream that night, and the root said to the villager: 'I am the goddess from Mei Island, my spirit was attached to the root. You can build a temple to place the root for worship there.' The villagers found it amazing and thus built a temple for the root. In years of drought, they would pray in the temple for rains. When there is epidemic, they would pray for health. When there are pirates, they would also pray to the goddess and all the pirates would go away at once. That is why the seagoing people would not be afraid even in case of adverse sea conditions as they know their ships or boats would not turn over under the protection of Mazu.[299]

Marine folklore has it that she is often seen standing on a cliff wearing red to alert returning sailors and fishermen from the treacherous waters ahead. It is also said that she appears as a red light in troubled ships just in time to calm a storm and rescue the sailors onboard. Seafarers were told that the invocation of her name would bring her to their rescue. Before typhoons, sailors would claim to see the bright red robes of Mazu on the water signaling the arrival of the impending storm. Mazu is said to appear as pure beam of light to sailors in need, though some have claimed to have seen the goddess herself riding on a chariot of clouds to save them. Mazu is also known to bless and protect babies and children and many women go to Mazu temples for infant names, scent bags and prayers for their children. Mazu is also called upon for protection, marriage, love, fortune and success.

During the Opium Wars of the Nineteenth Century, many Chinese were forced to leave their homes and travel overseas. They would appeal to Mazu for protection and safety and after arriving in a new place, would build a temple for Mazu in thanks for her guidance and protection. Mazu temples became the focus point for migrants to celebrate Chinese festivals, religious practice and community building, hence Mazu temples can be found in almost every overseas Chinese community. When the United States bombed Taiwan during WWII it is said that Mazu appeared at each of her 3,000 temples and if the temple was by the coast, she would sweep her cloak and whisk the falling bombs out to sea. If the temple was inland, she would catch the bomb with her scarf and gently place it on the ground, preventing it from exploding.

Worship of Mazu is often manifested through spirit mediums, usually females that lead rituals and offer healings, blessings and consultations. Mazu is also celebrated with processions of followers holding "Mazu Lanterns" and with candles, firecrackers and of course, incense. The Mazu belief and custom takes virtue, benevolence and love as its core and has been passed down generation by generation through sacrificial ceremonies, folk stories, dance and music. In 2009, the Mazu belief and custom was designated as "Intangible Cultural Heritage of Humanity" by the United Nations Educational, Scientific and Cultural Organization (UNESCO). Mazu culture includes overseas Chinese and relationships between China and foreign countries, the popular Mazu bun, the Mazu coat, Mazu noodles, Mazu ceremony, Mazu figures on boats, sacrifices before setting sail, Dajia Mazu Sightseeing Festival, Mazu's "fire joining", sacrificial ceremonies in spring and autumn, but most importantly the virtues of being true, good and her spirit of helping others, along with architecture, sculpture, painting, calligraphy, poems, antiques, folklore, mythologies, stories and beliefs about Mazu.

"Mazu, you are the goddess protecting the sea navigation channels, boats, ships and the sea transport all depend on your protection. You are so powerful, and you commit yourself to every call for help." - Record of Princess of the Sky Manifesting Herself 1281

Taiwanese Cannabis Culture

"In the beginning, the unimaginable vastness of the universe was contained within a single egg. Inside the egg, a giant named Pangu slowly developed over tens of thousands of years. One day, there was a rumble from within the egg. A crack stretched across the surface of its shell and soon, the egg burst open. The Big Bang. From within the egg's initial singularity, the giant, along with the rest of the nascent world, emerged."[300]

Taiwan has a long and ancient history that is entwined with cannabis from the earliest times. A stone age village in Taiwan dated to around 10,000 years ago contained pottery shards impressed with cannabis cords and tools for pounding cannabis fibers.[301] While the earliest signs of human activity found on Taiwan date to 30,000 years ago, the dating of the cannabis artifacts places them with the beginning of agriculture in the region, since rice was first cultivated in China around this same time. As far back as the 1970's the connection between cannabis and the rise of civilization has been noted as Carl Sagen stated: "It would be wryly interesting if in human history the cultivation of marijuana led generally to the invention of agriculture, and thereby to civilization."[302] The earliest humanoid fossil remains on the island are presumed to be 30,000 years old and their analysis may indicate that there may have been an unknown archaic species of humans who lived in Asia during the Pleistocene era.[303] This is also supported by Chinese texts and Taiwanese aboriginal oral traditions referencing pygmies on the island at some time in the past. The oldest artefacts on the island were found in the Eight Caves of the Immortals, the Baxin Caves (八仙洞), of the Paleolithic Changbin Culture, along the cliffs facing the Pacific Ocean in Taitung County. Many of the artifacts are similar to contemporary sites in Fujian. The biggest cave, Lingyan Cave, housed a temple while the smaller caves were filled with niches for placing cremation urns. Statues dominated the area, people practised religious ceremonies, and incense burned all year round. These first inhabitants lived in these caves from 30,000 until around 5,000 years ago.[304]

"We know there were as many as four other early humans living on Earth when modern humans were still confined to Africa. The Neanderthals lived in Europe, the Denisovans in Asia and the 'hobbit' Homo floresiensis in Indonesia: plus there was a mysterious fourth group from Eurasia that interbred with the Denisovans."[305]

The second identifiable migration to the island of Taiwan was undertaken by groups of Neolithic people from the southern East Asian mainland around 6,500 years ago, called the Dapenkeng Culture. Their language is believed to be the common ancestor to the Austronesian (Malayo-Polynesian) languages and they shared cultural qualities with the contemporary Chinese cultures across the Taiwan Strait including decorative hemp cord markings on the surface, or parallel markings on necks of pottery vessels.[306] From this culture locally differentiated cultures emerged that exemplify the resiliency of their cultural fluidity and broad-spectrum subsistence diversity leading to transformative evolutionary change. The Fengpitou (鳳鼻頭) culture in Penghu and the central and southern parts of the western side of the island, was characterized by fine red cord-marked pottery as was a culture that occupied the eastern coastal areas, and throughout the island there was a mixture of coastal foraging villages and large settlements practicing rice, millet and presumably cannabis farming.[307] This was an important factor in facilitating their expansion and exploration of the Philippines, Guam and New Guinea,[308] then later Eastern Polynesia, Tonga, Samoa, Western Polynesia, the Hawaiian Islands, New Zealand, and Easter Island. The Taiwanese indigenous peoples formerly called Taiwanese aborigines, Formosan people, Austronesian Taiwanese or Gāoshān people lived in relative isolation until the arrival of the Dutch East India Company and the Opium Wars.

"Opium smoking was, however, strongly condemned in China, since according to Confucian morality the smoker's body was not his own, to demolish exactly as he chose, but had been entrusted to him by his ancestors as their link with his descendants... Intelligent Chinese saw opium in extreme terms- as a social poison introduced by foreign enemies. To their two armed conflicts between 1838 and 1860 with Britain (later allied with France)- periods of open warfare linked by a turbulent armed truce- they have, reasonably enough, given the name, the Opium Wars."[309]

1624 was a turning point in Taiwan's cultural history. With the arrival of the Dutch East India Company came an end to the prehistory of Taiwan. The Dutch missionaries introduced the Sinckan Manuscripts creating a Romanized script and compiling a language dictionary introducing written language to the indigenous people of the island. The Dutch were followed by an influx of Han immigrants and refugees from the Fujian and Guangdong areas of mainland China, across the Taiwan Strait, with the transition of imperial power from the Ming dynasty to the Manchurian Qing dynasty. This migration and rule continued for the next three centuries and Taiwanese aborigines became incorporated into the wider global economy by a succession of competing colonial regimes from Europe and Asia. Over time many of the distinctive cultures gradually disappeared, creating an integrated cultural blend of Confucian Chinese and indigenous Taiwanese cultures. In 1839 began the First Opium war between the British Empire and the Qing Dynasty of China ending in 1842, then the Second Opium War from 1856 to 1860, leading to the forced legalization of opium in Taiwan and half of Taiwan's trade was comprised of the opium trade. In 1895 Taiwan was ceded to Japan by the Qing Dynasty and Taiwan began to shift from local to globalized culture and Japanese cosmopolitan westernization.

Taiwan is highly diversified in terms of religious belief, with the practices of Buddhism, Taoism, Christianity, Mormonism, Yiguandao, the Unification Church, Catholicism, Islam, Eastern Orthodoxy, Judaism, and Hinduism, as well as native sects such as Yiguandao and others. Taiwan's has a population of roughly 23 million people who most commonly practice a syncretism of Buddhism (Fo Jiao), Taoism (Dao Jiao) and Chinese Folk Religion, "three ways to one goal," the co-existence and syncretism of the three religions. Chinese folk religion includes Chinese ancestral worship, Mazu worship, Wang Ye worship and Zhai Jiao often with a Confucian worldview. Taiwan's folk religion combines faith and ritual with material pragmatism recognizing the need to be sincerely devotional to the gods and offer something in return. In a 2014 U.S. State Department's Bureau of Democracy, Human Rights and Labor report it was noted that up to 80% of the population of Taiwan believes in some form of folk religion, including shamanism, animism, and ancestor worship. It also noted that many consider themselves to be both Buddhist and Daoist, and incorporate the religious practices of other faiths.[310] One common deity is Tudigong (土地公) also known as The Village Deity or The God of the Soil. He is an old man with a long white beard with a black or gold hat, wearing a red or yellow robe, carrying a wooden staff in his right hand and a golden ingot in the left. He is the deity of wealth and fortune, honored in homes to ward off evil spirits. Buddhism is widespread throughout the island and self-avowed Buddhists may also be adherents of more localized faiths such as Yiguandao, which also emphasize Buddhist figures like Guanyin or Maitreya and espouse vegetarianism and Humanistic Buddhism is the major distinguishing trait of modern Taiwanese Buddhism. During the Japanese rule of Taiwan many schools of Japanese Buddhism came to Taiwan such as Kegon (華厳宗), Tendai (天台宗), Shingon Buddhism (真言宗), Rinzai school (臨済宗), Sōtō (曹洞宗), Jōdo shū (浄土宗), Jōdo Shinshū (浄土真宗) and Nichiren Buddhism (日蓮宗). More recently Vajrayana Buddhism has been introduced from the four major

Tibetan schools (Kagyu, Nyingma, Sakya and Gelug) and the Dali Lama has visited the island three times. The island's third-largest religion is I-Kuan Tao, founded on the Chinese mainland in the 1930's attempting reconcile Buddhism, Taoism and Confucianism and accepting other religions as valid equals. This diversity and freedom of religion is inscribed in the constitution of Taiwan.

Of the 23 million people in Taiwan, there approximately 360,000 indigenous people, distinguished into 14 different tribes, each with their unique tribal identity, culture and religious expression. Many have been heavily influenced by the Presbyterian Church since the times of first contact with the Dutch missionaries. Even with this Christian influence, most of the 14 indigenous tribes of Taiwan have traditions of shamanism, many going back before the arrival of the Chinese Han in the 15th Century. These shamans are mediums between humans and the gods and spirits through visual contact and possession, to pray for blessings, to heal sickness, to exorcise pestilence, to pray for fertility, ward off misfortune, or cast spells and incantations. Their rites are often performed during pilgrimages and temple festivals and they were the spiritual guides of the community.[311] Shamans were a democratized role that could be held by any regardless of social status or gender, but traditionally, most shamans were women. Among the Taiwanese Piawan tribe the shamans, called malada, are all exclusively female.[312] During the Qing Dynasty, shamans, in addition to local gods and goddesses, worshipped well-known deities such as Mazu, Ch'eng-huang (city gods), Ch'i-niang (the Seventh Female Immortal), Ho hsien-ku (the Female Immortal Ho), Shui-hsien (Deities of the Water) and Chiu-t'ien hsüan-nü (Mysterious Woman of the Nine Heavens).

"After 10 minutes of drum-beating and incense-burning by her assistants, Chang Yin donned a black, spotted robe and a pointed hat. She picked up a fan with her right hand and a silver flask of sorghum liquor with her left. Then, she sat in a chair before an altar piled with joss sticks, cans of beer, fruit, other snacks and images of deities. The session began. She appeared to slip into a trance. Ms. Chang is a jitong, a shaman who dispenses advice while said to be possessed by a spirit. Here, inside a modern office building next to Taipei's bustling main train station, she is carrying on a folk tradition that goes back hundreds of years in Taiwan and the Chinese mainland… The practice has not been totally abandoned, just updated. Ms. Chang, for example, regularly sends out text messages to about 300 clients. That virtual network has replaced the tightly knit village setting of old… Most often, Ms. Chang said, she is possessed by Ji Gong, a maverick Buddhist monk who lived in China in the 12th century and loved his meat and liquor. Thus, the cans of beer as offerings on the altar

and Ms. Chang's slurred speech as she channeled the tipsy monk… She said that these days the gods were more likely to be consulted on thorny personal relationships than on physical illness. 'So now they give a different type of guidance,' she said. 'The gods have changed along with the times and kept up with the trends.'"[313]

Taiwan is studded with temples and shrines everywhere. The majority of Taiwan's temples are folk shrines with a mixture of Taoist, Buddhist and folk deities that are honored by offerings of fruit, sweets, rice wine, ghost money and the ever present burning incense. There are numerous Buddhist temples, over 18,000 Taoist temples island-wide and Confucian temples are found in every major city in Taiwan. There are also temples dedicated to individual deities such as the god of medicine Pao Sheng who is the principal deity in over 100 Taiwanese temples and Mazu, the patron saint of Taiwan, with thousands of temples dedicated to her around the country.

The Taiwanese calendar has many traditional Chinese festivals involving traditional practices such as burning ghost money, lighting firecrackers, or wearing clothes of a certain color, often red. The Chinese New Year Festival is the biggest holiday celebrated in Taiwan and marks the start of the Chinese year. The Boat Festival, Taiwanese: Toan-ngó·-chiat; Mandarin: Duānwǔjié, celebrated also as the Korean Dano Festival, Vietnam's Tết Đoan Ngọ and Japan's Kodomo no Hi, on the fifth day of the fifth lunar month, is also known as the Double Fifth Festival. The main feature is the Dragon Boat races and Taiwanese dragon boat races arose from a hybrid of Chinese folk culture and pre-existing aboriginal boat-racing traditions. The Ghost Festival begins on the first day of the seventh lunar month when the gates of hell are wide open and an army of hungry ghosts comes out to haunt the livings, eat Chinese food, drink rice wine, and collect ghost money. The Chinese Ghost Festival is a month long event which takes place every year, during the seventh month and events are held at various temples throughout Taiwan during the entire month. Another festival, Liu Fang Ma Guolu (六房媽過爐), which celebrates the legend of Lin Meiyun (林美雲), a "barefoot doctor" that was murdered at a young age and then canonized as "Heavenly Holy Mother" by parading her image across the county and offering sacrifices. Several hundred thousand people now take part in the 360-year-old festival, which is unique to Yunlin and is intended to drive away malevolent spirits and bring good luck but has also the traditional elements while updating itself to respond to contemporary times. One participant in the festival observed: "People are devoted to the goddess and come up with great new ideas to prove their dedication. They put tech devices on the holy palanquin, like geographic information systems or GPS. This helps people follow the route of the march. You will also see hot dancers gyrating on cars to electronic music. Young people love to post news about the event on Facebook or Instagram."[314] But of all of Taiwan's festivals with their brilliant colors and exploding firecrackers none compares with the Mazu Holy Pilgrimage which recreates the journey of 19th century devotees who traveled every 12 years from Taiwan to the goddess' temple in Meizhou Island, off the coast of Fujian in China. The eight-day pilgrimage from Zhenlan Temple in Taichung to Fengtian Temple in Chiayi is internationally famous and recognized by UNESCO as a world intangible cultural heritage. An estimated 200,000 pilgrims, called xiangke, or "incense guests," walk up to 12 hours per day, carrying a statue of Mazu in a swinging sedan chair, covering more than 300 kilometers, through mountains and coastlands visiting more than 100 temples in route, while carrying flags and banners, playing gongs and cymbals and other musical instruments, dressed up in masks and costumes on Mazu's Excursion of Peace, 迎神赛会. Festivities include puppet shows, music, acrobatics, lion dances, dragon dances, Buddhist prayer rituals, and Daoist rites in this multifaceted religious and cultural extravaganza. Along the route, devotees of Mazu line the roads hoping to gain Mazu's blessing by touching her palanquin or lying prostrate on the road ahead of the procession so her icon is carried over their bodies. Millions of people join in, and the festival is said to be largest religious gathering in the world outside India. Afterwards, on the 23rd day of the third lunar month celebrations are held in every corner of the island especially the temples dedicated to Mazu to celebrate her birthday and more than 5 million gather for Mazu March Mania at the Mazu International Festival in central Taiwan's Taichung City. Mazu is worshiped primarily through shamans and mediums and while as noted before, most shamans of Taiwan are women, there is a very notable exception: the jitong (乩童) blood rites of the Tang Ki, who are very visible in the festivals of Mazu. These shamans achieve ecstatic states of consciousness through alcohol, betal nut, flagellation, piercing and other forms of self-mutilation that allow them to pass into other states of consciousness and allow themselves to be possessed by spirits so that they can be the medium of communication between the spirits and the devotees of the festival.[315] The Tang Ki came to Taiwan from the Fujian province in China bringing with them a democratized shamanism that utilized bodily mortification to achieve trance states quickly.

"Tang Ki are almost always dressed in a special garment resembling an apron, covered with intricate patterns. These leave the back exposed, and ready for the centerpiece of the Tang Ki's ritual, self-flagellations. Traditionally, the Tang Ki uses five weapons,

called *Wu Bao Fa Qi (五宝法器), the five treasured tools*. These are typically carried in a basket, pushed by a member of the temple group, ready for use. The *Wu Bao Fa Qi* are: a *Ci Qiu (刺球)*, a ball studded with nails attached to a string, a *Tong Gun (铜棍)*, a baton-shaped weapon also studded with nails, a *Yue Fu (月斧)* literally meaning 'moon axe', a *Qi Xing Jian (七星剑)*, a sword, and *Sha Yu Jian (鲨鱼剑)*, literally 'shark sword', a very serrated sword resembling the teeth of a shark. A *Tang Ki* may use just one, or some, of these weapons, but it is common to see all of them used. A *Tang Ki* ritual involves them moving around the area, usually directly in front of a temple, with unnatural and unpredictable steps, stop, and then repeatedly hit themselves on either the back or upper-forehead with one of their weapons. After a few seconds they will stop, and move again. It is at this point that they will change weapon, often by engaging in a brief dance with a temple group member, who will hand them the next weapon. They will then repeat the process, often until all weapons have been used. In addition to the five treasured tools, a *Tang Ki may… [use]* piercing, which may take the form of long and thin metal wires pushed through the skin on the arms or head, or a thicker bar being pushed through one or both cheeks… [or] walking along lines of firecrackers as they explode, or burning themselves with incense sticks. The drawing of blood is said to give the Tang Ki a 'kai mien' (開面), 'open face'… When the ceremony is coming to a close, the Tang Ki will be released. This may cause convulsions, and a Tang Ki will often be restrained by members of the temple group while the god is exiting them in order to protect them. Alternatively Tang Ki will often pass out, and be carried away to rest and recover."[316]

Cannabis in Taiwan is illegal. Cannabis and THC are listed as a category 2 narcotics by Narcotics Hazard Prevention Act in Taiwan, and is punishable by no less than seven years in prison, according to the Statue for Narcotics Hazard Control. Trafficking is punishable by death. CBD is not listed under restricted drugs.[317] There is a recent push towards legalization of medical and recreational cannabis by Taiwan's Green Party but it is an uphill effort. In spite of the harshness of Taiwan's drug policies and attitude towards cannabis, the classical formula Cannabis Seed Pill (Ma Zi Ren Wan 麻子仁丸), ranked number 40 out of the 301 most frequently prescribed TCM formulas for insurance reimbursement, with over 10,705 kg of concentrated dry extract prescribed in Taiwan in 2003 and 967 kg of concentrated dry extract from cannabis achenes prescribed for insurance reimbursement as a single-herb addition to formulas, ranking it as number 140 of 353 single herb extracts by weight.[318]

Death of Magu

There are various tales of Magu's death, perhaps reflecting various incarnations at various times and places. She lived by the water and was killed by either her father or her husband, placed in a coffin and thrown in a lake, or she ate raw snake meat and started spitting out blood as her tongue darted out and flicked like a snake's, then she died. These connections with the snake display a large element of clan totemism, the hereditary connection with the snake, which is also connected with the dragon. But the further implications are the chthonic references implying paleolithic origins of Magu herself in the cave dwelling underworld of the ancient past. What comes of these tales is that Magu transcends death, the waters she walks upon become healing waters, and her body she has left behind to become a resource for all so that they may be sheltered, clothed, nourished, comforted, and illuminated.

After Magu liberated the slaves working for her father, Magu was punished for her acts of compassion. Magu's father fed her raw snake meat hash and Magu became violently sick, vomiting blood and her tongue lashed out of her mouth like a serpent's tongue. Her father, terrified at what he had done, killed Magu. He placed her body in a stone coffin and threw the coffin into the lake. A Dragon King seeing what had transpired, came down and opened the coffin of Magu releasing her, and she floated to the surface of the waters and walked across the lake in the moonlight transforming its waters into a healing elixir. In the morning, a Daoist shaman found her body washed up upon the shore of the lake. There were cannabis plants growing around her where she lay. He took her body and built a stone pyre to lay it upon. He then built a temple around her shrine. The next morning when he returned, Magu's body was gone. He went down to the shoreline where he first found her body and found instead a grove of cannabis in full bloom and seed growing on the shoreline where her body had laid. He took the seeds of Magu and taught the people how to cultivate this precious plant ally and of her many uses. Magu had left her earthly body behind only to ascend to the Mountain Grotto of Taishan where she became the consort and concubine of her brother Wang Fangping. She mastered the arts quickly and went on to learn the alchemical secrets of the Dao and the Immortals. She learned of healing and elixirs, of massage and pleasure, the tantric arts of the gods, the flow and transmutation of energies. She learns of the secrets of the Xians, Bodhisattvas and the secrets of the White Tigress and Jade Lion. In Jianchang was a Mt. Magu during the Song period Hong Mai mentioned a Magu Cave near Mt. Qingcheng in Sichuan. Pilgrims to Taishan Mountain toss cannabis seeds along the trail, for

Ma Gu to bless them with health and prosperity, as they climb to the summit where resides Pan Gu, the creator. During the twilight mists of fog on the first and last days of the lunar month and on the third day of the third lunar month, Magu would walk across Magu Pond (Jiangzhu Pond), situated in a canyon at the foot of Tianzhu Peak. Fishing and hunting were prohibited in the area and those that did not heed the warning would often be lost or drown.

Snake Whip Cord of the Law

The Cord of Law, or Snake Whip, is a whip, the wooden handle carved into a snake's head with a flat braided hemp rope tongue attached. The Cord of Law is activated through invocations and mantras recited while lashing the space around the practitioner. It is used to clear a space of negative and malignant energies and malicious spirits or to purify and consecrate an area and clear it of hungry ghosts. It is also used in exorcisms to bind or dispel demons by wrapping the possessed one with the lashes of the whip or by whipping them to expel the demons.[319]

The Taoist Snake Whip (法索/淨鞭/法鞭/聖者/金鞭聖者) is one of the most used ritual items in Taoist Lu Shan Sect (閭山派).

Functions of a Taoist Snake Whip:[320]

- Getting rid of wandering spirits in the ceremonial area
- Deployment of spiritual armies (调营放兵)
- Recalling of spiritual soldiers and rewarding (收兵犒赏)
- Exorcism rituals (驱邪压煞)
- To summon heavenly deities hastily (急召萬神)
- To punish disobedient spirits

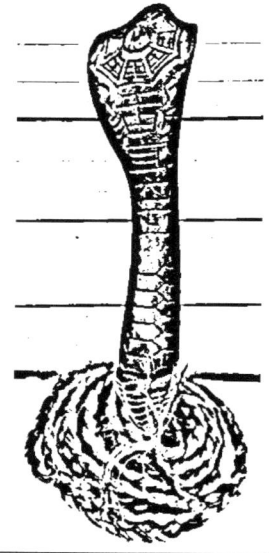

The origins of the snake whip are uncertain and clouded in the mists of time, but there are several old legends that do connect snakes and cannabis. There is a folk tale of the Emperor Lui Chi-nu, which tells of a day when Lui Chi-nu was out in the cannabis fields harvesting the plants and saw a snake in the field. Lui Chi-nu shot the serpent with an arrow to prevent it from biting him or anyone else working in the fields. The next day, he returned to the cannabis field to find two boys sitting and grinding cannabis leaves with a mortar and pestle. Lui Chi-nu asked the boys what they were doing and they told him they were making medicine for their master who had been wounded by an arrow shot by Lui Chi-nu. He asked the boys what they would do if they found Lui Chi-nu and the boys replied that they could not take revenge on Lui Chi-nu because he was destined to become the next emperor. Lui Chi-nu scolded them for their foolish talk while chasing them out of the field, leaving behind the medicine they had prepared. Lui Chi-nu gathered up the medicine and took it with him. Later, Lui Chi-nu was wounded in battle, and he applied the medicine the boys had made to the wound. The wound healed and Lui Chi-nu taught the people of China to prepare a medicine from cannabis leaves to heal wounds. Another tale relates that a farmer saw two snakes in a field and stopped to watch them. One of the snakes carried a bunch of cannabis leaves and flowers in its mouth to the other snake and placed it on an injury that the second snake had received. Afterwards, the farmer cut himself while working and put cannabis leaves on the cut to heal it as he had observed the snakes doing. The cut healed, and the farmer taught others in his village of this amazing remedy.[321] In yet another tale, the Taoist Herbalist Ci Guan was on a mystical island gathering herbs. As he walked along the path he came across two hemp ropes laying in the middle of the pathway. He reached down to pick them up and they turned into snakes. He was able to grab one as the other slithered of into the grass. The snake coiled around his neck and as it reared its head to strike Ci Guan, the snake looked into Ci Guan's eyes and became transfixed. Unable to move, the snake's eyes began to radiate in magical colours and the snake came under the control of Ci Guan, becoming a powerful protective weapon.[322] In a variant of this tale, the snake whip is the deified Snake Demon that Zhang Gong Sheng Jun subdued subordinated.[323]

"One day Lui was out in the fields cutting down some hemp, when he saw a snake. Taking no chances that it might bite him, he shot the serpent with an arrow. The next day... he found two boys grinding marijuana leaves... preparing a medicine to give to their master who had been wounded by an arrow... they could not take revenge on him because Liu Chi-nu was destined to become the emperor of China... they ran away, leaving behind the medicine. Sometime later Liu himself was injured and he applied the crushed marijuana leaves to his wound. The medicine healed him and Liu subsequently announced his discovery to the people of China and they began using it for their injuries."[324]

A Magic Spell for the Far Journey

"Without beginning, without end, without past, without future. A halo of light surrounds the world of the law. We forget one another, quiet and pure, altogether powerful and empty. The emptiness is irradiated by the light of the heart and of heaven. The water of the sea is smooth and mirrors the on in its surface. The clouds disappear in blue space; the mountains shine clear. Consciousness reverts to contemplation; the moon disk rests alone." - The Hui Ming Ching, The Book of Consciousness and Life, Ch. 8 trans. Richard Wilhelm

*"Four words crystallize the spirit in the space of energy.
In the sixth month white snow is suddenly seen to fly.
At the third watch the sun's disk sends out blinding rays.
In the water blows the wind of the Gentle.
Wandering in heaven, one eats the spirit-energy of the Receptive.
And the still deeper secret of the secret:
The land that is nowhere, that is the true home..."-."* - Secret of the Golden Flower Ch 8 trans. Richard Wilhelm

"*The man of superior virtue is not (conscious of) his virtue, And in this way he really possesses virtue. The man of inferior virtue never loses (sight of) his virtue, And in this way he loses his virtue. The man of superior virtue takes no action, but has no ulterior motive to do so. The man of inferior virtue takes action, and has an ulterior motive to do so. The man of superior humanity takes action, but has no ulterior motive to do so. The man of superior righteousness takes action, and has an ulterior motive to do so. The man of superior propriety takes action, And when people do not respond to it, he will stretch his arms and force it on them. Therefore when Tao is lost, only then does the doctrine of virtue arise. When virtue is lost, only then does the doctrine of humanity arise. When humanity is lost, only then does the doctrine of righteousness arise. When righteousness is lost, only then does the doctrine of propriety arise. Now, propriety is a superficial expression of loyalty and faithfulness, and the beginning of disorder. Those who are the first to know have the flowers of Tao but are the beginning of ignorance. For this reason the great man dwells in the thick, and does not rest with the thin. He dwells in the fruit, and does not rest with the flower. Therefore he rejects the one, and accepts the other.*" Dao de Ching Ch. 38 trans. Wing-Tsit Chan

"Because of the eagerness of my heart to liberate the world, I sincerely spoke a lot. Buddha also pointed directly to life and death to show what is most valuable. Lao-tzu also suggested that all trouble comes from the lower self, and transmitted the teaching of the valley spirit, but people could not recognize it. Now I will give a general explanation of the road of finding the truth: The pervasive principle of the Yellow Middle conveys the great changes of yin and yang. When one establishes the right state, that is the mysterious pass. You stabilize your breathing at midnight, noon, and in between. The light returns to the primal opening, ten thousand spirits become calm. The medicine produced from the river source is the one breath emerging. It passes through a screen and transforms into golden light; The single disk of the red sun incessantly shines with brilliance. Common people mistake the vitalities Kan (Water ☵) and Li (Fire ☲), Conveying them between the heart and the kidneys, producing separation. How can the human way meet the Heavenly Heart? If in accord with the celestial, the way is naturally met. Let go of the ten thousand attachments, so nothing comes to mind; this is the true infinity of the primordial. The great void is silent, signs are gone; At the pass of essence and life, you forget discriminating consciousness. After discriminating consciousness is forgotten, you see basic reality. The water-clarifying pearl appears, mysterious and unfathomable: Endless afflictions disappear all at once. The jade capital sends down a nine dragons' decree; Walking in the sky, you arrive at the gateway of Heaven: Controlling wind

and lightning, you make the thunder rumble. Focusing the spirit and steadying breath are for beginners; retreating to hide in secrecy is eternal calm. Two poems, which I used when I initiated Zhang Zhennu long ago, both contain the Great Way. After midnight and before noon doesn`t refer to the time, but to Kan (Water ☵) and Li (Fire ☲). Settling the breath means returning to the root and the Yellow Middle with each breath. Sitting means that the mind is unmoved. The mid-spine where the ribs join does not refer to vertebrae; it is the great road directly through to the jade capital. As for the double pass; this is difficult to put into words. Thunder in the earth rumbles, setting in motion rain on the mountain means the arising of true energy. The yellow sprouts emerging from the ground refer to the growth of the true medicine. These two little verses express everything you need to practice the Great Way. If you understand this, you will not be confused by others. In old times Confucius and his student Yanhui climbed Tai mountain and looked out over the Wu area (Jiangsu province). Yanhui was fascinated by the view of a white horse running in the far away distance. Confucius suddenly put his hand in front of Yanhui`s eyes to block his view, so that spiritual energy would not leak out of Yanhui`s eyes. How could one not turn around the light? Turning the light around is a matter of single-minded practice: just use the true breath to stabilize awareness in the central chamber. After a long time working with this you will naturally commune with the spirit and attain transmutation. Quieting the mind and stabilizing energy is the basis. When the mind is forgotten and the energy congeals, this is a sign of effectiveness. The emptiness of the mind and quietness of breath is the formation of the elixir. The unification of mind and energy is incubation. Clarifying the mind and seeing its essence is understanding the Way. You should each practice diligently; what a pity if you waste your time. If you do not practice for a day, then you are a ghost for a day; if you do practice for a single breath, then you are a realized immortal for a breath. More effort! More effort!"
Secret of the Golden Flower Ch. 7/13, Trans. Walther Sell and Junyong Wang

"The eight realization is awareness that the fire of birth and death is raging, causing endless suffering everywhere. We should take the vow to help everyone, to suffer with everyone and to guide all beings to the realm of great joy."[325]

"Dao does nothing and leaves nothing undone practicing wuwei. If the ruler observes this, ten thousand thing will transform themselves. When people get freedom, they begin to have desires; the unnamed unmanifest removes desire. Without desire there is quiet and under heaven all is settled." Dao de Jing Ch. 37

"True speech isn't beautiful. Beautiful speech isn't true. Expertise doesn't debate. Debate isn't expertise. Knowing isn't wealth, Wealth doesn't know. The holy person doesn't accumulate. Already, considers people's personal healing his own. Already, so as to support people's personal healing more. Nature's way benefits, and yet doesn't harm. The holy person's way acts, and yet doesn't contend." Dao de Ching Ch. 81 trans. Carl Abbott

"The sage never tries to store things up; the more he does for others, the more he has; the more he gives to others, the greater his abundance." Dao de Ching Ch. 81 trans. Gia-fu Feng and Jane English

"Faithful words are not pleasant. Pleasant, or specious, words are not faithful. The virtuous do not bandy arguments. Those who bandy arguments are not virtuous. The wise do not seek learning [from outside]. Those who do so are not wise. The Sage does not lay up hidden stores [of TAO], The more he employs it on behalf of others the more he has for himself. The more he imparts to others, the more his own stores increase. The TAO of Heaven confers benefit, and injures not. The TAO of the Sage acts, and does not strive." Dao de Jing h. 81 trans. Frederic Henry Balfour

"The Tao proceedeth by its own nature, doing nothing; therefore there is no doing which it comprehendeth not. If kings and princes were to govern in this manner, all things would operate aright by their own motion. If this transmutation were my object, I should call it Simplicity. Simplicity hath no name nor purpose; silently and at ease all things go well." Dao de Jing Ch. 37 trans. Alister Crowley

That which is the Dao cannot be named. All that we give names to is the Dao. True words are not beautiful and beautiful words are not true. The luminous void called, Taiyi, the Supreme One, Taima, the Great Cannabis Mother, created the heavens and the earth with Tian Men, the gates of heaven called, the Divine Ladle, the Big Dipper. As the Divine Ladle spins around and around, the equinoxes and solstices, planting and harvest times, can be determined by its position as it displays the spiral dance of creation. The luminous void is the Dao, the unity. Dao creates One. One is Heaven. Dao is Heaven. The One creates Two. Two is Earth. The Two produce Three, which create the Five. The Three are Humanity. Three create the myriad of things in physical matter through the immortal Ba Gua. Through the magick square the Eight Elements are controlled by the Five Stages of Change dictated by the formulating cycles of creation and destruction activated by the spiral sequence codified by numerology which is the Dao that gives pulse to the ever-expanding universe which is the binary code where the Two are the One which is Dao personified as De the One Divine of many names and many faces.

Zig Zag Zen Commandments of Lama Surya Das[326]

- Spiritual Practice is Perfect- Just Do It!
- Take Care. Watch your step. Be Careful.
- Just Say Maybe.
- Find a way to have your own spiritual practice and experience.
- Awaken your mind, open your heart; learn to see clearly and love.
- Go on this journey with a friend, even a guide, if possible.
- Lighten up while enlightening up. Cultivate joy. Don't take yourself too seriously, or it won't be much fun.
- See everything as impermanent and like a dream.
- Be mindful. Be vigilant and intelligent about your experiments.
- Don't cling to anything.
- Don't rely on mere words and concepts.
- Be good and do good.

Immortal Sister Cui Shaoxuan wrote:[327]

- The first crescent of the moon shows its form like a beauty's brow; paired with the light of the sun, its clear purity abounds. If you want to gain productive energy and congeal the jade broth, first seek the wax and wane, grab the golden wave.
- Where the source of the essence is clear; the fountain of life is firm; turn the waterwheel nine times, and the nine cauldrons' complete. The gold tiger and jade dragon meet together and join; the three flowers offer forth a little spirit immortal.
- Mind like still water, I am naturally at peace. Always calm yet ever alert, I make good progress. Having nurtured the raven to plumpness, I feed the rabbit so thin: spiritual mushrooms pop up on the blue-green peak.
- You should know there is also a heaven in the earth; To seek it single-mindedly is to seek immortality. One day when you thoroughly understand the meaning of yin and yang, you will find it is only before the energy of generation.
- Dark hair and ruddy face- how long do they last? In a moment grey hair are strewn about like thread. Opening the blinds, I glimpse the bloom of the apricot blossom: here is the scenery of spring- don't allow delay.
- I don't seek supporters, and do not study Chan- the world's changes in my eyes I let go on as they may. The alchemical path, you should know, goes directly upward- the mystic jewel is only in our hearts.

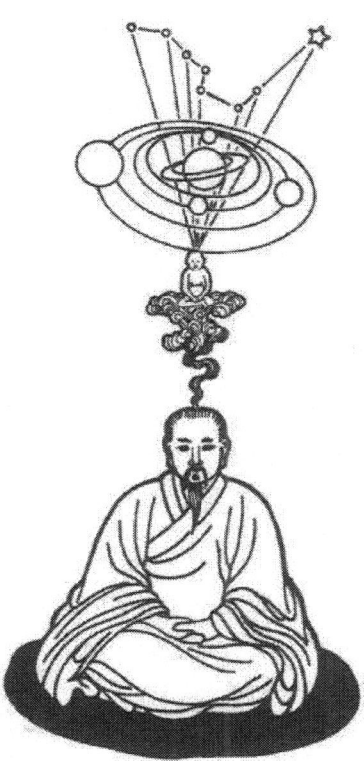

Celestial Goddesses of the East

Abkai Hehe- Sky Mother of the Manchu people, who gave birth to the universe and the first shamaness, then saved all creatures from the flood.

Bana-jiermu- Earth Mother of the Manchus, who oversees many other goddesses of sun, moon, cloud, rock, hot spring, or sea soul.

Baogu (Bao Gu)- A legendary healer and master of medicinal plants, who reportedly lived in the 300s CE.

Bixia Yuanjun (Pi-Hsia Yuan Chin)- The goddess of dawn, childbirth, and destiny, who brings health and good fortune to the newborn, and protection to mothers.

Can Nu (Cannü, or Cangu Nainai)- The Silkworm Mother, protector of silkworm culture, mothers, families, and healing. A magic horse skin whisked her to heaven, after which she returned as a silkworm and lived in a mulberry tree. Worshiped on the third day of the third month.

Chang'e (Chang O, Heng-o)- Stole the elixir of immortality and floated to the moon. In another adventure she came to earth, delivered a magic potion which killed a cruel emperor, and re-ascended to the moon.

Chen Jinggu (Lady Linshui)- A deified shamaness from the coast of Fujien, who founded a line of female adepts for healing, exorcising spirits, calling souls, conducting seasonal rites, making rain, aiding childbirth, and fighting enemies of the people.

Chokyidronme- A Tibetan Buddhist master of the 1400s, recognized as the embodiment of the meditation deity Vajravarahi. Also known as Samding Dorje Pagmo, she began a line of female tulkus, or reincarnate lamas, which continues to the present.

Chuang Mu (Ch'uang Mu, or Ch'ang Mu)- The goddess of the bedroom and of sexual delights.

Cinnabar Mother of Highest Prime- The imperial lady who resides in the third star of the Big Dipper constellation, who governs time and the six yin powers.

Dakinis- Enlightened goddesses of Tibet, whose name means "sky dancers."

Dechen Karmo- Mother of all the Buddhas.

Feng Bo Bo (Feng Po-Po)- A goddess of winds, storms, and moisture.

Five Shards Constellation- The unmoving spot around which the stars revolved, also called the "womb point" from which the universe was born.

Fufei- A daughter of the snake emperors Fu Xi and Nü Wa. She was lured into the water by the river's admiring spirit, where she became the goddess of the Luo River.

Gong Detian (Gong De Tian, or Kung-Te-Tien)- The goddess of Luck, who has a magic pearl that grants wishes.

Guanyin (Kuan Yin)- The goddess of universal compassion, a Buddhist bodhisattva, known as "She Who Hears the Cries of the World."

He Xiangu (He Xian Gu, He-Hsien-Ku, or Ho-Hsien-Ku)- One of the eight Daoist immortals, a woman who discovered the potion of immortality. Alleged founder of the Morning Cloud (Yunxia Pai) lineage of the Complete Perfection (Quanzhen) sect of Daoism.

Hou- A lion-like creature who was the mount of the earth's guardian queen.

Hu Tu (Hou-T'u)- Female deity of the earth, like Gaia. She was the ruler of magic and fertility, to whom the Emperor offered sacrifices on a square marble altar in the Forbidden City each summer solstice. Sometimes said to be male.

Jade Maiden- The first woman, who the first man, Peng Gu, discovered wandering the cosmos. The first couple then generated the lineage of divine ancestors.

Jade Maiden of Highest Mystery- A divine representative of the sun who engages in sexual relations with selected adepts.

Jade Maiden of Profound Wonder- The first woman. Later she became Eternal Mother Wusheng Laomu, the mother of Laozi, who gave birth to the sage by immaculate conception, taught him the Dao, and ascended bodily into heaven as a realized immortal.

Lan Cai-He (Lan Ts'ai-Ho)- One of the Eight Immortals, either an effeminate male dressed as a woman, or a very eccentric woman with a male voice, who carried a flute, a basket of fruit, and ruled over music.

Lao Jun (Lao Chün)- A holy mother of creation.

Lie Zu (Luozu, Lei-Zi, Lei-Tsu, Lei-Tzu, Hsi-Ling-Shih)- Wife of the Yellow Emperor, who discovered silk, cultivated silkworms and mulberry trees, and invented the loom.

Lo Shen- Goddess of rivers and ruler of water magic.

Luozu- A wife of the Yellow Emperor. She initiated silk production.

Magu- An ancient female immortal, also called "the Hemp Lady." Revered by the Complete Perfection sect of Daoism. Portrayed wearing a tiger-head pouch, a sword, and a head dress symbolizing the freedom of heaven, with wild hair and bird-like fangs.

Mago- Korean grandmother creatrix goddess.

Ma Ku. Goddess of springtime, honored in Spring rites.

Mamo- A wrathful Tibetan dakini who eats flesh.

Ma Xian Ku (Ma Hsian Ku)- A holy shamaness who protected her people.

Mat Chinoi- The serpent goddess who was mother of the Chinese people.

Mazu (Ma Tsu, or Tien Hou—the Queen of Heaven)- A girl from Fujian who traveled in spirit while asleep to save sailors at sea. She protested against an arranged marriage by starving herself to death, and continued saving sailors in the spirit.

Meng Po Niang (Mong-Po, Lady-Meng, Meng-P'o, Meng-Po-Niang-Niang, Mi-Hung-Tang)- The goddess who lives just inside hell's exit door, who gives the potion of forgetfulness to each soul departing for a new reincarnation.

Miaoshan- And incarnation of Guanyin, who refused orders to marry, was cast out of her family, yet later gave her eyes and arms for medicine to cure her father of a disease.

Nü Ji- An immortal lady who attained power through sexual practices.

Nü Wa (Nü Kwa, Nuwa)- Snake goddess, who with the male snake god Fuxi, created the world. She then saved the world from flood and collapse by repairing the sky.

Pan Jinlian (P'an-Chin-Lien)- The goddess of sex and prostitutes.

Prajanaparamita- The Great Mother, who is transcendent realization of emptiness—the realization which is the "mother" of Buddhahood.

Qi Gu (C'hi-Ku, or Tsi Ku)- A goddess of the outhouse. When women want to know the future, they go to the outhouse and ask Qi Gu.

Sien Zang (Sien Tsang)- Wife of the divine farmer Shennong. She wove the clouds that clothe the heavens.

Shin Mu- The mother of perfect intelligence. China's holy virgin.

Songzi Niangniang- The Lady Who Brings Children. In charge of conception, pregnancy, delivery, child welfare.

Suiren- A primordial teacher of indeterminate sex, who invented fire-making with wooden drills.

Sun Buer (Sun Pu-erh)- A Daoist master of the 1100s CE, seventh master of Complete Perfection (Quanzhen) sect of Daoism. Credited with many magical feats and wondrous teachings. Founded the Qingjing Pai sublineage (or the Lineage of Clarity and Stillness).

Sunu- A woman who helped the Yellow Emperor stimulate the crops by inventing and playing her twenty-five string qin instrument, to orchestrate the growing seasons.

Taimu, Lady- An ancestress of Fujian legend, who led her followers to open the land and became the earliest forebear of the Min people.

Taimu goddess- Primary mother of the Yue nationality, who moved to a cave on Mt. Lanshan, attained immortality, and rode to heaven on a nine-colored dragon horse.

Taishan [mountain] Goddess- The bringer of fertility and rain, patroness of Mount Tai, sister of the Jade Emperor, also called "Old Mother, " "Old Grandmother of Tai," "the Heavenly Immortal," "Green Jade Mother," or "Goddess of the Azure Clouds."

Tara- Tibetan goddess of unconditional awareness and compassion. Best known as either Green Tara or White Tara. White Tara is also known as "Tara of the Seven Eyes"—with eyes on her hands, feet, and forehead, to symbolize her all-seeing mercy.

Tenma goddesses- Twelve spirits of Tibet's mountain ranges, who protect the people and religion of Tibet.

Tian Mu (T'ien-Mu)- The goddess of lightning. Her husband, the dragon Lei Gong, supplies the thunder.

Tuoyalaha- Famous ancient shamaness of the Jurchen people, who stole fire from the fire god in a time of endless night, carried it in her mouth, and saved her people from freezing in the dark.

Tou Mou- Goddess of the polestar, who serves as the record-keeping scribe of the immortals, patroness of writing, and judge of all people.

Tru'ng Thac and Thu'ng Nhi- Two sisters who led a Vietnamese rebellion against Chinese rule in Han times, and were later deified.

Vajravarahi- A Tibetan female guardian spirit who defends practitioners of meditation from distractions. Usually portrayed with a pig's head protruding from her crown.

Wolado Mama- The cosmological star-planting goddess of the Manchu, who wears white wings and carries a bag of stars to create the constellations.

Wei Huacun (Wei Hua-ts'un-. An enlightened Daoist female master. After her death, she appeared to Yang Xi (Yang Hsi), and gave him the first texts of Shang-ch'ing (mystical Daoism). She is also a mountain goddess residing on the eminence of Lojiang in Fujian.

Wu- Female shamans.

Wusheng Laomu- The Eternal Mother, the mother of Laozi.

Xiang (Hsiang) River Goddesses- Two goddesses of the Xiang River, named Ehuang and Nüying, whose tears for the dead emperor Shun reportedly made the water patterns in bamboo. Evoked by southern shamenesses, and sometimes called the Maiden in the Mist of the Xiang River.

Xiao River Goddess- One of many river goddesses in the Yangze basin.

Xi He (Hsi Ho)- Empress and wife of the Yellow Emperor, Huangdi. She reportedly gave birth to the ten suns. Later she drove the sun as a chariot, though later myths changed the sex of the chariot driver.

Xi Shi (Hsi-Shih)- A goddess of cosmetics and perfumes, who was so beautiful that when the evil Prince Wu beheld her he fell into a stupor, which allowed the righteous exiled King Yue to regain the throne.

Xi Wang-mu (Hsi Wang-mu)- The Queen Mother of the West, great shamaness of the world pillar, gatekeeper of death, birth, healing, and immortality; also called The Primordial Ruler.

Yang- The patroness of shamans, one of the ten immortal sorcerers on Wu-shan, the Mount of Sorcerers.

Yangze River Goddess- A goddess evoked by southern shamanesses, as recorded in the Nine Hymns (Chiu Ko) of early 200s BCE.

Yao Chi (the Jasper Lady)- A goddess who guided emperor Yü in controlling the primordial flood. She could shape-shift to any creature's form.

Yao Chi Jinmu (Yao-chih chin-mu-. Golden Mother of the Jasper Pool, the Keeper of Paradise.

Yaoji- A patron goddess of Wushan, or Shamaness Mountain. Also, a daughter of the Queen Mother of the West, who brought women's writing to the embroidering women of Jianyong.

Yinjiang- The first shamanness, created by the Sky Mother Abkai Hehe, according to the Nian Manchu people.

Youying, Lady- Otherwise known as Lady Right Bloom of the Palace of Cloud Forest, a mountain goddess who was reportedly a daughter of the Queen Mother of the West.

Zhi Nu (Chih Nu, Zhinü)- A goddess of spinners, weavers and clouds. She wove both silk garments and clouds for the Lord of Heaven, but fell in love with a cowherd boy, who stole her clothes as she bathed. Her father, the Jade Emperor separated the lovers in constellations at opposite side of the sky. The lovers could unite only once a year, when magpies created a bridge across the Milky Way.

Zi Gu (Tzu-Ku, Tzu-Ku-Shen)- A goddess of toilets, who was murdered for jealousy while in the latrine. She haunted latrines thereafter, and became the patroness of spirit writing from beyond.

Bibliography

Andrews, George [ed] (1974). *Drugs and Magic*, IllumiNet.
Andrews, Grorge and Vinkenoog, Simon [eds] (1974). *The Book of Grass*, Penguin Books.
Abel, Ernest. L., (1980). *Marijuana, The First Twelve Thousand Years*. New York: Plenum Press.
Badiner, Allan [ed](2015). *Zig Zag Zen*, Synergetic Press.
Bennett, Chris, Osburn, Lynn and Judy (1995). *Green Gold the Tree of Life: Marijuana in Magic & Religion*, Access Unlimited.
Bennett, Chris (2010). *Cannabis and the Soma Solution*, Trine Day.
Booth, Martin (2015). *Cannabis, A History*, St. Martin's Publishing.
Burger, Bruce (1998). *Esoteric Anatomy: The Body as Consciousness*, North Atlantic Books.
Bynner, Witter (1944). *The Way of Life According to Lao Tzu*, Capricorn Books.
Campany, Robert Ford (2002). *To Live As Long As Heaven and Earth: Ge Hong's Traditions of Divine Transcendents*, University of California Press.
Carus, Paul (1915, 1995). *The Gospel of the Buddha*, Senate.
Chang, Kwang-chih (1986). *The Archaeology of Ancient China*, Yale University Press.
Chia, Mantak (1983). *Awaken Healing Energy Through the Tao*, Aurora Press.
Chia, M. and Wei, W.U. (2002). *Sexual Reflexology: The Tao of Love and Sex*, Universal Tao Publications.
Clarke, Robert C. & Merlin, Mark (2013). *Cannabis: Evolution and Ethnobotany*, University of California Press.
Cleary, Thomas (1993). *The Essential Tao : An Initiation into the Heart of Taoism Through the Authentic Tao Te Ching and the Inner Teachings of Chuang-Tzu*, Harper One.
Cleary, Thomas (1996). *Immortal Sisters: Secret Teachings of Taoist Women*, North Atlantic Books.
Conrad, Chris (1994). *Hemp, Lifeline to the Future, the Unexpected Answer for Our Environmental and Economic Recovery*, Creative Xpressions Publications.
Crowley, Aleister (1971). *Shih Yi: A critical and mnemonic paraphrase of the Yi King by Ko Yuen (Equinox III:8)*, H. P. Smith.
Crowley, Aleister (1976). *The Tao Teh King : A New Translation (Equinox III:8)*, Thelema Publications.
Crowley, Aleister (1980). *Khing Kang King : The Classic of Purity, Being Liber XXI*, Thelema Publications.
Crowley, Mike (2016). *Secret Drugs of Buddhism, Psychedelic Sacraments and the Origins of the Vajrayana*, Amrita Press.
Drakka, Jana (2016). *Rituals of Change*, Synergetic Press.
Eberhard, Wofram (1996). *A Dictionary of Chinese Symbols: Hidden Symbols in Chinese Life and Thought*, Routledge & Kegan Paul.

Estren, Mark [ed] (2017). *One Toke to God, 30 Essays by Noted Researchers into the Entheogenic Spirituality of Cannabis*, Cannabis Spiritual Center.

Febg, Gai-Fu, English, Jane and Lippe, Toinette (1997, 2011). *Tao Te Ching*, Vintage Books.

Gray, Stephen [ed] (2017). *Cannabis and Spirituality, An Explorer's Guide to an Ancient Plant Spirit Ally*, Park Street Press.

Griffith, Brian (2012). *A Galaxy of Immortal Women, the Yin Side of Chinese Civilization*, Exterminating Angel Press.

Hagar, Steve (2014). *Magic, Religion and Cannabis*; Abacus Books.

Hall, Manly P. (1924). *The Occult Anatomy of Man to Which is Added Occult Masonry*, Hall Publishing Company.

Hanh, Thich Nhat (1987) *Being Peace*, Parallax Press.

Hanh, Thich Nhat (1992). *The Diamond That Cuts Through Illusion*, Parallax Press.

Hanh, Thich Nhat (2007) *Two Treasures*, Parallax Press.

Henrich, Clark (2002). *Magic Mushrooms in Alchemy and Religion*, Inner Traditions.

Herrigel, Eugen (1953). *Zen and the Art of Archery*, Pantheon Books.

Hua, Hsuan (1978). *Listen to Yourself- Think Everything Over*, Guan Yin.

Hauang, Alfred (1998). *The Complete I Ching*, Inner Traditions.

Hwang, Helen Hye-Sook (2015). *The Mago Way, Re-discovering Mago the Great Goddess from East Asia*, Mago Books.

In-Sob, Zong (1979). *Folk Tales From Korea*, Evergreen.

Jackson, Simon (2009). *Cannabis and Meditation: An Explorer's Guide*, Headstuff Books.

Kerouac, Jack (1958). *The Dharma Bums*, Signet.

Kung, C.T. (1959). *Archeology in China*, University of Toronto Press.

Lai, His (2001). *The Sexual Teachings of the White Tigress, Secrets of the Female Taoist Masters*, Destiny Books.

Langer, Ellen (1989). *Mindfulness*, De Capo Press.

Leary, Timothy and Metzner, Ralph; Alpert, Richard. (1964). *The Psychedelic Experience: A Manual Based on the Tibetan Book of the Dead*, University Books.

Leary, Timothy (1966). *Psychedelic Prayers after the Tao Te Ching*, Poets Press.

Le Guin, Ursula (1998). *Lao Tzu : Tao Te Ching : A Book About the Way and the Power of the Way*, Shambhala.

Levi, Jean (2011). *The Complete Tao Te Ching with the Four Canons of the Yellow Emperor*, Inner Traditions.

MacHovec, Frank J. (1962). *The Book of Tao*, The Peter Pauper Press.

Marks, Howard (2001). *Book of Dope Stories*, Vintage.

Marshall, Peter (2001). *The Philosopher's Stone*, Macmillan Publishers.

Mitchell, Stephen (1998). *A New English Version Tao Te Ching*, HarperPerennial.

Needham, Joseph (1959). *Science and Civilization in China, Vol. 3, Mathematics and the Sciences of the Heavens and the Earth*. Cambridge University Press.

Needham, Joseph (1974). *Science and Civilization in China: Volume 5, Chemistry and Chemical Technology; Part 2, Spagyrical Discovery and Invention: Magisteries of Gold and Immortality*. Cambridge University Press.

Needham, Joseph. (1980). *Science and Civilization in China: Volume 5, Chemistry and Chemical Technology; Part 4, Spagyrical Discovery and Invention*. Cambridge University Press.
Okakura, Kakuzo (1964). *The Book of Tea*, Dover.
Oliver, Joan Duncan (2007). *Coffee with the Buddha*, Duncan Baird Publishers.
Onon, Urgunge (2011). *The Secret History of the Mongols*, Bolor Sudar.
Pepper, Jeff and Wang, Xiao Hui (2018, 2020). *Dao De Jing in Clear English*, Imagine 8 Press.
Ratsch, Christian (2001). *Marijuana Medicine, A World Tour of the Healing and Visionary Powers of Cannabis*, Healing Arts Press.
Regardie, Israel [ed](1968). *Roll Away the Stone, An Introduction to Aleister Crowley's Essays on the Psychology of Hashish*, Llewellyn.
Revolutionary Health Committee of Hunan Province (1977). *A Barefoot Doctor's Manual*, Cloudburst Press.
Rinpoche, Sogyal (2002). *The Tibetan Book of Living and Dying*, Rider.
Rosenthal, Ed (2010). *Ed Rosenthal's Marijuana Growers Handbook*, Quick American Publishing.
Ruck, Hoffman, Staples and Celdran (2007). *The Hidden World: Survival of Pagan Shamanic Themes in European Fairytales*, Carolina Academic Press.
Rudgley, Richard (1999). *The Encyclopedia of Psychoactive Substances*, McMillan.
Sagan, Carl (1977). *The Dragons of Eden, Speculations on the Origin of Human Intelligence*, Random House.
Schafer, E.H. (1963). *The Golden Peaches of Samarkand*, University of California Press.
Schuhmacher, S. and Woerner, G. (1994). *The Encyclopedia of Eastern Philosophy and Religion*, Shambhala.
Schultes, Richard Evans (1973). *Man and Marijuana*, American Museum of Natural History.
Screech, Timon(2009). *Sex and the Floating World, Erotic Images in Japan 1700-1820*, Reaktion Books.
Shah, Amina (1970). *Folk Tales of Central Asia*, Octagon Press.
Sherman, Carol and Smith, Andrew (1999). *Highlights, An Illustrated History of Cannabis*, Ten Speed Press.
Shi, David Borji (2016). *North Asian Magic, Spellcraft from Manchuria, Mongolia, and Siberia*, Yronwode Institution for the Preservation and Popularization of Indigenous Ethnomagicology (YIPPIE).
Suzuki, D. T. (1935). *Manual of Zen Buddhism*, Forgotten Books.
Suzuki, D. T. (1962). *The Essentials of Zen Buddhism*, Dutton.
Suzuki, D. T. (1970). *Zen and Japanese Culture*, Princeton University Press.
Suzuki, Shunryu (2970). *Zen Mind, Beginner's Mind*, Shambhala.
Theroux, Paul (1975). *The Great Railway Bazaar*, Ballantine Books.
Towler, Solala (2005). *Tales From the Tao: The Wisdom of the Taoist Masters*, Duncan Baird Publishers.

Tsunetomo, Yamamoto (1979). *Hagakure: The Book of the Samurai*, Kodansha International.
Unschuld, P.U. (1986). *Medicine in China: History of Pharmaceutics*, University of California Press.
Vavilov, N. I. (1992). *Origin and Geography of Cultivated Plants*, Cambridge University Press.
Wei, Ma Guang (2013). *Way of Infant Harmony, Path of Her Holiness Princess Ma Gu, Goddess of Cannabis*, Way of Infinite Harmony.
Walker, Barbara (1983). *The Woman's Encyclopedia of Myths and Secrets*, HarperSanFrancisco.
Walker, Brian (1995). *The Unknown Teachings of Lao Tzu: Hua Hu Ching*, HarperOne.
Wasson, R. Gordon (1971). *Soma: Divine Mushroom of Immortality*, Harcourt Brace Jovanovich.
Wen, Benebell (2016). *Tao of Craft, Fu Talismans and Casting Sigils in the Eastern Esoteric Tradition*, North Atlantic Books.
Wilhelm, Richard (1921). *The Chinese Fairy Book*, Frederick A. Stokes Company.
Wilhelm, Richard (1931). *Secret of the Golden Flower a Chinese Book of Life*, Harcourt Brace Jovanovich.
Wilhelm, Richard (1967). *The I Ching or Book of Changes*, Princeton University Press.
Yang, Lihui, An, Deming and Turner, Jessica Anderson (2008). *Handbook of Chinese Mythology*, Oxford University Press.
Yohannan, John D. (1956). *A Treasury of Asian Literature*, John Day Company.
Yu, Upasaka Lu Kuan (date unknown). *The Diamond Sutra- The Heart Sutra*, Buddhist Association of America.
Yutang, Lin (1948). *Famous Chinese Short Stories*, John Day Company.

Additional Dao de Jing Sources:
Yellow Bridge https://www.yellowbridge.com/onlinelit/daodejing.php
Chinese Text Project https://ctext.org/dao-de-jing
Wayism https://wayism.com/ttc-comparison-line-byline-ch01
Tao Te Ching Translation Comparison
https://ttc.tasuki.org/display:Code:gff,sm,jhmd,jc,rh
Translators Index Index to the Tao Te Ching (Dao De Jing) Translations
http://www.egreenway.com/taoism/ttclztrans3.htm
Terebess Asia Online (TAO) https://terebess.hu/english/tao/_index.html

Notes

[1] Wen, Benebell (2016). *Tao of Craft, Fu Talismans and Casting Sigils in the Eastern Esoteric Tradition*, North Atlantic Books, Berkeley. 2-6, 162 ,524

[2] Ma is also used in conjunction with the Sesame Seed due to its affinity with hempseed and exchangeability; also as Ma haung or Fo Ti: ephedra, which is associated with the Zoroastrian haoma and was found along side cannabis and opium residue in the archaeological excavations at the Indus Valley site at Mohenjo-Daro.

[3] Bennett, Chris, Osburn, Lynn and Judy (1995). *Green Gold the Tree of Life: Marijuana in Magic & Religion*, Access Unlimited. p. 121

[4] Walker, Barbara (1983). *The Woman's Encyclopedia of Myths and Secrets*, HarperSanFrancisco. p. 560- 627

[5] Hwang, Helen Hye-Sook (2015). *The Mago Way, Re-discovering Mago the Great Goddess from East Asia*, Mago Books. p. 104- 105

[6] Chang, Kwang-chih (1986). *The Archaeology of Ancient China*, Yale University Press. p.80

[7] Merlin, Mark (2017). *Archaeological Evidence for Ancient Cannabis Use*, in Estren, Mark [ed]*One Toke to God, 30 Essays by Noted Researchers into the Entheogenic Spirituality of Cannabis*, Cannabis Spiritual Center. p. 27

[8] Clarke, Robert C. & Merlin, Mark (2013). *Cannabis: Evolution and Ethnobotany*, University of California Press. p. 138

[9] Schultes, Richard Evans (1973). *Man and Marijuana*, American Museum of Natural History.

[10] Vavilov, N. I. (1992). *Origin and Geography of Cultivated Plants*, Cambridge University Press, Cambridge.

[11] Booth, Martin (2015). *Cannabis, A History*, St. Martin's Publishing.

[12] Chang (1986). p. 143

[13] Ruck, Carl (2017). *Cannabis Caves and Plays* in Estren, Mark [ed]*One Toke to God, 30 Essays by Noted Researchers into the Entheogenic Spirituality of Cannabis*, Cannabis Spiritual Center. p. 27

[14] Li, H. (1974). An Archaeological and Historical Account of Cannabis in China. *Economic Botany*, 28(4), 437-448. Retrieved February 15, 2021, from http://www.jstor.org/stable/4253540

[15] Fleming, Michael & Clarke, Robert (1998). *Physical evidence for the antiquity of Cannabis sativa L.* J. Int. Hemp Association. 5.

[16] Xi'an Banpo Museum 1963 publication. See also Liu, L. and Banpocun, Smith C. [ed] (2014) *Encyclopedia of Global Archaeology*, Springer. https://doi.org/10.1007/978-1-4419-0465-2_980

[17] Nelson, Robert A. (1996). *A History of Hemp* http://www.rexresearch.com/hhist/hhicon.htm

[18] Nelson, Robert A. (1996).

[19] Quoted in Ratsch, Christian (2001). *Marijuana Medicine, A World Tour of the Healing and Visionary Powers of Cannabis*, Healing Arts Press. p. 21

[20] Hwang, Hye Sook (2005). *Seeking Mago, the Great Goddess: A mytho-historic-theological reconstruction of Magoism, an archaically originated gynocentric tradition of East Asia (Korea, China, and Japan)*, Claremont Graduate University, PhD dissertation.

[21] Bennett, Chris (2010). *Cannabis and the Soma Solution*, Trine Day. p. 155- 199

[22] Chinese: 麻姑; pinyin: Mágū; Wade–Giles: Ma Ku; literally "Hemp Aunt"

[23] Wen (2016) p. 153

[24] Wen (2016) p. 152- 154

[25] "Mago (마고, 麻姑) is a cosmogonic goddess in Korean creation myths. Nogo or Nogu is the Ancient Goddess, Grandmother and Crone or Samsin, a triad deity." Issues in Studying Mago, the Great Goddess of East Asia: Primary Sources, Gynocentric History, and Nationalism", Helen Hye-Sook Hwang 2004 in "The Constant and Changing Faces of the Goddess", ed Deepak Shimkhada and Phyllis K. Herman

[26] Japanese Mako (麻姑) is usually a literary reference to the Chinese story about Ma Gu's long fingernails.

[27] According to the Budoji, Korean mytho-history began with the "Era of Mago." Hwang, Hye Sook (2004). *An Investigation of Gynocentric Unity in Mago, the East Asian Great Goddess, and Elsewhere*. Presented at the Conference of Pacific and Southwest Women's Studies, Scripps College, Claremont CA.

[28] Hemp cords were used to create the characteristic line designs on Yangshao culture pottery and the fibers were used to produce cloth prior to the introduction of cotton.

[29] Clark and Merlin (2016). p. 216

[30] Quoted in Schafer, E.H. (1963).*The Golden Peaches of Samarkand*, University of California Press. p. 195.

[31] https://www.goldenelixir.com/taoism/ill_xianren.html

[32] Quoted in Crowley, Mike (2016). *Secret Drugs of Buddhism, Psychedelic Sacraments and the Origins of the Vajrayana*, Amrita Press. p. 285

[33] China Kunyu Mountain Shaolin Martial Arts Academy http://www.chineseshaolins.com/the-kunyu-mountain.html#sthash.dQfM767u.dpuf

[34] Clarke, Robert C. (1995). Hemp (Cannabis sativa L.) Cultivation in the Tai'an District of Shandong Province, Peoples Republic of China. *Journal of the International Hemp Association* 2(2): 57, 60-65. http://druglibrary.net/olsen/HEMP/IHA/iha02201.html

[35] Harrison, Kathleen (2017). Who Is She, The Personification of Cannabis in Cultural and Personal Experience, in Gray, Stephen [ed] (2017). *Cannabis and Spirituality, An Explorer's Guide to an Ancient Plant Spirit Ally*, Park Street Press. p. 18- 37.

[36] https://www.wayofinfiniteharmony.org/about/

[37] Wang Jianghang recorded stories of 145 deified women in 215 BC.

[38] Griffith, Brian (2012). *A Galaxy of Immortal Women, the Yin Side of Chinese Civilization*, Exterminating Angel Press. p. 16- 18

[39] Griffith (2012). p. 45- 48, 64

[40] Griffith (2012). p. 81

[41] Clark, Robert C. and Merlin, Mark D. (2013). p. 62- 69

[42] Entheogen: From the Greek en- within and theo- god. A psychoactive plant that allows on to contact or connect with the inspiration of the god within.

[43] Henrich, Clark (2002). *Magic Mushrooms in Alchemy and Religion*, Inner Traditions.

[44] Ruck, Hoffman, Staples and Celdran (2007). *The Hidden World: Survival of Pagan Shamanic Themes in European Fairytales*, Carolina Academic Press.

[45] Universal Veil is the membrane that surrounds the baby mushroom and makes it appear like an egg. When the mushroom bursts through the veil, parts of it remain on various parts of the mushroom.

[46] Wasson, R. Gordon (1971). *Soma: Divine Mushroom of Immortality*, Harcourt Brace Jovanovich.

[47] Many ancient peoples believed that mushroom were born of thunder storms.

[48] Ruck, Hoffman, Staples and Celdran (2007).

[49] Clarke and Merlin (2016) p. 231- 232

⁵⁰ Shi, David Borji (2016). *North Asin Magic, Spellcraft from Manchuria, Mongolia, and Siberia*, Yronwode Institution for the Preservation and Popularization of Indigenous Ethnomagicology (YIPPIE) p. 5-7

⁵¹ Shi (2016) p. 20

⁵² Berger, Markus 2011. Ruderalis 101 in *Soft Secrets* Issue 1, 2011.

⁵³ Marshall, Peter (2001). *The Philosopher's Stone*, Macmillan Publishers.

⁵⁴ Wei, Ma Guang (2013). *Way of Infant Harmony, Path of Her Holiness Princess Ma Gu, Goddess of Cannabis*, Way of Infinite Harmony. p. 15

⁵⁵ Vavilov, N. I. (1992).

⁵⁶ *Ethnobotanical research on origin, cultivation, distribution and utilization of hemp (Cannabis sativa L.) in China*. http://nopr.niscair.res.in/handle/123456789/40123

⁵⁷ Quoted in Ratsch (2001). p. 21

⁵⁸ Brand, EJ and Zhao, Z (2017). *Cannabis in Chinese Medicine: Are Some Traditional Indications Referenced in Ancient Literature Related to Cannabinoids?* Front. Pharmacol. 8:108. doi: 10.3389/fphar.2017.00108

⁵⁹ Seshata, Cannabis in China, 2014, *Cannabis News*, Sensi Seeds, Amsterdam

⁶⁰ Seshata, Cannabis in China, 2014, *Cannabis News*, Sensi Seeds, Amsterdam

⁶¹ Lu, Y. X., Dong, P., Cui, X. G., Guo, J. S., and Wang, Y. (2007). *Differentiation and use of industrial hemp and drug cannabis*. Pharm. J. China 23, 1112–1114.

⁶² Brand EJ and Zhao Z (2017) *Cannabis in Chinese Medicine: Are Some Traditional Indications Referenced in Ancient Literature Related to Cannabinoids?* Front. Pharmacol. 8:108. doi: 10.3389/fphar.2017.00108

⁶³ Cleary, Thomas (1996). *Immortal Sisters: Secret Teachings of Taoist Women*, North Atlantic Books. p. 77.

⁶⁴ Bennet and Osburn (1995) p. 123

⁶⁵ Hanh, Thich Nhat (2007). *Two Treasures*, Parallax Press. p. 1

⁶⁶ Hanh, Thich Nhat (1987). *Being Peace*, Parallax Press. p. 88

⁶⁷ Bennet, Chris, Osburn, Lynn & Judy (1995). p. 124

⁶⁸ Wen (2016). p. 8

⁶⁹ Wen (2016) p. 295

⁷⁰ Wen (2016) p. 139

⁷¹ Wen (2016)p. 273- 275

⁷² Wen (2016) P. 52

⁷³ Szirom, Dr Tricia (2015). *Goddess Mago, Ma_Ku, Magu, Goddess of China, Korea and Japan*. https://ganja-goddess-blog.tumblr.com/post/97267895619/goddess-mago-maku-magu-goddess-of-china-korea

⁷⁴ Hawng (2015) p. 21

⁷⁵ Hawng (2015) p. 148

⁷⁶ Hawng (2015) p. 9

⁷⁷ Magohalmi, *Encyclopedia of Korean Folk Culture* https://folkency.nfm.go.kr/en/topic/detail/2040

⁷⁸ National Folk Museum of Korea

⁷⁹ Hawng (2015) p. 152

⁸⁰ Chamberlain, Laura Kristine (2002). Durga and the Dashain Harvest Festival: From the Indus to Kathmandu Valleys, *ReVision*, Summer 2002, vol. 25, no. 1, 24-3

⁸¹ Changsega, *Encyclopedia of Korean Folk Culture* https://folkency.nfm.go.kr/en/topic/detail/5402

⁸² Hwang (2005).

⁸³ Hall, Manly P. (1924). *The Occult Anatomy of Man to Which is Added Occult Masonry*, Hall Publishing Company.

[84] Russo, E. (2015). *Introduction to the Endocannabinoid System.* http://www.phytecs.com/wp-content/uploads/2015/02/Russo-Introduction-to-the-Endocannabinoid-System-corr-January-2015.pdf

[85] Carter. G.T., Javaher, S.P., Nguyen, M.H.V., Garret, S., Carlini, B.H. (2015). Re-branding Cannabis: The next generation of chronic pain medicine? *Future Medicine.* 5(1), 13-21.

[86] McPartland, J.M. (2008). The Endocannabinoid System: An Osteopathic Perspective. *The Journal of the American Osteopathic Association.* 108: 586-600; see also: Russo, E. (2004). Clinical Endocannabinoid Deficiency (CECD): Can this Concept Explain Therapeutic Benefits of Cannabis in Migraine, Fibromyalgia, Irritable Bowel Syndrome and Other Treatment-Resistant Conditions? *Neuroendocrinology Letters.* Nos.1/2, Feb-Apr Vol.25; see also: Aggarwal, S.K. (2012). Cannabinergic Pain Medicine: A Concise Clinical Primer and Survey of Randomized-controlled Trial Results. *Clinical Journal of Pain.* https://journals.lww.com/clinicalpain/pages/default.aspx; see also: Idris, A (2010). Cannabinoid Receptors as Target for Treatment of Osteoporosis: A Tale of Two Therapies. *Current Neuropharmacology.* 8(3): 243-253.

[87] Hagar, Steve (2014). *Magic, Religion and Cannabis*; Abacus Books. p. 53

[88] Han, Enomae, Isogai, Yamamoto, Hasegawa, Sang and Jang (2006).Traditional Papermaking Techniques revealed by Fiber Orientation in Historical Papers, *Studies in Conservation*, Number 51, 2006.

[89] Seshata, (2015). History of cannabis in North Korea, *Sensi Seeds.*

[90] Seshata (2015)

[91] Richter, Darmon (2015). On Smoking Weed in North Korea; *The Bohemian Blog*, 29 September 2013. https://www.exutopia.com/on-smoking-weed-in-north-korea/

[92] Hawng (2015). p. 23

[93] Hawng (2015) p. 48

[94] Ryu, Yonsei (1948). Shamanism: The Dominant Folk Religion in Korea, *Inter-Reiigio* 5, Spring 1984, Yonsei University.

[95] Koo, Se-Woong (2010). Religions of Korea Yesterday and Today, *SPICE Digest*, Fall 2010, https://spice.fsi.stanford.edu/docs/religions_of_korea_yesterday_and_today

[96] Based on material from *Chinese Buddhist Encyclopedia* [http://www.chinabuddhismencyclopedia.com/en/index.php?title=Chinese_Buddhist_Encyclopedia] and *Guide to Buddhism A-Z* [https://www.buddhisma2z.com/].

[97] Griffith (2012). p. 31

[98] Griffith (2012). p. 112

[99] Ratsch (2001) p. 23- 24

[100] Wen (2016) p. 320

[101] Gait, Christopher (1977). *The I Ching*, OTO Newsletter Volume I, No. 3, Winter Solstice, An. LXXIII E.N., Dec., 1977 E.V.

[102] Three Sovereigns and Five Emperors. (2008, May 10). *New World Encyclopedia*, . Retrieved 00:59, December 29, 2020 from https://www.newworldencyclopedia.org/p/index.php?title=Three_Sovereigns_and_Five_Emperors&oldid=706400.

[103] Quoted in Ratsch, Christian (2001). p. 23

[104] Eberhard, Wofram (1996). *A Dictionary of Chinese Symbols: Hidden Symbols in Chinese Life and Thought*, Routledge & Kegan Paul. p.272.

[105] Inspired by Eberhard, Wofram (1996). p.272.

[106] *Si Min Yue Ling* quoted in Lu, X., & Clarke, R. (2012). The cultivation and use of hemp (Cannabis sativa L .) in ancient China.

[107] Translated by Roth, Harold D. (1997), Evidence for Stages of Meditation in Early Taoism, *Bulletin of the School of Oriental and African Studies* 60.2: 295-314.

[108] Cleary, Thomas (1996) p. 19

[109] based on an exercise outlined in Allister Crowley, *Liber RV vel Spiritus*

[110] Lai, His (2001). *The Sexual Teachings of the White Tigress, Secrets of the Female Taoist Masters*, Destiny Books.

[111] Cleary, Thomas (1996)

[112] Hanh (2007) p. 2

[113] Hanh (2007) p. 28

[114] Wen (2016) p. 12- 13

[115] Wen (2016) p. 87

[116] Wen (2016) p. 524

[117] Chan, Alan (2018). Laozi, *Stanford Encyclopedia of Philosophy*, Edward N. Zalta (ed.), https://plato.stanford.edu/archives/win2018/entries/laozi/.

[118] Quoted in Ratsch (2001) p. 23

[119] 1.3 inches

[120] Wen (2016). p. 7- 8

[121] Wen (2016) p. 106

[122] Needham, Joseph (1974). *Science and Civilization in China: Volume 5, Chemistry and Chemical Technology; Part 2, Spagyrical Discovery and Invention: Magisteries of Gold and Immortality*. Cambridge University Press. p 130

[123] *Tara, Mother of All Buddhas*, The Maitreya Project. http://www.abuddhistlibrary.com/Buddhism/A%20-%20Tibetan%20Buddhism/Subjects/Tantra/Practices-%20%28Sadhanas%20and%20commentaries%29/Tara/Tara%20-%20The%20Mother%20of%20All%20Buddhas/Tara,%20the%20Mother%20of%20all%20Buddhas.htm

[124] Tara the Liberator, *The 21 Taras Thangka*. https://21tarasthangka.org/tara-the-liberator/#:~:text=%E2%80%9CThere%20are%20many%20who%20desire,beings%20in%20a%20woman's%20body.%E2%80%9D

[125] Quoted in Crowley, Mike (2016) p. 243

[126] Russo, E. B., Jiang, H. E., Li, X., Sutton, A., Carboni, A., del Bianco, F., Mandolino, G., Potter, D. J., Zhao, Y. X., Bera, S., Zhang, Y. B., Lü, E. G., Ferguson, D. K., Hueber, F., Zhao, L. C., Liu, C. J., Wang, Y. F., & Li, C. S. (2008). Phytochemical and genetic analyses of ancient cannabis from Central Asia. *Journal of Experimental Botany*, 59(15), 4171–4182. https://doi.org/10.1093/jxb/ern260

[127] Yang, Lihui, An, Deming and Turner, Jessica Anderson (2008). *Handbook of Chinese Mythology*, Oxford University Press. p. 195

[128] Classic of Tea written by Lu Yu in the Tang dynasty (618 - 907 A.D.).

[129] Brand EJ and Zhao Z (2017) *Cannabis in Chinese Medicine: Are Some Traditional Indications Referenced in Ancient Literature Related to Cannabinoids?* Front. Pharmacol. 8:108. doi: 10.3389/fphar.2017.00108

[130] Translation from Unschuld, P.U. (1986). *Medicine in China: History of Pharmaceutics*, University of California Press.

[131] Abel, Ernest. L., *Marijuana, The First Twelve Thousand Years*. New York: Plenum Press. 1980

[132] Brand EJ and Zhao Z (2017) Cannabis in Chinese Medicine: Are Some Traditional Indications Referenced in Ancient Literature Related to Cannabinoids? *Front. Pharmacol.* 8:108. doi: 10.3389/fphar.2017.00108

[133] Ryz NR, Remillard DJ, Russo EB (2017) Cannabis roots: a traditional therapy with future potential for treating inflammation and pain, *Cannabis and Cannabinoid Research* 2:1, 210–216, DOI: 10.1089/can.2017.0028.

[134] Seshata, Getting down to the roots of cannabis; 2014, *Sensi Seeds*, Amsterdam

[135] Seshata, Getting down to the roots of cannabis; 2014, *Sensi Seeds*, Amsterdam

[136] Rosenthal, Ed (2010). *Ed Rosenthal's Marijuana Growers Handbook*, Quick American Publishing, p. 238

[137] Russo E. B. (2007). History of cannabis and its preparations in saga, science, and sobriquet. *Chemistry & biodiversity*, 4(8), 1614–1648. https://doi.org/10.1002/cbdv.200790144

[138] Russo, E. B., Jiang, H. E., Li, X., Sutton, A., Carboni, A., del Bianco, F., Mandolino, G., Potter, D. J., Zhao, Y. X., Bera, S., Zhang, Y. B., Lü, E. G., Ferguson, D. K., Hueber, F., Zhao, L. C., Liu, C. J., Wang, Y. F., & Li, C. S. (2008). Phytochemical and genetic analyses of ancient cannabis from Central Asia. *Journal of experimental botany*, 59(15), 4171–4182. https://doi.org/10.1093/jxb/ern260

[139] Merlin, Mark (2017). Archaeological Evidence of Ancient Cannabis Use, in Estren, Mark [ed] (2017). *One Toke to God, 30 Essays by Noted Researchers into the Entheogenic Spirituality of Cannabis*, Cannabis Spiritual Center. p. 38- 39

[140] Bennett (2010) p. 189- 193

[141] Needham, Joseph (1974). *Science and Civilization in China: Volume 5, Chemistry and Chemical Technology; Part 2, Spagyrical Discovery and Invention: Magisteries of Gold and Immortality*. Cambridge University Press. p. 150- 154

[142] Liu, F.-H & Hu, H.-R & Du, G.-H & Deng, G. & Yang, Y.. (2017). Ethnobotanical research on origin, cultivation, distribution and utilization of hemp (Cannabis sativa L.) in China. 16. 235-242. http://nopr.niscair.res.in/handle/123456789/40123

[143] Ratsch 2001. p. 22

[144] Clarke, Robert C. and Gu, Wenfeng (1998). Survey of hemp (Cannabis sativa L.) use by the Hmong (Miao) of the China/Vietnam border region, *Journal of the International Hemp Association* No. 5 http://www.internationalhempassociation.org/jiha/jiha5101.html

[145] Her, Vincent K. (2005) Hmong Cosmology: Proposed Model, Preliminary Insights, *Milwaukee Hmong Studies Journal*, Volume 6, University of Wisconsin

[146] Wen (2016) p. 520, 528, 538

[147] Tapp, N. (1989). *Hmong Religion*. Asian Folklore Studies, 48(1), 59-94. doi:10.2307/1178534

[148] Clarke, Robert C. and Merlin, Mark D. (2016). p. 260

[149] Clarke and Gu (1998).

[150] Ibid.

[151] Ibid.

[152] Magagnini, Stephen (2017). Marijuana and Hmong farmers: Siskiyou County sheriff fights to control cannabis trade; December 22, 2017, *The Sacramento Bee*

[153] Shulman, Alayna (2017). Pot is literally a 'state of emergency' now in Siskiyou County; September 13, 2017, *Record Searchlight*, Reading CA

[154] Fuller, Thomas (2017). California's 'Green Rush' Takes Hmong Back to Their Opium-Growing Roots; June 3, 2017, *The New York Times*

[155] Clarke, Robert C. and Merlin, Mark D. (2016) p. 261.

[156] Cleary, Thomas (1996). p. 11-14.

[157] Digram of the Ascent and Decent of Yang and Yin in the Human Body, quoted in Griffith (2012) p. 187

[158] Dilgo Khyentse Rinpoche quoted in Rinpoche, Sogyal (2002). *The Tibetan Book of Living and Dying*, Rider. p. 395

[159] Hanh (2007) p. 2
[160] Wen (2016) p. 13-14, 152
[161] Wen (2016) p. 328, 332
[162] Wen (2016) p. 327, 330
[163] Wen (2016) p. 331, 327- 328.
[164] Wen (2016) p. 329.
[165] Rosenthal, Ed (2010). *Ed Rosenthal's Marijuana Growers Handbo*ok, Quick American Publishing.
[166] Hanh (1987) p. 22
[167] Wen (2016) p. 481- 482
[168] self.gutenberg.org/articles/eng/Yellow_Emperor
[169] Cleary, Thomas (1996).
[170] Huang Di 黃帝, , *ChinaKnowledge.de -An Encyclopedia on Chinese History, Literature and Art*; http://www.chinaknowledge.de/History/Myth/personshuangdi.html
[171] Major, J.S., Queen, S.A.; Meyer, A.S.; Roth, H.D. (2010). *The Huainanzi: A guide to the theory and practice of government in early Han China*. New York: Columbia University Press.
[172] Cleary, Thomas (1996). p. xxii- xxiv
[173] Liu, F.-H & Hu, H.-R & Du, G.-H & Deng, G. & Yang, Y.. (2017). Ethnobotanical research on origin, cultivation, distribution and utilization of hemp (Cannabis sativa L.) in China. 16. 235-242. http://nopr.niscair.res.in/handle/123456789/40123
[174] Griffith (2012). p. 41
[175] Wen (2016) p. 40-41, 51
[176] Anonymous 1 CE quoted in Andrews, George [ed] (1974). *Drugs and Magic*, IllumiNet. p. 65
[177] Cannabis Evolution and Ethnobotany, Clarke and Merlin, p. 220
[178] Needham, Joseph (1959). S*cience and Civilization in China, Vol. 3, Mathematics and the Sciences of the Heavens and the Earth*. Cambridge University Press.; Needham, Joseph (1974). *Science and Civilization in China*: Volume 5, Chemistry and Chemical Technology; Part 2, Spagyrical Discovery and Invention: Magisteries of Gold and Immortality. Cambridge University Press.; Needham, Joseph. (1980). *Science and Civilization in China*: Volume 5, Chemistry and Chemical Technology; Part 4, Spagyrical Discovery and Invention. Cambridge University Press.
[179] Nelson, Robert A. (1996).
[180] Clarke and Merlin (2016)
[181] Luk, Charles [trans.]. *Incense Praise Introduction to The Diamond Sutra*, Buddhist Association of America, San Francisco, CA.
[182] from *Taoism and the Arts of China* exhibition by The Art Institute of Chicago from November 4, 2000, to January 7, 2001, and at the Asian Art Museum of San Francisco from February 21 to May 13, 2001.
[183] Bennett (2010) p. 155- 199
[184] Needham, Joseph (1974). p. 154 4
[185] quoted in Lu, X., & Clarke, R. (2012). The cultivation and use of hemp (Cannabis sativa L .) in ancient China.
[186] *Archaeological Study of Textiles*, Textile Museum, Thailand 2006
[187] Seshata (2013). *Sensi Seeds*, Cannabis in Thailand 27/06/2013
[188] Ibid.
[189] *Silk Magazine* 2001, Textile Museum, Naresuan University, Phitsanulok, Thailand 2007
[190] Seshata, *Cannabis in Thailand*, 2013, Cannabis News, Sensi Seeds, Amsterdam

[191] Blair, Eric (2011). *History of Marijuana Use and Anti-Marijuana Laws in Thailand*, Thailand Law Forum, 07/11/2011

[192] Eric Blair (2011). *History of Marijuana Use and Anti-Marijuana Laws in Thailand*, Thailand Law Forum, 07/11/2011

[193] Bennett Chris (2005). Smoke of the Ages, *Cannabis Culture* 05/10/2005 https://www.cannabisculture.com/content/2005/05/10/4114/

[194] Shi (2016) p 9-11

[195] Hanh (1987) p. 54-55.

[196] Interview with Jana Drakka by Ilse Thompson 07/03/15 in *Zen and the Art of Harm Reduction.*

[197] Drakka, Jana (2015). *Buddhist Harm Reduction and Cannabis* in Badiner, Allan (2015) [ed]. *Zig Zag Zen*, Synergetic Press.

[198] https://cabhp.asu.edu/sites/default/files/reiman-research-to-practice.pdf

[199] Jackson, Simon (2009). *Cannabis and Meditation: An Explorer's Guide*, Headstuff Books.

[200] Drakka, Jana (2016). *Rituals of Change*, Synergetic Press.

[201] Hanh (2007) p. 3

[202] Wen (016) p. 109, 525

[203] Wen (2016) p. 18-23, 336

[204] https://www.lieske.com/5e-intro.htm

[205] Crowley 2016. p. 261

[206] Jack Kornfield interviewed by Robert Forte in Badiner (2015) p. 49

[207] Villalba, Dokusho (2015). *Dissolving the Roots of Suffering*, trans. McNicholls, Stuart in Badiner (2015) p. 30

[208] Carus, Paul (1915, 1995). *The Gospel of the Buddha*, Senate

[209] Conrad, Chris (1994). *Hemp, Lifeline to the Future, the Unexpected Answer for Our Environmental and Economic Recovery*, Creative Xpressions Publications. p. 188

[210] Mitchell, Jon (2014). Cannabis: the fabric of Japan, *The Japan Times*, April 19, 2014.

[211] Paulhus, Brett (2004). *Hemp & Japanese Culture*. https://rense.com/general50/hemp4.htm

[212] Bennett (1995) p. 128- 129

[213] Conrad (1994) p. 8

[214] Bennett (1995) p. 129

[215] Clarke and Merlin (2016) p. 277

[216] Interview with Pon (Yamada Kaiya) December 1995 issue of *Jiyu Ishi*

[217] Hurtado, David (2013). *Japan, the Land of Imperial Hemp and the Rising Sun in the 21ST Century – Part 1*; 2013, *Sensi Seeds.*

[218] Hurtado, D. (2013). *Japan, the Land of Imperial Hemp and the Rising Sun in the 21ST Century – Part 2*; 2013, *Sensi Seeds.*

[219] Conrad (1994) p. 188

[220] Screech, Timon(2009). *Sex and the Floating World, Erotic Images in Japan 1700-1820,* Reaktion Books

[221] Conrad (1994) p. 188

[222] Clarke and Merlin (2016) p. 273- 274

[223] Clarke and Merlin (2016) p. 275

[224] Clarke and Merlin (2016) p. 274

[225] http://www.japanhemp.org/en/asanoha.htm

[226] *Hemp in Japan: the Samurai*, The Hash, Marijuana and Hemp Museum, Amsterdam

[227] Ratsch (2001) p. 28

[228] Martijn, Growing interest in hemp and medical cannabis in Japan; 2016, *Sensi Seeds*, Amsterdam

[229] Jun Hongo, Jun (2015). Japan's First Lady Touts Revival of Hemp Culture, *Wall Street Journal*, Dec 15, 2015.

[230] Mitchell, Jon (2014). Cannabis: the fabric of Japan; *Japan Times* April 19, 2014.

[231] Quoted in Walt, Paul (1982). Shinto and Buddhism: Wellsprings of Japanese Spirituality, Asia Society's Focus on Asian Studies, Vol II, No. 1, *Asian Religions*, Fall 1982.

[232] Sherman, Carol and Smith, Andrew (1999). *Highlights, An Illustrated History of Cannabis*, Ten Speed Press. p. 13. See also Able, Ernest (1980). *Marijuana - The First Twelve Thousand Years*, Springer.

[233] Wen (2016) p. 42-43
[234] Wen (2016) p. 146-147
[235] Wen (2016) p. 148- 149
[236] Wen (2016) p. 158
[237] Wen (2016) p. 169- 174
[238] Wen (2016) p. 298- 299
[239] Wen (2016) p. 251
[240] Wen (2016) p. 109- 111
[241] Wen (2016) p. 312
[242] Hanh (2007) p. 3

[243] Smith, Huston (1964). Do Drugs Have Religious Import?, *Journal of Philosophy*, Vol LVI, No. 18, Oc 1 1964. Quoted in Regardie, Israel [ed](1968). *Roll Away the Stone, An Introduction to Aleister Crowley's Essays on the Psychology of Hashish*, Llewellyn. p. 30

[244] Watts, Alan (1962). *The Joyous Cosmology*, Pantheon Books. Quoted in Regardie, Israel [ed](1968). *Roll Away the Stone, An Introduction to Aleister Crowley's Essays on the Psychology of Hashish*, Llewellyn. p. 30, 38

[245] Leary, Timothy quoted in Regardie (1968) p. 30- 31, 38.

[246] Crowley, Aleister quoted in Regardie (1968) p.43.

[247] Taken from *Kindness, Clarity, and Insight*, by The Fourteenth Dalai Lama His Holiness Tenzin Gyatso, translated and edited by Jeffrey Hopkins, co-edited by Elizabeth Napper. Snow Lion Publications, 1984.

[248] Brand, E.J. and Zhao, Z (2017) Cannabis in Chinese Medicine: Are Some Traditional Indications Referenced in Ancient Literature Related to Cannabinoids? Front. *Pharmacol*. 8:108. doi: 10.3389/fphar.2017.00108

[249] Ratsch (2001) p. 53
[250] Meo, Nick (2005). *San Francisco Chronicle*, October 28, 2005
[251] Theroux, Paul (1975). *The Great Railway Bazaar*, Ballantine Books
[252] Gilboa, Amit (1998). Cambodia: smoker's paradise, *Cannabis Culture*, November 1, 1998
[253] Jackson, Will (2015). *The Phnom Penh Post* May 29, 2015
[254] Rudgley, Richard (1999). *The Encyclopedia of Psychoactive Substances*, McMillan.
[255] Ratsch (2001) p. 52
[256] Jackson, Will (2015). *The Phnom Penh Post* May 29, 2015
[257] Harfenist, Ethan and Murray, Bennett (2015). The high life, *The Phnom Penh Post* May 29, 2015
[258] Ratsch (2001) p. 50
[259] Hanh (2007) p. 3-4
[260] Wen (2016) . p. 13-14, 152, 327- 331
[261] Wen (2016). p. 35
[262] Lai (2001) p. 120

[263] Bennett, Chris (2019). Cannabis in Ancient China, Part 1: Ma, plant of the Tao, *Cannabis Culture*. https://www.cannabisculture.com/content/2019/06/22/cannabis-in-ancient-china-part-1-ma-plant-of-the-tao/

[264] The Jiayi Cemetery, Turpan, China, contained the Tomb of a shaman buried wrapped in a well-preserved shroud of female cannabis plants.

[265] Campany, Robert Ford (2002). *To Live As Long As Heaven and Earth: Ge Hong's Traditions of Divine Transcendents*. University of California Press.

[266] Ch'u Tz'u (5-1 BCE), *The Songs of the South*, quoted in Andrews, George and Vinkenoog, Simon [eds] (1974). *The Book of Grass*, Penguin Books p. 65-72

[267] Wen (2016) p. 207, 215, 232

[268] Wen (2016) p. 147

[269] Bello, Joan (2017). *Marijuana and the Body-Mind*, in Gray (2017) p. 60-61.

[270] Dussault, Dee (2017). *For the Love of the Leaf: Ganja-Enhanced Yoga for the Modern Practitioner*, in Gray (2017) p.119

[271] Viet, Nguyen Van (1999). *The uses of Cannabis hemp in Vietnam: History and present situation*, National University of Hanoi, Center for Vietnamese and Intercultural Studies, The Project for Ancient Civilizations in Vietnam, Hanoi.

[272] Van Viet, Nguyen (1999).

[273] Ibid.

[274] Kulke, Hermann (1974). *The Deva Raja Cult*, Cornell University. https://ecommons.cornell.edu/bitstream/handle/1813/57575/108.pdf?sequence=1&isAllowed=y

[275] Griffith (2012) p. 214

[276] http://www.microprojects-vietnam.org/VietnamDrinkingWater/religions-of-vietnam

[277] https://vwam.com/vets/tribes/ethnicminorities.html

[278] Clarke and Gu (1998).

[279] Harrigan, Serena Lee (2008). *Dress of the Lolo, Pathen, Hmong and Yao of Northern Vietnam in 2005-2006: Reflections of Cultural Continuity and Change*, Textile Society of America Symposium Proceedings. Paper 97

[280] Ibid.

[281] Ibid.

[282] Viet, Nguyen Van (1999). *The uses of Cannabis hemp in Vietnam: History and present situation*, National University of Hanoi, Center for Vietnamese and Intercultural Studies, The Project for Ancient Civilizations in Vietnam, Hanoi.

[283] Fleming & Clarke (1998).

[284] Zhixu, Chen (1290-ca.1368), *Jindan dayao (Great Essentials of the Golden Elixir)*.

[285] *Gold Pavilion Classic* (330 CE) quoted in Griffith (2012) p. 186

[286] Hanh (2007) p. 4

[287] Cleary (1996) p. 84- 86

[288] Yingning, Chen, Commentary on *Gathering the Mind*, Bu-er, Sun (12th Century) in Cleary (1996) p. 8

[289] Bu-er, Sun (12th Century). *Unexcelled True Scripture of Inner Experiences of Jadelike Purity*, in Cleary (1996) p. 50

[290] Wen (2016) P. 23

[291] Wen (2016) P. 24-32

[292] Wen (2016) P. 25-29

[293] Griffith (2012) p. 280

[294] Wen (2017) p. 314

[295] Griffith (2012) p. 129

[296] Wen (2016) P. 316

[297] Clarke & Merlin (2016)
[298] https://georgehbalazs.com/wp-content/uploads/2019/06/MoNiang.pdf
[299] Gui, Tang Shi; *Mazu – the Protecting Goddess of the Sea* https://georgehbalazs.com/wp-content/uploads/2019/06/Mazu-Goddess-of-the-Sea.pdf
[300] In The Beginning, *Island Folklore* March 15, 2018. https://islandfolklore.com/in-the-beginning/
[301] Abel, Ernest L. (1980). *Marihuana: the first twelve thousand years*. Plenum Publishers. http://druglibrary.org/schaffer/hemp/history/first12000/1.htm; see also Chang, K. (1968). *The Archaeology of Ancient China*, Yale University Press p. 111-12; and Kung, C.T. (1959). *Archeology in China*, University of Toronto Press p. 131.
[302] Carl Sagan(1977). *The Dragons of Eden, Speculations on the Origin of Human Intelligence*, Random House. p 191 footnote.
[303] Hung, H., & Carson, M. (2014). Foragers, fishers and farmers: Origins of the Taiwanese Neolithic. *Antiquity*, 88(342), 1115-1131. doi:10.1017/S0003598X00115352
[304] Yu-be, Chen (2020). Anthropology Matters on Taiwan: Research Methodologies, the earliest arrivals, and more... Taiwan Memory Exhibition, National Central Library. https://tme.ncl.edu.tw/en/archaeology
[305] Ibid.
[306] Ibid.
[307] Hung, H., & Carson, M. (2014). Foragers, fishers and farmers: Origins of the Taiwanese Neolithic, *Antiquity*, 88(342), 1115-1131. doi:10.1017/S0003598X00115352
[308] Hsu, Phoenix and Lin, Ko (2020) DNA from Guam's indigenous peoples traced to Taiwan: study, *Focus Taiwan* 12/24/2020. https://focustaiwan.tw/culture/202012240009
[309] Beeching, Jack (1977). *The Opium Wars*, quoted in 8 p. 79- 82.
[310] The Way of the Gods – Folk Religion in Taiwan. *The News Lens* 07/21/2016.
[311] Sui, Cindy (2009). Taiwan's shamanistic traditions undergo revival, *Taiwan Today* 12/18/2009.
[312] Wen-Jing, Liang (2020). Witchcraft that Connects Humans and Nature - A Look into Taiwanese Indigenous Shaman Culture, *Indigenous Sight* 04/23/2020. https://insight.ipcf.org.tw/en-US/article/281
[313] Adams, Jonathan (2008). Shaman Channels 12th Century but Adapts to 21st, *New York Times* 12/06/2008.
[314] The Way of the Gods – Folk Religion in Taiwan, *The News Lens* 07/21/2016.
[315] Ibid.
[316] http://www.godsoftaiwan.com/Tang-Ki.html
[317] Cheng-feng, Wu and Chung, Jake (2020). Medicinal cannabis a category 2 narcotic: ministry, Taipei Times May 11, 2020.
[318] Chien, T. M. (2006). Analysis of crude drug preparations used in traditional Chinese medicine in Taiwan national health insurance (2002-2003). Chinese Medical University.
[319] Wen (2016) P. 150
[320] http://taoist-sorcery.blogspot.com/2015/09/the-taoist-snake-whip.html
[321] Able, Ernist L. (1980). Marijuana the First Twelve Thousand Years, University of Michigan Press.
[322] http://taoist-sorcery.blogspot.com/2015/09/zhang-gong-sheng-jun.html
[323] http://taoist-sorcery.blogspot.com/2015/09/the-taoist-snake-whip.html
[324] Clarke & Merlin (2016). p. 242
[325] Hanh (2007) p. 4-5
[326] Das, Lama Surya (2015). *The Zen Commandments*, in Badiner (2015) p. 184- 193
[327] Cleary (1996) p. 63- 66

Made in the USA
Columbia, SC
12 February 2022